# Berkeley's Argument for Idealism

Samuel C. Rickless presents a novel interpretation of the thought of George Berkeley. In *A Treatise Concerning the Principles of Human Knowledge* (1710) and *Three Dialogues Between Hylas and Philonous* (1713), Berkeley argues for the astonishing view that physical objects (such as tables and chairs) are nothing but collections of ideas (idealism); that there is no such thing as material substance (immaterialism); that abstract ideas are impossible (anti-abstractionism); and that an idea can be like nothing but an idea (the likeness principle). It is a matter of great controversy what Berkeley's argument for idealism is and whether it succeeds. Most scholars believe that the argument is based on immaterialism, anti-abstractionism, or the likeness principle. In *Berkeley's Argument for Idealism*, Rickless argues that Berkeley distinguishes between two kinds of abstraction, 'singling' abstraction and 'generalizing' abstraction; that his argument for idealism depends on the impossibility of singling abstraction but not on the impossibility of generalizing abstraction; and that the argument depends neither on immaterialism nor the likeness principle. According to Rickless, the heart of the argument for idealism rests on the distinction between mediate and immediate perception, and in particular on the thesis that everything that is perceived by means of the senses is immediately perceived. After analyzing the argument, Rickless concludes that it is valid and may well be sound. This is Berkeley's most enduring philosophical legacy.

# Berkeley's Argument for Idealism

Samuel C. Rickless

OXFORD
UNIVERSITY PRESS

# OXFORD
## UNIVERSITY PRESS

Great Clarendon Street, Oxford, OX2 6DP,
United Kingdom

Oxford University Press is a department of the University of Oxford.
It furthers the University's objective of excellence in research, scholarship,
and education by publishing worldwide. Oxford is a registered trade mark of
Oxford University Press in the UK and in certain other countries

© Samuel C. Rickless 2013

The moral rights of the author have been asserted

First published 2013
First published in paperback 2016

Published in the United States of America by Oxford University Press
198 Madison Avenue, New York, NY 10016, United States of America

British Library Cataloguing in Publication Data
Data available

Library of Congress Cataloging in Publication Data
Data available

ISBN 978-0-19-966942-4 (Hbk.)
ISBN 978-0-19-877758-8 (Pbk.)

*For my father*
*Elwood Abraham Rickless*
*and my father-in-law*
*Norton Nelkin*
*would that I could bring you the joy that you brought me*

# Preface

I was first exposed to George Berkeley's idealism as a teaching assistant in Robert Adams's upper division history of modern philosophy course at UCLA in 1993. The course represented an extraordinary learning experience for me, and I am deeply grateful to Bob for bringing the work of seventeenth- and eighteenth-century philosophers to life in a way that will never be equaled. Bob treated every philosopher he discussed (Descartes, Spinoza, Malebranche, Locke, Leibniz, Berkeley, Hume, and Kant) with respect and admiration: he laid out the arguments, discussed their strengths and weaknesses, and then encouraged his students (and his TA) to think through them on their own. I hope that this book, even if only in small measure, lives up to the ideals of interpretation and understanding that Robert Adams embodies.

The first course I taught on the history of philosophy was a standard survey of British Empiricism from Locke to Hume. It became obvious to me that a great deal of philosophical commentary treats Berkeley as a way-station between Locke and Hume, and treats his idealist and anti-materialist arguments as momentarily mesmerizing but ultimately either blatantly fallacious or just plain silly. On Berkeley's behalf I thought this a trifle unfair, but by and large I found Locke's materialism so attractive that it didn't seem worth it to quibble with the mostly negative commentary on Berkeley's pleasure–pain argument, his argument from perceptual relativity, and his Master Argument. After a few years of working on what I took to be the clearest reconstruction of Berkeley's reasons for accepting an idealistic metaphysics, I came to believe that most scholars had misidentified the central arguments of the *Three Dialogues Between Hylas and Philonous* (1713), that a correct reconstruction of these arguments reveals that Berkeley almost certainly wrote the first of these dialogues to shore up the sketchy arguments for idealism that appear in the first four sections of *A Treatise Concerning the Principles of Human Knowledge* (1710), and that the most important conceptual tool at the heart of Berkeley's case for idealism is the distinction between mediate and immediate perception first discussed in his *An Essay Towards a New Theory of Vision* (1709).

In the summer of 2007, I sat down to write what I thought would be a long article or short book reconstructing Berkeley's argument for idealism. By April 2008, I had a draft of the manuscript that was longer than I had expected. At first, I thought I had accurately identified what I took to be the main fallacy in the argument. But after benefiting from very helpful and constructive feedback from numerous sources over several years, I realized that what I took to be a fallacy was in fact a useful illustration rather than an invalid argument. This opened up the possibility that Berkeley's argument is valid, even sound. I now take this possibility very seriously, and I hope that you, dear reader, will do so too.

My intellectual debts in the service of this project are many. I have presented some of the ideas in this book to different audiences: the History of Philosophy Roundtable at UCSD (on various occasions), a faculty colloquium at UC Santa Barbara (May 2006), the Third Biennial Margaret Dauler Wilson Conference (UCSD, June 2006), the Southwest Seminar in Early Modern Philosophy (UCSD, February 2007), a meeting of the International Berkeley Society at the Eastern APA (December 2007), an International Berkeley Society conference (Newport, June 2008), a faculty colloquium at Cornell University (September 2009), an International Berkeley Society conference commemorating the 300th anniversary of the publication of the *Principles* (Neuchâtel, April 2010), the Thomas Rukavina Lecture on the History of Philosophy at Gonzaga University (April 2010), a colloquium at Charles University (Prague, July 2010), a colloquium at UCSD (April 2011), an International Berkeley Society conference (Zürich, June 2011), and an Author Meets Critics session on Georges Dicker's *Berkeley's Idealism: A Critical Examination* at the Central APA (February 2012). I thank all the organizers of these events and the members of the audiences for their questions and comments, particularly Timo Airaksinen, Tony Anderson, Dick Arneson, Margaret Atherton, Bertil Belfrage, Laura Berchielli, Dominique Berlioz, Talia Bettcher, Martha Bolton, Seth Bordner, Shoshana Brassfield, Wolfgang Breidert, Tad Brennan, David Brink, Dick Brook, Janet Broughton, Tony Brueckner, Geneviève Brykman, Craig Callender, John Carriero, Sébastien Charles, Andrew Chignell, Jonathan Cohen, Steve Daniel, Georges Dicker, Matti Eklund, Kevin Falvey, Keota Fields, Gail Fine, Melissa Frankel, Dan Garber, Carl Ginet, Richard Glauser, Petr Glombicek, Sean Greenberg, Rick Grush, Heta Gylling, Jani Hakkarainen, Matt Hanser, Michael Hardimon, Marc Hight, Benjamin Hill, James Hill, Harold Hodes, Paul

Hoffman, Tom Holden, Matthew Holtzman, Laurent Jaffro, Nick Jolley, Monte Johnson, Dan Kaufman, Nancy Kendrick, Mark Kulstad, Sukjae Lee, Tom Lennon, Ruth Mattern, Ed McCann, Jeff McDonough, Genevieve Migely, Dick Miller, Alan Nelson, Larry Nolan, Walter Ott, George Pappas, Silvia Parigi, Ville Paukkonen, Kenny Pearce, Derk Pereboom, Luc Peterschmitt, Wayne Pomerleau, Lewis Powell, Timothy Quandt, David Raynor, Michael Rescorla, John Russell Roberts, Thomas Rukavina, Don Rutherford, Nathan Salmon, Katia Saporiti, Erik Schmidt, Daniel Schulthess, Claire Schwartz, Robert Schwartz, Lisa Shapiro, Gila Sher, Sydney Shoemaker, Nicholas Silins, Pietr Szalek, Tom Stoneham, Erin Taylor, Clinton Tolley, John Troyer, Jim Van Cleve, Eric Watkins, John Whipple, Catherine Wilson, and Ken Winkler. My apologies to those scholars whose contributions to this project I may have inadvertently omitted. For corresponding with me about various issues related to the project, I thank Margaret Atherton, Martha Bolton, Seth Bordner, Steve Daniel, Georges Dicker, Melissa Frankel, Richard Glauser, Marc Hight, James Hill, Laurent Jaffro, George Pappas, Kenny Pearce, David Raynor, Katia Saporiti, and Catherine Wilson. Had it not been for their probing questions and generous comments, this book might never have seen the light of day. I am particularly grateful to those philosophers whose views are criticized in the pages of this book but who have shown me nothing but grace, kindness, and good humor, namely Martha Bolton, Steve Daniel, Georges Dicker, George Pappas, Tom Stoneham, and Ken Winkler.

I gratefully acknowledge permission from the publisher to use material from the following publication:

Chapter 3: "The Relation Between Anti-Abstractionism and Idealism in Berkeley's Metaphysics," *British Journal for the History of Philosophy* 20 (2012): 723–40.

Completing this project would not have been possible if I had not received the support of students, colleagues, friends, and family. I am grateful to Erin Frykholm, who as a graduate student served as my research assistant in summer 2005, tracking down sources and summarizing secondary literature. The UCSD philosophy department and administration granted me a two-quarter sabbatical leave in fall 2007 and winter 2008, most of which I used to write the first draft of the manuscript. In summer 2007, my family and I spent a glorious two weeks at Whitehall, the house on the outskirts of Newport, Rhode Island that Berkeley designed and in which he lived from 1729 to 1733, while he was waiting to hear whether King George II and the English Parliament would deliver the funds he was seeking to build a college in Bermuda. I served as docent, giving tours and watching over the property, all with the kind permission of the officers of the International Berkeley Society and the delightful representatives of The National Society of The Colonial Dames of America in The State of Rhode Island and Providence Plantations, notably Nancy Bredbeck and Margo Stapleton. My friends, Eduardo Arredondo, Meghan Bach, David Foldi, Nancy Foldi, Jill Green, Lindsay Grubensky, Mike Grubensky, Lauren Macdonald, Elissa McBride, Kelly Moore, Mike Moore, Jennifer Phelps, Jerry Phelps, Laurie Pieper, Zoltan Sarda, Doug Schauer, Kelly Schauer, Damon Silvers, Tiveeda Stovall, and Roxyanne Young helped keep me sane as I lost myself in the intricate details of Berkeley's arguments. The love and support of my family was beyond compare: my wife's stepmother, Sue Metzner, and her husband, David Metzner, sent me sweet gifts and care packages from Vermont and beautiful western Massachusetts; my mother-in-law, Nancy Morais, her husband, Lee Morais, my sister-in-law, Karen Nelkin Brandao, and my brother-in-law, John Brandao, welcomed me into their homes with smiles, warmth, and hope; my mother, Regina Sarfaty Rickless, my sister, Sarah Baker, and my brother-in-law, Matt Baker, sent me words of encouragement; my daughters, Sophie and Alice, laughed at my jokes, read *Harry Potter* with me, made chocolate chip scones and lemon bars, and took it in their stride when I insisted that the sensible world might be nothing but an intricate collection of ideas; and my wife, colleague, and soul-mate, Dana Kay Nelkin, read every word of the book, provided me with precious feedback and insightful comments, kept my spirits up throughout the reviewing process, and brings magic to every moment of my life.

# Contents

# Note to the Reader

All references to Berkeley's writings are to *The Works of George Berkeley, Bishop of Cloyne*, edited by A. A. Luce and T. E. Jessop, 9 vols. (London: Thomas Nelson, 1948–57). Passages are cited by a "W," followed by the relevant volume number, followed by a colon, followed by the relevant page number. Thus, "W4: 134" refers to page 134 of the fourth volume of the *Works*. In the works that have been divided into sections, such as the *Notebooks* (also known as *Philosophical Commentaries*, abbreviated as "N"), *An Essay Towards a New Theory of Vision* (abbreviated as "NTV"), *A Treatise Concerning the Principles of Human Knowledge* (abbreviated as "PHK"), the Introduction to the *Principles* (abbreviated as "I"), *The Theory of Vision . . . Vindicated* (abbreviated as "TVV"), and *A Defence of Free-Thinking in Mathematics* (abbreviated as "DFM"), I have also cited the work by its abbreviation and section number. In addition, I have abbreviated the *Three Dialogues Between Hylas and Philonous* as "DHP," followed by the number of the relevant dialogue, and *Alciphron* as "ALC," followed by the number of the relevant dialogue, a colon, and the relevant section number. Thus, a passage from "ALC 4:9; W3: 152" may be found in the ninth section of the fourth dialogue of *Alciphron*, on page 152 of the third volume of the *Works*.

# Introduction

Idealism is the view that sensible objects (such as tables and chairs, apples and pears) and their sensible properties (such as shape and color) are nothing more than mind-dependent entities, i.e., things that depend for their existence on the existence of some mind or minds.[1] Immaterialism is the view that there is no such thing as material substance, that there is no senseless, unperceiving thing in which sensible properties inhere. George Berkeley is an idealist, for he holds quite explicitly that sensible objects are nothing but collections of ideas, and that ideas cannot exist unperceived; and he is also an immaterialist, for he maintains that matter is necessarily non-existent.

Among the various philosophical positions one could take on the nature of the sensible world, idealism and immaterialism are surely the most widely derided and dismissed. David Hume, in many other ways Berkeley's intellectual successor, captured this attitude for posterity in characterizing Berkeley's arguments for these views as "admit[ting] of no answer

---

[1] For many, idealism is the thesis that the only kinds of things there are in the world are minds and ideas. Call this view "ID2" and the sense of idealism described in the text "ID1." Berkeley infers ID2 from ID1 on the strength of the following argument: if sensible objects are nothing but collections of ideas and the only kinds of things there are in the world are minds, ideas, and sensible objects, then the only kinds of things there are in the world are minds and ideas. Given that ID2 follows in this way from ID1, it makes sense to identify ID1 as idealism *par excellence*.

Some materialists might argue, or be brought to accept (as Hylas does at the end of DHP 1; W2: 206), that "[a]ll material things... are in themselves insensible." On such a view, there are unthinking, mind-independent, insensible things (namely, material substances); and if this is so, then (ID2) does not follow from (ID1). Berkeley's reaction to this view is that it is contrary to common sense inasmuch as it leads to skepticism (DHP 1; W2: 206), and that, in conjunction with the belief (widely accepted by materialists) that our ideas of material substances represent (and hence, resemble) those substances, it contravenes the axiomatic "likeness principle," namely, that "an idea can be like nothing but an idea" (PHK 8; W2: 44). (There is more discussion of the likeness principle in the chapters to follow.)

and produc[ing] no conviction."[2] Nowadays few philosophers (and even fewer non-philosophers) are willing to endorse the ideality and immateriality of such things as tables and stones.[3] Perhaps this is because the view seems so easy to refute. As James Boswell reports in *The Life of Samuel Johnson* (1791):

> After [Johnson and I] came out of the church, we stood talking for some time together of Bishop Berkeley's ingenious sophistry to prove the non-existence of matter, and that every thing in the universe is merely ideal. I observed, that though we are satisfied his doctrine is not true, it is impossible to refute it. I shall never forget the alacrity with which Johnson answered, striking his foot with mighty force against a large stone, till he rebounded from it, 'I refute it *thus*.'[4]

Charitable scholars of Berkeley are fond of pointing out, rightly, that Johnson's famous toe-poke does not establish the falsity of idealism, for Berkeley has the resources to explain why, within an idealistic metaphysics, it makes perfect sense for the kinaesthetic sensation of driving one's foot towards a stone should be followed by the sensation of hardness (and pain). But when they are asked to explain *why* Berkeley is convinced of the truth of idealism and immaterialism, scholars, perhaps surprisingly, provide very different answers. Some argue that Berkeley takes idealism to be self-evident, that anyone who considers and understands the relevant proposition can see that it is true. Others, by far the majority, claim (in my view, rightly) that Berkeley accepts idealism on the strength of a deductive argument. But scholars who think that Berkeley reasons his way to idealism have reached no consensus on the argument they take to lie at the foundation of his metaphysical system. For some, Berkeley comes to accept idealism on the strength of his prior acceptance of immaterialism. Others take this to be the reverse of the truth: as they see it, Berkeley's defense of immaterialism depends on his prior acceptance of idealism. A significant number of commentators claim that Berkeley's acceptance of idealism depends on his denial of the scholastic and Lockean doctrine of abstraction, according to which it is possible for the mind to separate ideas that are joined in experience and to consider ideas apart from their particular determinations. But these scholars do not agree on the *way* in which Berkeley's idealism is supposed to depend on his anti-abstractionism.

---

[2] See Hume (1999, 203, fn. 32).
[3] Adams (2007) is a notable exception.
[4] See Boswell (1791/2008, 248).

Yet others do not find Berkeley's reasons for idealism in his hostility to materialism or abstractionism: rather, they find these reasons in his acceptance of the likeness principle, according to which an idea can be like nothing but an idea.

The main purpose of this book is to settle this debate by providing a complete logical reconstruction of Berkeley's argument for idealism. As I argue, Berkeley's argument depends neither on his immaterialism nor on the likeness principle.[5] Moreover, the argument both depends on and entails anti-abstractionist principles, without succumbing to the fallacy of circularity. The key to Berkeley's argument for idealism lies in his distinction between mediate and immediate sense perception, a distinction with which Berkeley scholars are familiar, but that none has identified as lying at the heart of his reasons for holding that sensible objects are mind-dependent.

An accurate reconstruction of Berkeley's argument for idealism solves the following historical puzzle. Berkeley first announces his acceptance of idealism in *A Treatise Concerning the Principles of Human Knowledge* (PHK: 1710), and a mere three years later repeats his acceptance of the same doctrine in *Three Dialogues Between Hylas and Philonous* (DHP: 1713). Many of the arguments that appear in PHK are reproduced in DHP, clothed in different rhetorical garb. It continues to puzzle scholars *why* Berkeley published two works so similar in content a mere three years apart. According to many, Berkeley's use of the dialogue form was motivated by the desire to make his ideas more palatable and accessible. I believe that this is only part of the story. As I argue below, sometime between 1710 and 1713 Berkeley realized that the argument for idealism in PHK is inadequate. As it stands, the argument is little more than an argument sketch, based on premises that need further articulation and defense. The logical analysis undertaken in this book shows that Berkeley wrote DHP, particularly DHP 1, with the aim of filling out the insufficiently philosophically persuasive argument of PHK.

---

[5] It may be that Berkeley relies on the likeness principle to establish the more general claim that all *unthinking things* are mind-dependent (=ID2; see note 1 above). The claim I defend below is that Berkeley does not rely on the likeness principle to establish the narrower claim that all *sensible things* are mind-dependent (=ID1; see note 1 above). It should be noted that even if Berkeley were incapable of establishing (ID2), it would still be an enormous philosophical achievement to establish (ID1). For the (narrower) claim that sensible things (such as tables and chairs) are mind-dependent flies in the face of received philosophical wisdom, both the wisdom of Berkeley's day and the wisdom of our own times.

Before describing the plan of this study, I would like to draw attention to its main methodological features. The logical reconstruction offered in this book presupposes, as I have said, that Berkeley's main support for idealism takes the form of a deductive argument. In saying this, I do not mean to suggest that this argument exhausts the sources of support that Berkeley identifies as favoring idealism over its main philosophical alternatives. Much of what Berkeley writes in PHK and DHP is devoted to explaining the relative explanatory advantages of idealism over materialism, to attacking the coherence and truth of materialism, or to addressing apparent difficulties that arise for those who accept idealism. All of this is designed to strengthen Berkeley's overall case for idealism by providing indirect support for it. (This kind of support is indirect because the truth of idealism does not follow from the fact that its main theoretical competitor is false or incoherent, that it has significant explanatory virtues, or that it can parry serious objections.) But this study supposes, on the basis of textual evidence discussed in the pages to follow, that Berkeley offers us a direct, deductive argument for idealism based on premises he assumes his philosophical contemporaries could not reasonably reject. This is the argument I am interested in reconstructing, in large part because its soundness would leave Berkeley's philosophical opponents no alternative but to accept that idealism is true.

The plan of the book is as follows. In chapter 1, I discuss the distinction that lies at the heart of Berkeley's argument for idealism: the difference between mediate and immediate perception. Berkeley first introduces this distinction (in print) in his *Essay Towards a New Theory of Vision* (NTV: 1709), and continues to rely on it in his later works on vision, including the fourth dialogue of *Alciphron* (ALC: 1732) and *The Theory of Vision, Vindicated and Explained* (TVV: 1733). As Berkeley scholars agree, the distinction plays an integral role in the main argument of NTV, an argument designed to establish (1) that (and how) the distance, magnitude, and situation of objects are perceived by sight, and (2) that the objects of sight and touch are both numerically distinct and different in kind. But scholars disagree about the nature of the distinction. For some[6] it is fundamentally epistemic, for others[7] it is fundamentally psychological.

---

[6] See, e.g., Dicker (1982; 1992; 2006).
[7] See, e.g., Pitcher (1977), Winkler (1989), Atherton (1990), and Pappas (2000).

As I argue, the latter position is correct, but not for the reasons given by the scholars who support it.

In chapter 2, I argue that a proper understanding of the nature of the distinction between mediate and immediate perception helps us solve a textual conundrum at the heart of Berkeley's theory of perception. In some places, Berkeley suggests that sensible objects are immediately perceived. But in other places, Berkeley seems to commit to the thesis that sensible objects are only mediately, and not immediately, perceived. Upon reflection, it turns out that the truth is complicated: for Berkeley some sensible objects are immediately perceived, while others are only mediately perceived. This explains the appearance of contradiction in the texts cited on both sides of the debate.

In chapter 3, I analyze the argument for idealism sketched in the opening sections of PHK. I begin by criticizing the reasons that have been given for thinking that Berkeley finds idealism self-evident.[8] I go on to argue that Berkeley does not attempt to base idealism on immaterialism; in fact, Berkeley's opposition to materialism is founded on a premise that would make it unnecessary for him to argue from immaterialism to idealism.[9] I argue further that Berkeley's idealism does not simply fall out of the (argument for) anti-abstractionism defended in the Introduction to PHK.[10] I also claim that Berkeley's reasons for invoking the likeness principle do not extend to providing ways of filling in his argument for idealism.[11] The true function of the likeness principle in Berkeley's theory lies rather in combating versions of the representative theory of perception adopted by many of his immediate predecessors and contemporaries (including Descartes and Locke).

Ultimately, careful scrutiny of the early sections of PHK reveals a sketch of two Simple Arguments for idealism. The First Simple Argument (found in PHK 4) has two premises and a conclusion that follows from them:

*First Simple Argument*
  Sensible objects are perceived by sense.
  Anything that is perceived by sense is an idea.
So, Sensible objects are ideas.

---

[8] See Fogelin (2001).
[9] See Allaire (1963; 1982; 1995), Cummins (1963), Watson (1963), Hausman (1984), and Wilson (1995).
[10] See Pappas (1985), Atherton (1987), and Bolton (1987).
[11] See Winkler (1989).

The Second Simple Argument (which is implicit in PHK 1) also has two premises and a conclusion that follows validly from them:

> *Second Simple Argument*
> Sensible objects are collections of sensible qualities.
> All sensible qualities are ideas.
> So, Sensible objects are collections of ideas.

Given that it is far from self-evident, and that it would beg the question against many of Berkeley's materialist contemporaries to claim, that everything that is perceived by sense is an idea (= second premise of the first Simple Argument) or that sensible objects are nothing more than collections of sensible qualities (= first premise of the second Simple Argument), it is no surprise that PHK was widely derided (even as it was also widely misunderstood) upon its publication.

It is commonly thought that, in addition to the argument(s) for idealism that can be found in the early sections of PHK, Berkeley offers a "Master Argument" for idealism in PHK 23 that does not rely on previously established assumptions. The thought is that the ideality of sensible objects is somehow supposed to follow from the fact that it is impossible to conceive such objects existing unconceived. In the last section of chapter 3, I argue that Berkeley does not mean the Master Argument to be an autonomous argument for idealism. Properly analyzed, the Master Argument relies on the assumption (call it the "Idea Schema") that every object of conception is an idea, an assumption Berkeley takes himself to have established in the early sections of PHK. After the publication of PHK, as I argue, Berkeley comes to realize that there is no adequate defense of the Idea Schema in PHK, and it is in part in order to defend the Idea Schema that Berkeley writes DHP 1.

In chapter 4, I provide a complete reconstruction of the sophisticated argument for idealism in DHP 1 that fills out the two Simple Arguments and the Master Argument that appear in PHK. Critical to the sophisticated argument, but not to the earlier arguments, is the distinction between mediate and immediate perception that is drawn in NTV and that appears, with insufficient emphasis, in PHK. There are two parts to Berkeley's reasoning. In the first part, Berkeley argues that sensible objects are nothing but collections of sensible qualities. In the second part, he argues that sensible qualities are nothing but mind-dependent ideas. From these two claims it then follows directly that sensible objects are nothing but collections of ideas, and hence that sensible objects are all mind-dependent. While much scholarly attention has been lavished on the argument for the claim that sensible qualities (such as color and shape) are ideas, hardly any attention has been paid to the case for the claim that sensible objects are nothing but collections of qualities. This is unfortunate, because the argument for the latter claim is just as crucial as the argument for the former: if either one of Berkeley's two main claims is false, the DHP argument for idealism collapses.

Here is the basic structure of the argument for the claim that sensible objects are collections of qualities. Berkeley begins (as he does in PHK) by defining a sensible object as an object that is perceived by means of the senses. He then argues that anything that is perceived by means of the senses is *immediately* perceived, and then points out that the objects of *immediate* sense perception are nothing but sensible qualities and collections thereof. From these premises (i.e., that sensible objects are perceived by sense, that anything perceived by sense is immediately perceived, and the objects of immediate sense perception are nothing but sensible qualities and collections thereof), it follows that sensible objects are nothing but sensible qualities or collections thereof. But sensible objects (such as tables and chairs) are surely not to be identified with *individual* sensible qualities. Therefore sensible objects are nothing but collections of sensible qualities.

There is a great deal of controversy surrounding the basic structure of Berkeley's argument for the claim that every sensible quality is nothing but an idea. For most, Berkeley's reasons for accepting this claim lie (at least partly) in principles about perceptual variation (such as that the same object can be perceived as large from one angle but small from another, sweet by one palate but bitter by another). But, as I argue, this is a mistake.[12] Rather, Berkeley's argument for the claim that sensible qualities are ideas depends on the distinction between primary qualities (such as shape, size, motion, solidity, and extension) and secondary qualities (colors, smells, sounds, tastes, and tangible qualities). Berkeley begins by identifying all secondary qualities with hedonic sensations (pleasures or pains), notes that hedonic sensations are all mind-dependent ideas, and concludes that secondary qualities are ideas. Then, on the strength of the claim that

---

[12] Here I agree with Muehlmann (1992).

secondary qualities are mentally, and hence metaphysically, inseparable from primary qualities, Berkeley concludes that primary qualities must also be mind-dependent ideas. It then follows directly that all sensible qualities, both primary and secondary, must be mind-dependent ideas. At no point in this argument does Berkeley rely on any facts about perceptual variation. These facts (as Berkeley himself recognizes in PHK) establish no more than that materialists are not entitled to suppose that sensible objects have the sensible qualities we perceive them to have.

This reconstruction of Berkeley's argument for the claim that sensible qualities are ideas brings out two important points beyond the fact that Berkeley does not base his argument for idealism on facts about perceptual variation. First, the argument is only as good as the argument for the claim that secondary qualities are hedonic sensations. For many, this is exactly where the argument is weak. As I will argue, this is exactly where the argument is strong. Second, the argument both relies on, and entails, anti-abstractionist conclusions. For, on the one hand, the argument relies on the fact that primary and secondary qualities are mentally inseparable; and, on the other hand, the argument, when combined with the argument for the claim that sensible objects are nothing but collections of qualities, establishes the crucial anti-abstractionist conclusion that the idea of existence (at least in the case of sensible objects) cannot be mentally separated from the idea of being perceived.

Is Berkeley's argument for idealism successful? Sophisticated and impressive as it is, the argument is potentially vulnerable to the fallacy of equivocation. Fundamental to the argument are two claims: that all sensible objects are perceived by sense, and that everything that is perceived by sense is immediately perceived. From these two claims it follows that all sensible objects (including, of course, tables and chairs) are immediately perceived, *as long as the phrase "perceived by sense" is treated univocally*. However, as I point out in the Conclusion, the relevant phrase can be understood in two ways. On one reading (call it the "Whole" interpretation), to say that an object is perceived by sense is to say that it is perceived *wholly* by sense, i.e., that it is perceived by sense and not by means of any other mental faculty. On another reading (call it the "Part" interpretation), to say that an object is perceived by sense is to say that it is perceived *in part but not wholly* by sense, i.e., that it is perceived by sense and also by means of another mental faculty. The worry is that the claim that sensible objects are perceived by sense is only uncontroversially true on the "Part" interpretation, while the claim that everything that is perceived by sense is immediately perceived is only uncontroversially true on the "Whole" interpretation. So if the two claims are read in such a way as to be *uncontroversially* true, Berkeley's argument for idealism commits the fallacy of equivocation.

As I will argue, Berkeley struggled with this problem, though not in these terms, for a number of years, taking different positions in three key works, NTV, DHP, and TVV. In NTV, Berkeley adopts the "Part" interpretation, at a time before he has developed a complete argument for idealism. In DHP, Berkeley retains the "Part" interpretation, but also recognizes that this interpretation renders it false to claim that everything perceived by sense is immediately perceived. His solution is to say that the falsity of this principle does not matter, for the only sorts of circumstances in which the principle is false presuppose the truth of idealism. But in TVV Berkeley sees that this solution won't do, and consequently abandons the "Part" interpretation for the "Whole" interpretation. The problem at this point is not the falsity of the principle, but rather the controversial nature of the claim that sensible objects are perceived by sense. For it is hardly obvious to materialists that sensible things (such as tables and chairs) are perceived *wholly* by sense. Still, Berkeley's move to the "Whole" interpretation both saves his argument from unsoundness and poses a significant challenge to his materialist opponents. For it is now up to them to explain both that and how it is possible for us to perceive such things as tables and chairs at least in part by means of a mental faculty other than the senses.

I conclude that Berkeley's argument for idealism, though not a knock-down argument, achieves some measure of dialectical success, inasmuch as it renders it difficult for his intellectual contemporaries and successors to hold the view that sensible objects are mind-independent. This is Berkeley's most enduring philosophical legacy.

# 1

# Mediate and Immediate Perception

The main purpose of the *Essay Towards a New Theory of Vision* (NTV) is to explain how human minds perceive distance, magnitude, and situation by sight. Berkeley's explanation turns on a distinction that will play a crucial role in his subsequent (sophisticated) proof of idealism, namely the distinction between mediate and immediate perception. My aim in this chapter is to explicate this distinction and clarify the role it plays in Berkeley's theory of perception.

I begin by discussing the function of the mediate/immediate distinction in the argumentative context of NTV. I then consider and criticize four different accounts of the relevant distinction. According to one prominent psychological account (defended by Winkler (1989) and Atherton (1990)) immediate perception amounts to perception without suggestion or inference. According to a different equally influential psychological account (defended by Pappas (2000)), immediate perception is roughly perception without intermediary or suggestion. On yet another psychological account (defended by Pitcher (1977)), Berkeley operates with two inequivalent ways of characterizing immediate perception: one similar to Winkler's (i.e., perception without suggestion or inference), another similar to the first part of Pappas's (i.e., perception without intermediary). All three of these psychological accounts contrast with epistemic accounts that *define* immediate perception as the kind of perception that can deliver knowledge of the existence and nature of what is perceived. According to Dicker (1982; 1992; 2006), Berkeley relies on such an epistemic account while also relying on a psychological account (i.e., perception without inference), sometimes conflating the two accounts to the detriment of his arguments for idealism and immaterialism. As I will argue, Berkeley understands immediate perception to be no more than perception without intermediary, a conception that may be *equated* with the conception of perception without suggestion and that *entails* (though it is not entailed by) the conception of perception without inference.

# 1  The Main Argument of the *New Theory of Vision*

In NTV, Berkeley argues that distance, magnitude, and situation are mediately, but not immediately, perceived by sight. I will concentrate on the perception of distance, in large part because Berkeley's position on the perception of magnitude and situation resembles his position on the perception of distance.

Berkeley begins by arguing that distance is not immediately perceived by sight:

It is, I think, agreed by all that distance, of itself and immediately, cannot be seen. For distance being a line directed end-wise to the eye, it projects only one point in the fund of the eye, which point remains invariably the same, whether the distance be longer or shorter. (NTV 2; W1: 171)

This argument is echoed in DHP and in ALC:

Phil: Is not *distance* a line turned endwise to the eye?
Hyl: It is.
Phil: And can a line so situated be perceived by sight?
Hyl: It cannot.
Phil: Doth it not therefore follow that distance is not properly and immediately perceived by sight?
Hyl: It should seem so. (DHP 1; W2: 202)

Euph: Tell me, Alciphron, is not distance a line turned endwise to the eye?
Alc: Doubtless.
Euph: And can a line, in that situation, project more than one single point on the bottom of the eye?
Alc: It cannot.
Euph: Therefore the appearance of a long and of a short distance is of the same magnitude, or rather of no magnitude at all, being in all cases one single point.
Alc: It seems so.
Euph: Should it not follow from hence that distance is not immediately perceived by the eye?
Alc: It should. (ALC 4.8; W3: 150)

There are several points to notice about the argument. The first point is that, in NTV and ALC, but not in DHP, Berkeley drops the reference to *proper* perception, while keeping the reference to *immediate* perception. The concept of a proper or special object of perception derives from Aristotle, who defines it thus:

> I call by the name of special object of this or that sense that which cannot be perceived by any other sense than that one and in respect of which no error is possible; in this sense color is the special object of sight, sound of hearing, flavor of taste.[1]

As Aristotle sees it, an object of perception that is not proper or special to a single sense is a common sensible:

> [Of the kinds of objects that are perceptible in themselves] one consists of what is special to a single sense, the other of what is common to any and all of the senses...Common sensibles are movement, rest, number, figure, magnitude; these are not special to any one sense, but are common to all.[2]

The fact that Berkeley does not ever explicitly define what he means by *proper* perception, combined with the fact that the Aristotelian distinction between proper and common sensibles is well known to Berkeley and his contemporaries, strongly suggests that Berkeley simply takes over the proper/common distinction from Aristotle. On this view, then, for an object O to be *properly* perceived by means of sense S is for O to be perceived by means of S and for O to be unperceivable by means of any sense other than S.[3]

The question then arises whether Berkeley takes immediate perception to be definitionally equivalent to proper perception. If the answer is yes, then the reference to proper perception in the DHP version of the argument is redundant. If the answer is no, then there is no straightforward redundancy; but there may still be extensional redundancy on Berkeley's view if immediate perception is both necessary and sufficient for proper perception. (We will return to this issue below.) For the moment, I will drop the reference to proper perception because Berkeley himself does so.

The second and more important point is that the DHP version of the argument, strictly understood, is invalid. The argument is this:

> Distance is a line turned endwise to the eye.
> A line turned endwise to the eye cannot be perceived by sight.

---

[1]   *De Anima* 418a11–14 (Barnes 1984, vol. 1, 665).

[2]   *De Anima* 418a10–11, 418a17–19 (Barnes 1984, vol. 1, 665).

[3]   On this, see Pappas (2000, 170–1).

So, Distance is not immediately perceived by sight.

The problem is that the conclusion does not follow from the premises.

There are two ways to read the relevant passage without supposing that Berkeley's reasoning is fallacious. The first is to suppose that Berkeley misstates his conclusion as the claim that distance is not *immediately* perceived by sight, when he really means to endorse the conclusion that distance is not perceived by sight. In that case the argument would look like this:

> Distance is a line turned endwise to the eye.
> A line turned endwise to the eye cannot be perceived by sight.
> So, Distance is not perceived by sight.

The second is to suppose that Berkeley misstates his second premise as the claim that a line turned endwise to the eye cannot be perceived by sight, when he really means to endorse the assumption that a line turned endwise to the eye cannot be *immediately* perceived by sight. In that case, the argument would look like this:

> Distance is a line turned endwise to the eye.
> A line turned endwise to the eye cannot be immediately perceived
>    by sight.
> So, Distance is not immediately perceived by sight.

As between these two alternatives, it is clear that the latter is superior to the former. For Berkeley's first purpose in NTV is to show "the manner wherein we perceive by sight the distance . . . of objects" (NTV 1; W1: 171); and, as he emphasizes, "it is plain that distance is in its own nature imperceptible, and yet it is perceived by sight" (NTV 11; W1: 173). So Berkeley denies the conclusion of the first way of restating the argument, and is therefore most charitably read as meaning to put forward the second way of restating it.

A third important point concerns the support Berkeley finds for the argument's premises. As is well known, Berkeley's definition of distance is orthodox and closely resembles the definition provided by his contemporary, William Molyneux, in his *Dioptrica Nova*:

*Distance* of it self, is not to be perceived; for 'tis a Line (or a Length) presented to our Eye with its End towards us, which must therefore be only a *Point*, and that is *Invisible*.[4]

---

[4]  See Molyneux (1692, 113).

But this passage suggests more than just agreement on definitions: Molyneux provides an *argument* for the conclusion that distance *of itself* is invisible, a conclusion that corresponds to Berkeley's conclusion that distance is not an immediate object of sight. Molyneux reasons that a line that is turned endwise to the eye presents itself to the organ of sight as a point, that points are invisible, and hence that such a line is *of itself* invisible. Berkeley reasons similarly in NTV and ALC, claiming that a line turned endwise to the eye, whether long or short, projects a single point on the fund of the eye (i.e., the retina), that a single point is of "no magnitude at all," and hence is immediately invisible.

Berkeley's argument is best read as follows:

O can be immediately perceived by sight only if what O projects on the retina has magnitude.

A line turned endwise to the eye projects a point on the retina.

Points have no magnitude.

So, A line turned endwise to the eye cannot be immediately perceived by sight.

The driving assumption behind Berkeley's reasoning is that something becomes immediately visible only if what it projects on the retina has magnitude. The justification for the latter claim presumably lies in scientific experiment, which finds a straightforward lawlike connection between immediate invisibility and either no projection or dimensionless projection on the retina.[5]

So Berkeley's argument, properly understood, rests on the empirical assumption that it is a necessary condition for the immediate perception of an object that the object project something with magnitude on the retina. However, whether this assumption is justified depends at least in part on what Berkeley means by "immediate perception."

To gain a proper understanding of Berkeley's distinction between mediate and immediate perception, it helps to look at how he deploys the distinction in the rest of NTV. Having established that distance is not immediately perceivable by sight, Berkeley infers from the fact that we see distance that distance must be mediately perceived by sight:

---

[5] For a similar interpretation with a slightly different emphasis (namely, a discussion of Berkeley's solution of the problem of the inverted retinal image at NTV 88–100; W1: 206–12), see Atherton (1990, 144–8). For a different interpretation, see Armstrong (1960).

Now, from sec. 2 it is plain that distance is in its own nature imperceptible, and yet it is perceived by sight. It remains, therefore, that it be brought into view by means of some other idea that is it self immediately perceived in the act of vision. (NTV 11; W1: 173)

As Berkeley suggests, for something O to be mediately perceived by sense S is for O to be perceived by immediately perceiving something other than O.

Berkeley provides several analogies designed to help the reader understand the concept of mediate perception. For example, he writes:

It is evident that when the mind perceives any idea, not immediately and of it self, it must be by the means of some other idea. Thus, for instance, the passions which are in the mind of another are of themselves to me invisible. I may nevertheless perceive them by sight, though not immediately, yet by means of the colours they produce in the countenance. We often see shame or fear in the looks of a man, by perceiving the changes of his countenance to red or pale. (NTV 9; W1: 172–3)

Berkeley's point here is not that we do not see the mental states of other people; rather it is that we see these mental states only mediately, i.e., by immediately seeing something (namely, facial coloring) that these mental states "produce." This suggests the following definition of mediate perception:

X mediately perceives O by sense S = there is something (call it "M") such that (i) O causes M and (ii) X immediately perceives M by sense S.

But this understanding of mediate perception is too narrow for Berkeley's purposes. This comes through in another passage in which Berkeley relies on the same analogy:

For I ask any man what necessary connexion he sees between the redness of a blush and shame? And yet no sooner shall he behold that colour to arise in the face of another, but it brings into his mind the idea of that passion which hath been observed to accompany it. (NTV 23; W1: 176)

What this passage makes clear is that the relation between O and M that is required for the mediate perception of O via the immediate perception of M need not be causation (or any other relation of necessary or a priori connection); it could be nothing more than a contingent and a posteriori relation arising from customary or habitual mental association.

Let us then adopt the following provisional sketch of a reconstruction of Berkeley's understanding of mediate perception:

(MP)   X mediately perceives O by sense S = there is an object M and
relation R such that (i) M is related by R to O and (ii)
X immediately perceives M by sense S.

The question that has occasioned such controversy among Berkeley
scholars is which restrictions, if any, must be placed on the nature of the
relation R for (MP) to count as true by his lights.

We can make some headway on this score by looking at Berkeley's own
theory of how distance is mediately perceived by sight. Berkeley contrasts
his own theory with the geometric theory adopted by most of his contemporaries (including Descartes and his followers). According to the
geometric theory, the mind perceives distance by sight in two ways,
depending on whether two eyes are used (binocular vision) or one eye is
used (monocular vision). In the case of binocular vision, the Cartesians
hold that the distance of a point P (when P is not too far away) is perceived
by perceiving the angle formed by the two optic axes (where one optic
axis is the straight line that lies between P and the center of one eye and the
other optic axis is the straight line that lies between P and the center of
the other eye). As Berkeley writes:

But when an object is placed at so near a distance as that the interval between the eyes
bears any sensible proportion to it, the opinion of speculative men is that the two optic
axes...concurring at the object do there make an angle, by means of which,
according as it is greater or lesser, the object is perceived to be nearer or farther off.
(NTV 4; W1: 171–2)

In the case of monocular perception, the Cartesian view is that the distance
of a point P is perceived by perceiving the angle formed by the line that lies
between P and the left edge of the pupil and the line that lies between
P and the right edge of the pupil: the greater the angle, the greater the
divergency of the lines and the nearer the object's apparent distance; the
lesser the angle, the lesser the divergency of the lines and the farther the
object's apparent distance. As Berkeley puts it:

There is another way mentioned by optic writers, whereby they will have us judge of
those distances, in respect of which the breadth of the pupil hath any sensible bigness:
And that is the greater or lesser divergency of the rays, which issuing from the visible
point do fall on the pupil, that point being judged nearest which is seen by most
diverging rays, and that remoter which is seen by less diverging rays...And after
this manner it is said we perceive distance when we look only with one eye. (NTV 6;
W1: 172)

These passages strongly suggest that, in the case of both binocular and monocular vision, Berkeley takes the Cartesians to agree with him that distance cannot be immediately seen, that distance can be seen, and hence that distance is only mediately perceived by sight. Berkeley locates the nature of his disagreement with the Cartesians in the identity of the mediating object M and in the nature of the mediating relation R. According to the Cartesians, in both binocular and monocular perception, M is an angle formed by two lines that meet at O, and the relation R that obtains between this angle and the perceived distance of O is necessary and a priori. As Berkeley emphasizes:

There appears a very necessary connexion between an obtuse angle and near distance, and an acute angle and farther distance. It does not in the least depend upon experience, but may be evidently known by any one before he had experienced it, that the nearer the concurrence of the optic axes, the greater the angle, and the remoter their concurrence is, the lesser will be the angle comprehended by them. (NTV 5; W1: 172)

Berkeley's main objection to this geometric theory of mediate perception of distance by sight is that, whereas the mediate visual perception of O by means of M requires that M be immediately perceived by sight, the angle formed by the two Cartesian lines that meet at O is not seen (whether mediately or immediately) by those who use one eye or both eyes to judge O's distance:

But those lines and angles, by means whereof some men pretend to explain the perception of distance, are themselves not at all perceived, nor are they in truth ever thought of by those unskillful in optics . . . In vain shall any man tell me that I perceive certain lines and angles which introduce into my mind the various ideas of distance, so long as I my self am conscious of no such thing. (NTV 12; W1: 173)

The reference to consciousness in this passage indicates that Berkeley is taking for granted an important assumption that his Lockean and Cartesian contemporaries also accept, namely the view that the mind is conscious of whatever it perceives, i.e., that there is no such thing as unconscious perception. This is the doctrine of the transparency of the mental.[6] His argument against the geometric theory of distance perception, at bottom, is that, whereas the mind must perceive, and hence must be conscious of, the mediating element in any mediate perception, the mind is not in fact

---

[6] See Pitcher (1977, 21–2).

conscious of any of the lines and angles that function as the mediating elements in the mediate perception of distance on the geometric theory.

Berkeley's solution is to hypothesize the following mediating elements in the monocular and binocular perception of distance: (i) the sensation that attends the alteration of "the disposition of our eyes, by lessening or widening the interval between the pupils" (NTV 16; W1: 174), (ii) the extent to which the object is perceived confusedly (NTV 21; W1: 175), and (iii) the sensation that attends the effort of straining the eye to prevent confused perception (NTV 27; W1: 176–7). In the case of binocular vision, Berkeley supposes (i) that we judge objects to be nearer when we perceive the sensation that attends the lessening of the interval between the pupils, and that we judge objects to be farther when we perceive the sensation that attends the widening of the interval between the pupils. In the case of binocular and monocular vision, Berkeley supposes (ii) that the more confused the perception of an object, the nearer it appears, and the less confused the perception, the farther the object appears, and (iii) that the more acute the sensation that attends the effort of straining the eye to prevent confused perception, the nearer the relevant object appears, and the less acute the relevant sensation, the farther the object appears. In each of these cases, as Berkeley emphasizes, the mediating elements in the perception of distance are themselves perceived (even if they are not the objects of *attention*, which is a kind of mentally focused perception). It is primarily in this respect that Berkeley finds his own theory vastly superior to the geometric theory of the Cartesians.[7]

Berkeley makes a point of contrasting his theory of the mediating relation R with the geometric account of the nature of R. On the geometric theory, R is simply the entailment relation. For example, it follows directly from the principles of geometry that the more obtuse the angle formed by the two optic axes at P, the nearer O is to the viewing subject, while the more acute the angle formed by the two optic axes at P, the farther O is to the viewing subject. But on Berkeley's theory R is identified with the relation of "suggestion," where suggestion is itself

---

[7] Berkeley mentions two further reasons for preferring his theory of distance perception to the geometric theory. The first is that his own theory can explain phenomena that the geometric theory cannot explain (see NTV 29–40; W1: 177–86). The second is that his own theory correctly predicts phenomena that the geometric theory does not predict (see NTV 41; W1: 186 and TVV 71; W1: 275–6).

characterized as a contingent and a posteriori relation established by custom or habit:

[D]istance is suggested to the mind by the mediation of some other idea which is it self perceived in the act of seeing. (NTV 16; W1: 174)

[B]ecause the mind has by constant experience found the different [mediating sensations] to be attended each with a different degree of distance in the object, there has grown an habitual or customary connexion between those two sorts of ideas, so that the mind no sooner perceives the [mediating sensation], but it withal perceives the different idea of distance which was wont to be connected with that sensation; just as upon hearing a certain sound, the idea is immediately suggested to the understanding which custom had united with it. (NTV 17; W1: 174)

Understanding Berkeley's theory of distance perception and why he finds it better than the available alternatives helps us understand what Berkeley means by "mediate" and "immediate" perception. In the first place, as Berkeley sees it, if the geometric theory were true, the mind would perceive distance *mediately*. And the fact that Berkeley classifies the geometric theory as an account of *mediate* distance perception indicates that he does not treat the fact that R is contingent and a posteriori as a *definitional* requirement on mediate perception. Second, the fact that Berkeley insists that the mediating element M in any case of mediate perception be *immediately* perceived, combined with the fact that Berkeley sees his own theory of distance perception as a theory of mediate perception, indicates that he must take sensations that attend the lessening or widening of the interval between the pupils, sensations of visual confusion, and sensations that attend the effort to strain the eyes, to be objects of *immediate* perception.

With these constraints in mind, I now turn to an examination of the most influential accounts of Berkeley's conception of the nature of the distinction between mediate and immediate perception.

## 2 How *Not* to Understand the Distinction

Most scholars who have discussed the issue hold that Berkeley's distinction between mediate and immediate perception is psychological and non-epistemic. According to Pitcher, Berkeley provides two different ways of making the distinction: on one conception, immediate perception is perception without intermediary, on the other, it is perception without suggestion or inference. According to Winkler and Atherton, the first of these two conceptions reduces to the second, and hence Berkeley operates with only one conception of immediate perception, namely perception without suggestion or inference. By contrast, according to Pappas, there is no way to reduce one conception to the other, and Berkeley does not conceive of perception mediated by inference as a form of mediate perception at all. Rather, as Pappas sees it, Berkeley's conception of immediate perception amounts roughly to perception without intermediary or suggestion. Diametrically opposed to this view is the interpretation offered by Dicker, who finds Berkeley sometimes relying on a psychological distinction according to which immediate perception reduces to perception without inference. What is particularly distinctive about Dicker's view, however, is his claim that Berkeley also sometimes draws the mediate/immediate distinction in exclusively epistemic terms, and that Berkeley relies on such an epistemic distinction to establish various metaphysical results, including idealism and immaterialism. My purpose in this section is to evaluate these interpretations, sorting through them to find what is accurate and what is inaccurate to Berkeley's intentions.

Pitcher finds Berkeley distinguishing between mediate and immediate perception in two different, inequivalent ways. According to the first way of drawing the distinction, "immediate perception of something . . . is a sensuous awareness of it that is devoid of any 'intellectual' element, such as an interpretation of the object or a belief about it," while mediate perception "requires that the person immediately perceives something and then acquires, by some kind of mental process (e.g., by inference or . . . 'suggestion') a relevant belief."[8] Pitcher illustrates the distinction as follows. Suppose that I am looking at a glowing poker that has just been removed from a roaring furnace. As Pitcher sees it, Berkeley's view is that, in one sense, I immediately perceive the poker's red color but only mediately perceive the poker's heat. The redness of the poker is something I immediately perceive because I do not undergo a mental process of suggestion or inference that issues in the belief that the poker as red. By contrast, the heat of the poker is something I mediately perceive because I undergo a mental process (of suggestion or inference) that issues in the belief that the poker is hot. Pitcher calls this kind of mediate perception

---

[8] Pitcher (1977, 9–10).

"mediate perception with inference," though it would be more accurate to describe it as "mediate perception with inference or suggestion."

According to the second way of drawing the distinction, "immediate perception of something is the perception of it without the perception of any [distinct] intermediary," while "mediate perception of something is the perception of it by first perceiving a distinct intermediary."[9] Pitcher illustrates the distinction as follows. Suppose that a lookout sees a bubbling oil slick on the surface of the ocean and infers that there is a damaged submarine below the surface. As Pitcher sees it, Berkeley's view is that, in a new and different sense of "mediate" and "immediate," the lookout immediately perceives the oil slick but only mediately perceives the submarine. The oil slick is something the lookout immediately perceives because "there is no third thing between him and the oil slick that he must first perceive in order to perceive the oil slick." By contrast, the submarine is something the lookout mediately perceives because "he sees it by first perceiving an intermediary—something wholly distinct from it—namely, the bubbling oil slick." Pitcher calls this (second) kind of mediate perception "mediate perception with intermediary."

Pitcher claims that mediate perception with inference or suggestion is not equivalent to mediate perception with intermediary, even though every case of mediate perception with intermediary is also a case of mediate perception with inference or suggestion. The reason for the lack of equivalence is that it is possible to mediately perceive an object with inference without also mediately perceiving it with intermediary. Pitcher defends this claim by means of the following example:

Suppose you have been told by a friend that she has lost her black Persian cat, Gremlin, and that she is worried about the animal because he has injured his right front paw and limps badly. The next day, seeing a black Persian cat, obviously lost, limping badly on its right front paw, you sagely infer that the cat is none other than Gremlin. Since you made a (correct) inference from what you saw and arrived at a belief about it, clearly you mediately saw Gremlin with inference [or suggestion]. But it is not the case that you saw it only by first perceiving some intermediary— some third thing, distinct from Gremlin. You, therefore, immediately saw Gremlin without intermediary.[10]

But the example is problematic. To see why, consider that the very same case could be described as a case of mediate perception with intermediary.

---

[9] Pitcher (1977, 10).    [10] Pitcher (1977, 10–11).

For we can think of the cat's distinctive limp as one thing and the cat's identity (namely, the fact that it is Gremlin) as another. Under this description, you perceive Gremlin's identity by first perceiving an intermediary (namely, Gremlin's distinctive limp) that is wholly distinct from Gremlin himself. (Gremlin's limp is neither numerically identical to nor a part of Gremlin.) Thought of in this way, Pitcher's Gremlin example does not prove that there can be mediate perception with inference in the absence of mediate perception with intermediary.

In Pitcher's defense, it might be noted that Gremlin's limp counts as a "thing" only in an extremely general sense of the word. A limp is not a substance or even a scattered object (such as an oil slick); unlike an animal, or a rock, or an oil slick, Gremlin's limp is ontologically dependent on something (namely, Gremlin) for its existence. So, if the word "thing" is read strictly (i.e., as referring to ontologically independent entities) and the relevant intermediaries in cases of mediate perception with intermediary are stipulated to be "things" in the strict sense, then the perception of Gremlin's identity via perception of his limp is not, in fact, a case of mediate perception with intermediary. This all seems perfectly correct. But then it seems that Pitcher's distinction between "mediate perception with inference or suggestion" and "mediate perception with intermediary" is a distinction without a difference. In particular, there is no evidence to suggest that Berkeley himself conceives of the intermediaries that play a role in mediate perception as ontologically independent entities (i.e., as "things" in the strict sense). Worse, there is evidence to suggest exactly the opposite. For, as we have seen, Berkeley's own account of how we mediately perceive distance by sight allows sensations (namely, the sensations attending the widening or lessening of the distance between the pupils, and the sensations attending the straining of the eye to avoid confusion) to function as intermediaries. And yet, for Berkeley, sensations are dependent for their existence on some mind (even if they are not always dependent for their existence on a *particular* mind—see PHK 48; W2: 61).

For all Berkeley tells us, then, it may well be that, at least for him, every case of mediate perception with inference (or suggestion) is also a case of mediate perception with intermediary, and vice versa. Given that Berkeley himself does not tell us that he is working with two different ways of distinguishing between mediate and immediate perception and for all intents and purposes takes himself to employ the same distinction whenever he uses the terms "mediate" and "immediate" to refer to it, one reasonable interpretive hypothesis is that Berkeley's conception of perception with intermediary simply reduces to his conception of perception with inference or suggestion.

This is what some scholars, most notably Winkler (1989, 149–51) and Atherton (1990, 68–9, n. 12), have concluded. Winkler finds evidence at the beginning of DHP for the claim that Pitcher's two characterizations of Berkeley's conception of mediate perception come to the same thing. In a passage to which we shall return, Philonous introduces the notion of mediate perception as perception with intermediary:

*The "Two Questions" Passage*
Are those things only perceived by the senses which are perceived immediately?
  Or may those things properly be said to be *sensible*, which are perceived mediately, or not without the intervention of others? (DHP 1; W2: 174)

Twenty-seven lines later, Philonous has managed to push Hylas to answer the first question positively, seemingly on the basis of the fact that mediate perception amounts to perception with inference:

*The "Once For All" Passage*
To prevent any more questions of this kind, I tell you once for all, that by *sensible things* I mean those only which are perceived by sense, and that in truth the senses perceive nothing which they do not perceive immediately: for they make no inferences. (DHP 1; W2: 174–5)

Winkler (1989, 150) concludes that "both Hylas and Philonous take perception without intervention to be the same as perception without inference":

The two characterizations of immediate perception come to the same thing because intervention is understood not spatially, but in terms of perception itself. To perceive one object through the intervention of another is to perceive the first in virtue of perceiving the second. One object is perceived without inference or suggestion. The other is perceived or known only because it is inferred from (or suggested by) the first.[11]

As I argue below, Winkler is right to claim that Berkeley identifies perception without intervention (i.e., without intermediary) with perception without inference or suggestion. But the passages Winkler cites in defense of this interpretation are insufficiently probative. To see why, it is sufficient to note, as Winkler (1989, 150, n. 8) himself recognizes, that Berkeley explicitly distinguishes between suggestion and inference in TVV 42:

[11]   Winkler (1989, 151).

To perceive is one thing; to judge is another. So likewise, to be suggested is one thing, and to be inferred another. Things are suggested and perceived by sense. We make judgments and inferences by the understanding. (TVV 42; W1: 265)

Berkeley here takes for granted a distinction that his Lockean and Cartesian contemporaries also accepted, namely that between the faculty of sensation and the faculty of understanding, insisting that suggestion is the work of the former, while inference is the work of the latter. It follows from this distinction that perception without inference is not to be identified with perception without suggestion, and also that perception without inference does not entail perception without suggestion. In fact, as we have seen, one of the important differences between Berkeley's theory of distance perception and the geometric theory of distance perception is that, whereas on the geometric theory the relevant relation R that obtains between M and O is the relation of entailment (and hence necessary and a priori), on Berkeley's theory R is simply the relation of suggestion (and hence contingent and a posteriori). So Berkeley clearly holds that the mediate perception of distance with suggestion obtains in the absence of mediate perception of distance with inference.

Suppose now, along with Winkler, that Berkeley identifies "perception without intervention" with "perception without inference." This certainly seems to be the message of the "Once For All" passage, in which Hylas infers that "the senses perceive nothing which they do not perceive immediately" from the fact that "the senses make no inferences" (DHP 1; W2: 174–5). The problem, of course, is that the distinction between inference and suggestion means that Hylas's inference simply does not go through: from the fact that the senses make no inferences, it simply does not follow that the senses perceive nothing mediately. If, as Berkeley says in TVV 42, suggestion is the work of the senses (rather than the understanding), then it is possible for the senses to perceive things mediately *via suggestion* even though the senses cannot perceive things mediately *via inference*.

There are therefore two problems with the "Once For All" passage. The first is that the passage suggests, not that Berkeley equates perception without intermediary with perception without inference or suggestion, but rather that Berkeley equates perception without intermediary with perception without inference *tout court*. The second is that, on this reading of the passage, Hylas's inference (which Berkeley clearly means the reader to endorse) from the fact that the senses make no inferences to the claim that the senses perceive nothing mediately is straightforwardly invalid. So the passage fails to show that Berkeley equates perception without intermediary with perception without inference or suggestion. Worse, the passage suggests exactly the opposite. The "Once For All" passage therefore complicates, rather than simplifies, the relevant interpretive task. If Winkler is right (as I believe he is) that Berkeley identifies immediate perception with perception without inference or suggestion, it is not for the textual reasons he gives.

Thus far, we have considered two psychological accounts of Berkeley's theory of mediate perception. According to Pitcher, Berkeley sometimes takes mediate perception to be perception with intermediary, and sometimes takes mediate perception to be perception with inference or suggestion. According to Winkler and Atherton, Berkeley simply identifies these two conceptions, taking mediate perception to be perception with intermediary, where perception with intermediary reduces to perception with inference or suggestion. But these are not the only psychological accounts on offer. Pappas, for one, has proposed that Berkeley takes mediate perception to be perception with intermediary or suggestion. There are two distinctive features of Pappas's view: first, there is the claim that Berkeley does not reduce perception with intermediary to perception with suggestion; second, there is the claim that Berkeley does not treat perception mediated by inference to be a kind of mediate perception at all.

Pappas begins by citing the "Two Questions" passage and NTV 9 as support for the claim that Berkeley identifies immediate perception with "perception which does not require or proceed through a perceived intermediary."[12] The definition of immediate perception that Pappas attributes to Berkeley on the strength of these two passages is disjunctive: "immediately perceiving something is either immediately seeing it, or immediately touching it, or immediately hearing it, or immediately tasting it, or immediately smelling it."[13] And Pappas characterizes Berkeley's conception of immediate seeing (touching/hearing/tasting/smelling) as follows:

S immediately sees (touches/hears/tastes/smells) O = (i) S sees (touches/ hears/tastes/smells) O, and (ii) it is false that S would see (touch/hear/

---

[12] Pappas (2000, 148–9).      [13] Pappas (2000, 160).

taste/smell) O only if S were to perceive R, where R is not identical to O.[14]

But Pappas also cites NTV 16 in support of the claim that Berkeley adopts a slightly stronger (i.e., more restrictive) conception of immediate perception, according to which "immediate perception ... would be that perception not [dependent on or brought about by an element of] suggestion."[15] Pappas's final characterization of Berkeley's conception of immediate seeing (touching/hearing/tasting/smelling) thus requires the addition of a third clause:

> S immediately sees (touches/hears/tastes/smells) O = (i) S sees (touches/hears/tastes/smells) O, (ii) it is false that S would see (touch/hear/taste/smell) O only if S were to perceive R, where R is not identical to O, and (iii) it is false that S would see O only if O were to be suggested to S by R.

In sum, Pappas understands Berkeley to be working with the following definition of immediate perception:

> S immediately perceives O = S immediately sees or touches or hears or tastes or smells O (with immediate seeing/touching/hearing/tasting/smelling defined as above).[16]

The first problem with this definition is that it inverts the order of definition. Berkeley does not seek to define perception in terms of seeing/touching/hearing/tasting/smelling; rather, he seeks to define seeing/touching/hearing/tasting/smelling in terms of perception. To see an object is to perceive it by sight, to touch it is to perceive it by touch, to hear it is to perceive it by hearing, and so on. It is the notion of perception, not the notion of seeing/touching/hearing/tasting/smelling, that is fundamental to Berkeley's metaphysics and epistemology.

We can avoid this problem by changing the letter, while keeping the spirit, of Pappas's definition. The way to do this is to define immediate

---

[14] Pappas (2000, 149–50).    [15] Pappas (2000, 151).

[16] Pappas (2000, 151 and 158–9) finds Berkeley's definition wanting in several respects, and proposes epicycles to handle the problems on Berkeley's behalf. But he acknowledges that the addition of these epicycles does not result in a theory that Berkeley would have recognized as his own, given that Berkeley "never considered the problem cases and never was moved to amend" the definition described in the text (Pappas 2000: 160).

perception in terms of perception, rather than in terms of seeing/touching/ hearing/tasting/smelling, somewhat along the following lines:

> S immediately perceives O = (i) S perceives O, (ii) it is false that S would perceive O only if S were to perceive R, where R is not identical to O, and (iii) it is false that S would perceive O only if O were to be suggested to S by R.

This revised definition preserves the basic idea that animates Pappas's original definition, namely that, according to Berkeley, immediate perception is a matter of (i) perception that is (ii) without intermediary and (iii) without suggestion.

Is the revised definition accurate to Berkeley's intentions? One worry is that Pappas's reconstruction of Berkeley's definition of immediate perception includes redundancy by virtue of the fact that clause (ii) entails clause (iii). Pappas claims that the worry is unfounded, for the entailment holds in reverse:

> Consider a perception which is reached by an act of suggestion. It occurs, as mediate perception, only if some other perception occurs. Mediate perception is then some perception that would occur only if some other perception were to occur. In contrast, immediate perception would not be dependent on some other perception. The no suggestion notion [i.e., clause (iii)], then, implies that already on hand [i.e., clause (ii)]. Nevertheless, the no suggestion notion is richer, because it includes a new element [namely, clause (iii)] which . . . we should add to [the definition].[17]

Pappas claims that clause (iii) entails clause (ii), but that clause (ii) does not entail clause (iii). Consequently, Pappas finds it justified to add clause (iii) to the definition of immediate perception, acknowledging that, strictly speaking, clause (ii) is unnecessary.

In fact, however, exactly the reverse is true, as Pappas's own reasoning reveals. Suppose there is a perception that is reached only by an act of suggestion. Such a perception would be one that would occur only if another perception were to occur. Contrapositively, if it is false that perception P would occur only if another perception were to occur, then it is false that P would occur only if it were suggested by another perception. That is to say, if clause (ii) is true, then clause (iii) is true. The idea is simple. If there is suggestion, then there is an intermediary. If there is no intermediary, then there is no suggestion. So it is in fact clause

---

[17] Pappas (2000, 152).

(iii), not clause (ii), that is redundant. On Pappas's reconstruction, then, Berkeley's conception of immediate perception reduces to perception without intermediary.

Now consider clause (ii). As Pappas sees it, Berkeley equates the claim that S perceives O without intermediary with the claim that it is false that S would perceive O only if S were to perceive R, where R is not identical to O. But Pappas himself finds this equation problematic, even by Berkeley's own lights. The problem concerns the perception of idea clusters. As Pappas explains:

> Imagine a case in which an observer immediately [perceives] several visual ideas at once, perhaps a cluster of visual shapes. We want to say that she immediately [perceives] both the cluster and the individual ideas that make it up. But [Berkeley's definition of perception without intermediary] causes a problem. For it is true that the observer would [perceive] the cluster only if she were to [perceive] something other than the cluster, viz., its elements or components. The converse is also true; the observer would [perceive] the several ideas in the cluster only if she were to [perceive] the cluster.[18]

On Pappas's account of Berkeley's definition of *perception without intermediary*, it follows from the fact that the observer would perceive the cluster only if she were to perceive one of its elements that the observer does not perceive the cluster without intermediary. But then, on Pappas's account of Berkeley's definition of *immediate perception*, it follows directly that the observer does not immediately perceive the cluster. Similarly, on Pappas's account of Berkeley's definition of *perception without intermediary*, it follows from the fact that the observer would perceive one of the cluster's elements only if she were to perceive the cluster itself that the observer does not perceive any of the cluster's elements without intermediary. But then, on Pappas's account of Berkeley's definition of *immediate perception*, it follows directly that the observer does not immediately perceive any of the cluster's elements. The problem is that these two results (namely, that the observer does not immediately perceive the cluster and that the observer does not immediately perceive any of the cluster's elements) run counter to what "we want to say" about the case.

Pappas's way of avoiding this difficulty is to stipulate it away. He proposes that Berkeley's definition of perception without intermediary be revised as follows:

---

[18] Pappas (2000, 151).

> S perceives O without intermediary = it is false that S would perceive O only if S were to perceive R, where R is not identical to O *and where R is not an element or part of O, or a group of elements or parts of O, nor is O of R.*[19]

But there is a price to be paid for stipulating away the cluster counter-example in this way. To see this, consider how perception *with* intermediary would need to be defined if Pappas's revised account of perception *without* intermediary were adopted. The definition would look like this:

> S perceives O with intermediary = it is true that S would perceive O only if S were to perceive R, where R is not identical to O and where R is not an element or part of O, or a group of elements or parts of O, nor is O of R.

Now imagine that R★ *is* an element of cluster O★ and that it is precisely *by* perceiving R★ that an observer S★ perceives O★. Under these conditions, R★ functions as the *means* by which S★ perceives O★. If this situation were to occur, Berkeley would no doubt say that S★ perceives O★ *with* intermediary (namely, R★). Yet, according to Pappas's revised account of perception without intermediary, Berkeley would have to say that S★ perceives O★ *without* intermediary.

The problem is that it is a mistake to try to capture Berkeley's account of perception without intermediary in terms of the falsity of a counterfactual conditional. Berkeley himself does not use counterfactual locutions to elucidate the concept of perception without intermediary. Rather, he uses the "by" or "by means of" locution, a locution that he leaves completely unanalyzed. So, for example, as he writes: "[Distance] is brought into view *by means of* some other idea that is it self immediately perceived in the act of vision" (NTV 11; W1: 173—emphasis added). Or, as Philonous says early in DHP: "In reading a book, what I immediately perceive are the letters, but mediately, *or by means of these*, are suggested to my mind the notions of God, virtue, truth, etc." (DHP 1; W2: 174—emphasis added). There is in fact no more reason to suppose that a counterfactual analysis of Berkeley's conception of perception without intermediary succeeds than there is to suppose that a counterfactual analysis of the "by" locution succeeds generally.[20]

---

[19] Pappas (2000, 151).

[20] For alternative ways of handling the "by" locution that do not involve counterfactuals, see Thomson (1977) and Bennett (1988; 1998).

Finally, consider the notable absence of the notion of inference from Pappas's reconstruction of Berkeley's conception of mediate or immediate perception. In defense of this view, Pappas cites a passage from the "Julius Caesar" example towards the end of DHP 1. Hylas begins the exchange by insisting that, in looking at a picture of Julius Caesar, he perceives Caesar by sight. Philonous counters that Hylas's "thoughts are directed to" Caesar only by virtue of reason and memory, not by virtue of sight, for someone "who had never known any thing of Julius Caesar" would not see the picture as a picture of Caesar. Rather, such a person would see nothing more than "some colours and figures with a certain symmetry and composition of the whole" (DHP 1; W2: 203–4). Although this passage appears to suggest that Philonous thinks that Hylas mediately perceives Caesar by sight via inference, Pappas claims that the continuation of the exchange establishes exactly the opposite. As Philonous puts it:

Consequently, it will not follow from [the Caesar case] that anything is perceived by sense which is not immediately perceived. Though I grant we may, in one acceptation, be said to perceive sensible things mediately by sense: that is, when, from a frequently perceived connexion, the immediate perception of ideas by one sense *suggests* to the mind others, perhaps belonging to another sense, which are wont to be connected with them. (DHP 1; W2: 204)

As Pappas reads this passage, Berkeley identifies mediate perception with perception that is dependent on suggestion, and contrasts perception via suggestion with perception via inference. This reading meshes well with TVV 42, in which Berkeley distinguishes suggestion, which is the work of sense, from inference, which is the work of reason. The conclusion Pappas draws is that, on Berkeley's view, mediate perception does not involve inference.

For those who think that Berkeley countenances the possibility of mediate perception via inference, the "Caesar" passage (at DHP 1; W2: 204) is indeed troublesome. (We will return to it later.) But, as Pappas recognizes, there are also passages in which Berkeley appears to acknowledge the possibility of mediate perception via inference (in addition to those passages in which Berkeley acknowledges the possibility of mediate perception via suggestion). But Pappas thinks that these passages can be explained away.

Pappas explicitly considers only one such passage, which appears in DHP 2. The relevant statement belongs to Philonous:

*The "Perception of Matter" Passage*
Either you perceive the being of Matter immediately or mediately. If immediately, pray inform me by which of the senses you perceive it. If mediately, let me know by what reasoning it is inferred from those things which you perceive immediately. (DHP 2; W2: 221)

Pappas's reaction to the passage is this:

> Nor need [the "Perception of Matter" passage] be read as an endorsement of the claim that mediate perception includes or has as an ingredient an element of inference. Its last sentence can just as easily be read as asserting that if something is mediately perceived, then if we know something about it, we do so by means of an inference.[21]

Pappas finds such an interpretation consistent with a "conservative approach" to the text. But Pappas's interpretation is inconsistent with the most straightforward reading of the final sentence. Philonous says, quite clearly, that the mediate perception of matter (if it were to occur) would involve (a) the immediate perception of something (call it "M") by sense, and (b) an inference from the existence of M to the existence of matter. Such a reading of the last sentence fits neatly into our previous sketch of Berkeley's conception of mediate perception, namely (MP):

(MP)  X mediately perceives O by sense S = there is an object M and relation R such that (i) M is related by R to O and (ii) X immediately perceives M by sense S.

Perhaps more could be said on behalf of Pappas's gloss of the last sentence of the "Perception of Matter" passage, if it were not for the fact that this is not the only passage in which Berkeley implicitly or explicitly countenances the possibility of mediate perception via inference. There is, in the first place, the "Once For All" passage (see above), in which Hylas (under pressure from Philonous) infers from the fact that the senses "make no inferences" that "the senses perceive nothing which they do not perceive immediately." As we have seen, the "Once For All" passage clearly suggests that the absence of perception by means of inference is *sufficient* for the absence of mediate perception, and hence implies that Berkeley classifies perception by means of inference as one form (in fact, perhaps problematically, the *only* form) of mediate perception. Pappas's reaction to this passage is that "[w]e should be

---

[21] Pappas (2000, 156).

wary of attributing to Berkeley a definition [of immediate perception] which is only put in Hylas' terms and which is not agreed to by Philonous."[22] But this is surely to place more emphasis on the ideological differences between Hylas and Philonous than the context of the relevant passage warrants. Hylas states the propositions of the "Once For All" passage only because Philonous has badgered him to accept them. And then there are the following passages, one from the end of DHP 1 and one from ALC 4:9:

*The "Sense or Reason" Passage*
Whatever we perceive, is perceived either immediately or mediately: by sense, or by reason and reflexion. (DHP 1; W2: 205)

To me it seems that a man may know whether he perceives a thing or no; and, if he perceives it, whether it be immediately or mediately; and, if mediately, whether by means of something like or unlike, necessarily or arbitrarily connected with it. (ALC 4:9; W3: 152)

In the "Sense or Reason" passage, Philonous, who speaks for Berkeley, makes the same point that Hylas had earlier been brought to make, namely that perception by means of "reason and reflection" is necessary and sufficient for mediate perception. And in the passage from ALC 4:9, Euphranor, who also speaks for Berkeley in this context, claims that there are four different kinds of mediate perception, each a form of perception with intermediary, depending on whether the mediating element M is like, unlike, necessarily related to, or arbitrarily related to the mediately perceived object O. But, in general, at least for Berkeley, X is necessarily related to Y only when X is a cause of Y or Y is a cause of X. And the mental faculty that enables us to collect causes from effects and effects from causes is the faculty of inference. As Berkeley puts it in TVV:

We infer causes from effects, effects from causes, and properties one from another, where the connection is necessary. (TVV 42; W1: 266)

So, in countenancing a form of mediate perception in which the mediating element is necessarily related to the mediately perceived object, Berkeley's spokesmen clearly allow for the possibility of mediate perception via inference.[23]

---

[22] Pappas (2000, 170).

[23] Pappas also claims that "attribution of the above psychological notion of immediate perception [namely, the notion of perception without inference] to Berkeley ignores the way in which Berkeley himself characterizes that notion in NTV. That characterization . . . proceeds in terms of lack of perceived intermediaries and lack of suggestion, and no mention is

The provisional conclusion to be drawn from our investigation of Berkeley's concept of mediate perception at this point is that Berkeley identifies mediate perception of O with perception by means of a mediating element M that is itself immediately perceived, and that the relation R between M and O that makes mediate perception of O possible can be either contingent and a posteriori (as in Berkeley's own suggestion-based account of the mediate perception of distance by sight) or necessary and a priori (as in the geometric inference-based account of the same phenomenon).

However, there is one scholar who argues that, in addition to conceiving of mediate perception in psychological terms (specifically, as perception via inference), Berkeley also conceives of mediate perception in epistemic terms, sometimes confusing the psychological conception with the epistemic conception in ways that lead him to commit the fallacy of equivocation in some of his central arguments. Before moving on to provide a complete account of Berkeley's conception of mediate perception that makes the best sense of all the relevant texts, let us see what can be said on behalf of such an interpretation.

Consider the famous "Coach" passage from DHP 1. The passage occurs in the context of an exchange that begins with Hylas questioning a proposition to which he had earlier agreed, namely the claim that "the senses perceive nothing which they do not perceive immediately" (DHP 1; W2: 174). Using the picture-of-Caesar example described above, Hylas insists that he perceives Caesar mediately by sight. Philonous demurs, insisting that Caesar is perceived, not by sight, but by reason and memory. Philonous then concludes that "it will not follow from [the Caesar example] that any thing is perceived by sense which is not immediately perceived" (DHP 1; W2: 204). He continues:

*The "Coach" Passage*
Though I grant we may in one acceptation be said to perceive sensible things mediately by sense: that is, when from a frequently perceived connexion, the

---

there made of inference" (Pappas 2000, 170). But this is a mistake. As we have seen, part of the point of NTV is to contrast Berkeley's suggestion-based account with the geometric inference-based account of the perception of distance by sight. In the early sections of NTV, Berkeley argues that distance is not *immediately* seen, concludes from the fact that distance *is* seen that distance is *mediately* seen, presents his own suggestion-based account and the geometric inference-based account as the only live proposals for how distance is seen, and hence presupposes that *both* of these accounts (including the inference-based account) count as theories of the *mediate* perception of distance by sight.

immediate perception of ideas by one sense suggests to the mind others perhaps belonging to another sense, which are wont to be connected with them. For instance, when I hear a coach drive along the streets, immediately I perceive only the sound; but from the experience I have had that such a sound is connected with a coach, I am said to hear the coach. It is nevertheless evident, that in truth and strictness, nothing can be *heard* but *sound*: and the coach is not then properly perceived by sense, but suggested from experience. So likewise when we are said to see a red-hot bar of iron; the solidity and heat of the iron are not the objects of sight, but suggested to the imagination by the colour and figure, which are properly perceived by that sense. In short, those things alone are actually and strictly perceived by any sense, which would have been perceived, in case that same sense had then been first conferred on us. As for other things, it is plain they are only suggested to the mind by experience grounded on former perceptions. (DHP 1; W2: 204)

Dicker (1982, 51) argues that the "Coach" passage reveals that Berkeley holds (as Dicker claims, erroneously) that "we do not really hear the coach," and that Berkeley arrives at this mistaken conclusion on the basis of the following argument:

    (i)    Whatever is perceived by sense is immediately perceived.

    (ii)   The coach is not immediately perceived.

So, (iii)  The coach is not perceived by sense.

As Dicker reads it, this argument equivocates on the notion of immediate perception. Dicker claims that Berkeley works with two different notions of immediate perception: a psychological notion (immediate perception$_p$) that is tantamount to perception without inference, and an epistemic notion (immediate perception$_e$) that he characterizes as follows:

X is immediately perceived$_e$ = $_{df}$ X is perceived in such a way that its existence and nature can be known solely on the basis of one's present perceptual experience.

The problem, as Dicker sees it, is that if the phrase "immediately perceived" is read in the psychological sense, then (i) is true but (ii) is false; unfortunately, if the same phrase is read in the epistemic sense, then (ii) is true but (i) is false. The only way to ensure that (i) and (ii) are both true is to interpret the phrase psychologically in (i) and epistemically in (ii). But in that case, the argument becomes straightforwardly invalid. If Dicker is right, there is no way out: Berkeley's argument for the claim that the coach is not perceived by sense is unsound.

In response to this criticism, Pappas claims that Dicker has misread the "Coach" passage by ignoring Berkeley's reference to *proper* perception:

> Berkeley is not here saying that the coach and piece of hot iron are not perceived by sense, as Dicker says, but rather that they are not *properly* perceived by sense . . . And, of course, Berkeley is right: the coach and hot piece of iron are not *properly* immediately perceived, for there is no one sense by the sole means of which they are perceived . . . Since Dicker has mis-identified the conclusion Berkeley is aiming at in this passage, his argument that Berkeley needs immediate perception_e breaks down.[24]

As Pappas reads him, then, Berkeley does not argue from (i) and (ii) to (iii), but rather from (i*) and (ii*) to (iii*):

(i*)   Whatever is *properly* perceived by sense is *properly* immediately perceived.

(ii*)   The coach is not *properly* immediately perceived.

So, (iii*)   The coach is not *properly* perceived by sense.

And, claims Pappas, if "immediately perceived" is read in the psychological sense in both (i*) and (ii*), then both premises are true and the argument is sound. There is therefore no need for Berkeley to ensure the truth of the second premise by reading "immediately perceived" in the epistemic sense.[25]

But this criticism of Dicker misses the mark. Although it is true that Berkeley claims that the coach is not *properly* perceived, he *also* claims or implies that the coach is not *immediately* perceived. For example, Philonous says that "when I hear a coach drive along the streets, immediately I perceive *only* the sound." From the fact that the *sound* of the coach is the *only* thing that is *immediately* perceived, it follows directly that *the coach itself* (which is being contrasted with the sound) is *not immediately* perceived. Moreover, when Philonous says that "the solidity and heat of the iron are not the objects of sight, but suggested to the imagination by the colour and figure," he means, quite clearly, that, by virtue of being *suggested* to the mind, the iron's solidity and heat are *mediately*, and hence *not immediately*, perceived. Despite the references to *proper* perception, then, the "Coach" passage must be read as endorsing (ii) in addition to (ii*). For all Pappas tells us, then, Dicker's criticism of Berkeley's argument stands.

---

[24] Pappas (2000, 170–1).

[25] Dicker has recently accepted Pappas's criticism. He writes: "I now think that Pappas is probably right to hold that Berkeley is not denying that the coach is perceived by sense" (Dicker 2006, 532).

But Pappas is right at least this far: Dicker is wrong to attribute to Berkeley an epistemic notion of immediate perception on the strength of his analysis of the "Coach" passage. Dicker claims that (ii) is false when "immediately perceived" is read in the psychological sense, that (ii) is true when "immediately perceived" is read in the epistemic sense, and hypothesizes that Berkeley does not see (ii)'s falsity because he conflates the psychological and epistemic senses of the relevant phrase. But is (ii) indeed false when "immediately perceived" is read in the psychological sense? Here is what Dicker says:

> [B]y (ii) Berkeley must mean to assert that the coach has to be (very rapidly but consciously) inferred from the sound; much as rain may be inferred from thunderclouds, or fire from smoke. But (ii), taken in this sense, is simply *false*; it is just false that the coach has to be . . . inferred, however rapidly, from the sound. Upon hearing the sound of an airplane (to modernize Berkeley's example), we do not *infer* that it is the sound of an airplane. We immediately take it to be the sound of an airplane—with no inference or reasoning in any ordinary sense involved. If we stick to the definition of "immediately perceived$_p$," then the airplane (the coach) is perceived (heard) just as immediately as the sound.[26]

As this passage makes clear, Dicker's claim that (ii) is false when "immediately perceived" is read in the psychological sense rests on his characterization of "immediately perceived$_p$" as "perceived without inference." Dicker's point is that, when "immediately perceived" is read in the psychological sense, (ii) states that the coach is not perceived without inference, i.e., that it is only by means of an *inference* that the coach is perceived. It is *this* that Dicker finds erroneous. But, as we have already seen, Berkeley explicitly allows for mediate perception via suggestion, where suggestion is a mental process that he explicitly *contrasts* with inference (e.g., at TVV 42). So from the fact that the coach (airplane) is not mediately perceived *via inference* it does not follow that the coach (airplane) is not mediately perceived *via suggestion*. And, indeed, as Philonous himself says in the "Coach" passage, the coach example is a case in which, "from a frequently perceived connexion, the immediate perception of ideas [such as sound] by one sense [here, hearing] suggests to the mind others [such as solidity] perhaps belonging to another sense [here, vision and touch], which are wont to be connected with them." As Philonous also puts it, "the coach is . . . suggested from experience."

[26] Dicker (1982, 51).

Whatever suggestion amounts to elsewhere in Berkeley's writings (more on this below), the kind of suggestion that Berkeley has in mind in this passage is clearly a contingent a posteriori relation, completely distinct from the necessary a priori relation of entailment that underwrites the mental process of inference. The upshot is that if "immediately perceived" is read in the psychological sense that Berkeley has in mind (a sense distinct from the sense of "immediately perceived$_p$," that Dicker mistakenly foists on him), then (ii) is not false, but true (at least by Berkeley's lights): the fact that the coach is mediately, rather than immediately, perceived simply follows from the fact that it is suggested to the mind by the sound that we hearers are wont to connect with it. There is therefore no reason to suppose that Berkeley would have been motivated to read "immediately perceived" in the epistemic sense in order to preserve the soundness of his argument. So Dicker's criticism gives us no good reason to believe that Berkeley operates with anything other than a psychological conception of immediate perception.

Dicker claims that there are passages from DHP 1 other than the "Coach" passage that are best read in accordance with the hypothesis that Berkeley conflates a psychological with an epistemic conception of immediate perception. Here is one:

*The "No Sensing of Causes" passage*
Phil: It seems then, that by *sensible things* you mean those only which can be perceived immediately by sense.
Hyl: Right.
Phil: Doth it not follow from this, that though I see one part of the sky red, and another blue, and that my reason doth thence evidently conclude there must be some cause of that diversity of colours, yet that cause cannot be said to be a sensible thing, or perceived by the sense of seeing?
Hyl: It doth.
Phil: In like manner, though I hear a variety of sounds, yet I cannot be said to hear the causes of those sounds.
Hyl: You cannot.
Phil: And when by my touch I perceive a thing to be hot and heavy, I cannot say with any truth or propriety, that I feel the cause of its heat or weight. (DHP 1; W2: 174)

And here is another, which refers back to the "No Sensing of Causes" passage:

Hyl: I own the very sensation of resistance, which is all you immediately perceive, is not in the *body*, but the cause of that sensation is.

Phil: But the causes of our sensations are not things immediately perceived, and therefore not sensible. This point I thought had been already determined. (DHP 1; W2: 191)

As Dicker (1982, 59; 1992, 204) argues, the latter passage reveals that Berkeley reasons from the assumption that the causes of our sensations are not immediately perceived to the conclusion that these causes are not sensible things (i.e., things perceived by the senses). In order for this conclusion to follow, Berkeley must assume (as he does at the beginning of "No Sensing of Causes" passage) that whatever is perceived by the senses is immediately perceived. So Berkeley, it seems, argues as follows:

(1) Whatever is perceived by the senses is immediately perceived.

(2) No causes of our sensations are ever immediately perceived.

So, (3) No causes of our sensations are ever perceived by the senses.

Again, as Dicker reads it, this argument equivocates on the notion of immediate perception. The problem is that if the phrase "immediately perceived" is read in the psychological sense (even according to *Pappas's* definition), then (1) is true but (2) is false; unfortunately, if the same phrase is read in the epistemic sense, then (2) is true but (1) is false. The only way to ensure that (1) and (2) are true is to interpret the phrase psychologically in (1) and epistemically in (2). But in that case, the argument becomes straightforwardly invalid.

Dicker justifies his claim that (2) is false on Pappas's definition of immediate perception by pointing out that, so read, (2) is inconsistent with adverbial causal realism, according to which "to perceive O is to be appeared to by O, and being appeared to by O consists in O's causing one to be appeared to some way, in the manner appropriate to perception."[27] Thus, if Pappas's definition of immediate perception were accurate to Berkeley's intentions, then it could not "serve Berkeley's purpose of giving a completely general refutation of causal realism," including adverbial causal realism.[28]

In response, Pappas admits that (2) is false on his own reconstruction of Berkeley's conception of immediate perception, but rightly points out that Berkeley is not in fact interested in refuting all conceivable forms of causal realism:

---

[27] Dicker (1992, 207).     [28] Dicker (1992, 207).

The sorts of causal realist theories Berkeley was motivated to refute by means of the arguments Dicker analyzes were theories that held that in every perceptual experience at least one idea...is immediately perceived. Berkeley never considered anything like adverbial causal realism, for it was not considered part of the competition, by Berkeley or anyone else (perhaps excepting Arnauld) at this point in time.[29]

But it is only on the strength of Berkeley's interest in refuting *all* forms of causal realism that Dicker finds reason to read him as adopting an epistemic conception of immediate perception on which (2) comes out true. Take away the interest in refuting adverbial causal realism and you thereby take away any reason to suppose that Berkeley is working with anything other than a psychological conception of immediate perception.[30]

However, correct as it is, Pappas's response to Dicker's criticism does not go to the heart of the matter. Both Dicker and Pappas claim that (2) comes out false if "immediately perceived" is read as "immediately perceived$_p$." In defense of this claim, Dicker provides the following cases:

---

[29] Pappas (2000, 172).

[30] In a recent reply to Pappas's criticism, Dicker admits that Berkeley did not anticipate contemporary adverbialism, but continues to insist that "Berkeley is attacking all forms of causal realism," in the sense that "Berkeley's attack on causal realism is so general that it would bear on adverbial theories as much as on theories which countenance perceptual intermediaries" (Dicker 2006, 524–5). As Dicker reads DHP 1, Hylas is a "philosophical novice whose initial realism is far too general and indeterminate to be characterized as a theory that 'in every perceptual experience at least one idea...is immediately perceived'." So, argues Dicker, in arranging for Philonous to refute Hylas, Berkeley is interested in refuting "causal realism as it might be understood by any thoughtful person, not just by philosophically sophisticated people" (Dicker 2006, 528). As Dicker sees it, a thoughtful but philosophically unsophisticated interlocutor might attack (2) by saying: "Sensations could be merely states of the self, or ways the self senses or is appeared to. Sensations need not necessarily be conceived as phenomenal individuals that could serve as perceptual intermediaries or as alternative objects of immediate perception. But if they are not conceived in that way, then [any psychological definition of immediate perception would allow causes] to be immediately perceived." Dicker concludes that it is only by adopting an epistemic conception of immediate perception that Berkeley would be able to defend (2) against this sort of attack.

But is the causal realist view that includes the thesis that sensations are "states of the self, or ways the self senses or is appeared to" the kind of view that Berkeley had it in mind to attack in DHP 1? Surely not. The claim that sensations are ways the self senses was no more part of the competition in 1713 than was adverbial causal realism. Not only is this the kind of claim that would not have occurred to a thoughtful but philosophically unsophisticated person; it is also the kind of claim that had not occurred to Berkeley's Lockean and Cartesian contemporaries. So, again, there is no reason to suppose that Berkeley would have felt the need to rely on anything other than a psychological conception of immediate perception in order to support the claim that the causes of our sensations are not immediately perceived.

Suppose that you are having salty, crispy sensations, which you rightly take to be caused by a potato chip in your mouth. Must you then *infer* that the cause of these sensations is a potato chip? Plainly not. You can just immediately take them to be produced by a potato chip.[31]

Upon hearing loud bangs on New Year's Eve, I immediately perceive$_p$ the explosions which are then the causes of my auditory experiences.[32]

Now it may indeed be *true* that the mind need not infer, at the time of eating, that such and such sensations are being produced by a potato chip (as opposed to, say, a French fry), and that the mind need not infer, on New Year's Eve, that the loud sounds are being produced by explosions (as opposed to, say, a car backfiring). But the relevant question is not whether it is *true* that the mind can perceive the causes of its sensations without inference; the relevant question is whether *Berkeley accepts it as true* that the mind can perceive the causes of its sensations without inference. And to me it seems consistent with everything Berkeley says that the answer to the relevant question is "no." In the "No Sensing of Causes" passage, Philonous (i.e., Berkeley) points out that the cause of the fact that one part of the sky is blue while another part is red (namely, the sun) is perceived only as the result of an inference. He then proceeds to generalize, inferring by parity of reasoning that the mind cannot perceive the causes of sounds, heat, or weight without inference. Dicker claims that there is no parity of reasoning here:

Philonous' attempt to generalize from the case of seeing different colors in the sky is fallacious. When I see part of the sky red and part of it blue, normally just after sunset, I may be said to *infer* that the cause of this diversity is the sun, because I can no longer *see* the sun, which is now below the horizon. One cannot conclude from this case that awareness of the causes of one's sensations is always inferential.[33]

But in relation to the issue of whether Berkeley takes (2) to be true on the psychological conception of immediate perception, whether Philonous's generalization is *justified* is really neither here nor there. All that matters is that Berkeley *takes* it to be justified.[34] I conclude that Dicker has given us

---

[31] Dicker (1982, 61).

[32] Dicker (1992, 205).

[33] Dicker (1982, 61).

[34] Dicker might reply that it is simply *obvious*, and hence should also have been obvious *to Berkeley*, that we can perceive the causes of our sensations non-inferentially. But, in the first place, it is a fallacy to infer from the fact that X is obvious *to us now* that X seemed obvious *to Berkeley then*. And further, what Dicker finds obvious is hardly so. Consider the following

no good reason to suppose that Berkeley *needs* to appeal to an *epistemic* concept of immediate perception in order to secure the main argumentative aim of DHP.

Dicker's thesis that Berkeley conflates immediate perception$_p$ with immediate perception$_e$ would be stronger if he were able to adduce independent evidence for the claim that Berkeley adopts an epistemic conception of immediate perception. And, indeed, Dicker claims that such independent evidence exists. In a passage that appears in DHP 3, Philonous discusses the case of a man who sees an oar, with one end in the water, as crooked:

*The "Crooked Oar" passage*
But his mistake lies not in what he perceives immediately and at present (it being a manifest contradiction to suppose he should err in respect of that) but in the wrong judgment he makes concerning the ideas he apprehends to be connected with those immediately perceived: or concerning the ideas that, from what he perceives at present, he imagines would be perceived in other circumstances. (DHP 3; W2: 238)

Dicker focuses on the phrase in parentheses, claiming that "Berkeley is here operating with an extremely strong *epistemic* concept of immediate perception, on which it is a necessary truth that one cannot be mistaken about anything that one immediately perceives."[35] But the fact that P is a necessary a priori truth (or that P's negation is self-contradictory) does not entail that P is *definitionally* true. In particular, it does not follow from the fact that one *cannot* (on pain of contradiction) be mistaken about anything that one immediately perceives that the very *concept* of immediate perception is or includes immediate perception$_e$. For all that the "Crooked Oar" passage tells us, it may be that Berkeley takes it to be necessary and a priori that perception of O without intermediary (i.e., immediate perception$_p$ of O) is sufficient for knowledge of O. Why would he think this? Presumably

picture, which coheres with everything Berkeley says and explains why people (such as Dicker) might *falsely assume as obvious* that they perceive the causes of their sensations without inference. When a subject S hears loud bangs on New Year's Eve, S infers (from the fact that it is New Year's Eve and the fact that similar such bangs were caused by fireworks on past New Year's Eves) that the causes of the bangs are fireworks. S does not notice that he is making an inference because the mental transition from assumptions to conclusion is extremely quick. So S assumes (wrongly, as it happens) that he hears the causes of the bangs without inference. In fact, his perception of the causes of the bangs is mediated by his perception of the bangs.

[35] Dicker (1992, 207). See also Dicker (2006, 529).

on the grounds that it is necessary and a priori that whatever is immediately perceived without intermediary is directly and wholly present to the mind, and that there is simply no room for the mind to be mistaken about what is directly and wholly present to it. As Berkeley puts the point in the *Principles*:

Colour, figure, motion, extension and the like, considered only as so many *sensations* in the mind, are perfectly known, there being nothing in them which is not perceived. (PHK 87; W2: 78)

For Berkeley it is simply a fundamental truth that when a sensation is directly and wholly present to the mind, there is nothing in the sensation that could possibly be hidden from the mind. And if every aspect of a sensation is necessarily manifest to the mind, then it is also a fundamental truth that the mind cannot make a mistake about what the sensation is like. This result is substantive, not definitional. So the "Crooked Oar" passage does not suggest that Berkeley is operating with an epistemic *concept* of immediate perception.[36]

## 3  How to Understand the Distinction

In the previous section, I canvassed four different ways of identifying the nature of Berkeley's distinction between mediate and immediate perception. The provisional conclusion of this investigation is that mediate perception is, first and foremost, perception with intermediary, and, correspondingly, that immediate perception is perception without intermediary (see the "Two Questions" passage). As the very appellation "mediate" connotes, there is a mediating element in every case of mediate perception that Berkeley describes. Thus, when I perceive your emotions mediately by sight, I see them by seeing the colors in your countenance (NTV 9, 10, 23, 65; W1: 172–3, 173, 176, 195); when I perceive distance mediately by sight, I see it by experiencing certain sorts of sensations in the act of vision: the sensation that

---

[36] Dicker (2006, 529, n. 10) cites two other passages in defense of his claim that Berkeley sometimes operates with an epistemic conception of immediate perception: "The real objects of sight we see, and what we see we know" (TVV 20; W1: 258), and "Do you not perfectly know your own ideas?" (DHP 1; W2: 206). But, again, from the fact that I know what I see and that I know my own ideas it does not follow that my very *concept* of (immediate) perception is epistemic. It could simply be necessary and a priori that the very nature of the relation I bear to my own ideas (namely, that they are directly and wholly present to me) makes it impossible for me to be mistaken about them.

attends the lessening or the widening of the interval between the pupils (NTV 16; W1: 174), the sensation of visual confusion (NTV 21; W1: 175), or the sensation that attends the effort to strain the eye to prevent confused perception (NTV 27; W1: 176–7); when I perceive the solidity and heat of a bar of iron by sight, I see it by seeing its color and shape, and when I perceive the coach that is rattling along the cobblestones outside my house by hearing, I hear it by hearing the rattling sounds (see the "Coach" passage); and when I perceive the ideas you communicate to me in conversation by hearing, I hear them by hearing the sounds of the words you utter (NTV 51; W1: 190).

Moreover, mediate perception of O via intermediary M requires the existence of a real relation R between M and O. If the geometric account of seeing distance were correct, R would involve the necessary and a priori deduction or inference of distance from seen lines and angles (NTV 4–7; W1: 171–2). In Berkeley's own account of seeing distance, R involves a contingent and a posteriori association of M with O established on the basis of custom or habit (NTV 17, 21, 26). On a third account that Berkeley canvasses and dismisses in NTV, R would consist in the relation of resemblance or similarity (NTV 147; W1: 231). (Part of the point of NTV, after all, is to establish the Heterogeneity Thesis, from which it follows that immediately visible ideas do not resemble the tangible ideas (such as distance, magnitude, and situation) that they enable subjects to mediately see.)

The distinction between mediate and immediate perception, then, is psychological, not epistemic, though Berkeley believes that anti-skeptical epistemic consequences follow from the fact that certain ideas are immediately (rather than mediately) perceived. The interpretive difficulties in this area, such as they are, concern the relation between Berkeley's *general* characterization of mediate perception as perception with intermediary and his more specific characterization of mediate perception as perception with suggestion and as perception with inference. At times, Berkeley contrasts suggestion with inference (TVV 42; W1: 265). Elsewhere, Berkeley implies that perception with inference is the *only* kind of mediate perception (the "Once For All," "Perception of Matter," and "Sense or Reason" passages). And yet Berkeley himself describes the mediate perception of distance by sight as a form of perception with suggestion (NTV 16; W1: 174). There is no way to preserve complete interpretive consistency here. Does this mean that Berkeley's views on the nature of mediate and immediate perception are irremediably confused?

The answer, I believe, is that, although Berkeley's views *are* confused, they are not *irremediably* so. Strictly speaking, it is impossible for *everything* that Berkeley says about mediate and immediate perception to be true. And yet, as I will now argue, it is possible to extract a consistent interpretation of Berkeley's views from all relevant texts holistically considered, an interpretation I venture to affirm he would recognize as his own were the issue put before him now.

The consistent interpretation to which I refer is built on a proper understanding of Berkeley's account of suggestion, which itself requires an understanding of the basic elements of Berkeley's theory of mind.[37] As Berkeley sees it, the mind (or spirit) is an active, indivisible, unextended, immaterial, and incorruptible substance that supports (that is, perceives) ideas (PHK 141; W2: 105–6 and DHP 3; W2: 231). Though the mind is partless, it is endowed with six basic mental faculties that operate about the ideas it perceives: sensation, reflection, imagination, reason, memory, and will.[38]

Sensation is a faculty by which the mind passively receives (from something that is external to the mind) a set of simple, clear, distinct,

---

[37] The interpretation of Berkeley's theory of mind that follows is, I believe, standard (or, at least, consistent with much of the scholarly literature on the subject). It is not meant to be compendious. But it should be noted that there are two prominent accounts of Berkeley's theory of mind with which my interpretation is *not* consistent. These accounts have been articulated and defended by Daniel (2001a; 2001b; 2007) and Muehlmann (1992). On both of these accounts, the mind is not a substance. For Daniel's Berkeley, the mind is activity (or a congeries of activities) of a certain sort; for Muehlmann's Berkeley, the mind is a congeries of perceptions. Detailed discussion of these proposals would take us too far afield. For criticisms of Muehlmann's and Daniel's proposals, see Hight and Ott (2004) and Roberts (2007, 7–8). For a reply, see Daniel (2007).

[38] It might be suggested that Berkeley thinks of memory as a sub-faculty of the imagination. But this suggestion does not sit well with the following passage from *Siris* 303 (W5: 140): "Sense supplies images to memory. These become subjects for fancy [i.e., imagination] to work upon. Reason considers and judges of the imaginations. And these acts of reason become new objects of the understanding. In this scale, each lower faculty is a step that leads to one above it." Berkeley here thinks of the faculties of sense, memory, imagination, and reason as hierarchically related, with sense as the lowest faculty and reason the highest. It cannot be that this hierarchy represents sense as a sub-faculty of memory, memory as a sub-faculty of imagination, and imagination as a sub-faculty of reason. For Berkeley makes clear in many places that sensing is not a kind of remembering, and that imagining is not a kind of reasoning. So what the hierarchy reveals is that Berkeley thinks of sense, memory, imagination, and reason as four separate faculties, with the deliverances of each lower faculty made available to the operation of the faculties above it in the hierarchy: thus, memory applies to the idea of sense, imagination applies to the ideas of memory, and reason applies to the ideas of imagination.

and regular ideas through vision, touch, hearing, taste, and smell. Passive reception, in this sense, is perception of ideas that is not dependent on one's will (PHK 29; W2: 53 and DHP 3; W2: 235). Berkeley claims that these ideas are produced in us by God (PHK 25–33; W2: 51–5). Simple ideas of sense are not the only sorts of ideas that the mind passively receives. Some simple, passively received ideas are the product of reflection, a form of introspection directed towards "the passions and operations of the mind" (PHK 1; W2: 41).

Having acquired ideas by means of sense and reflection, the mind can retain them in memory. Once an idea is stored in memory, it can be actively revived at will or, as Berkeley puts it, "barely represent[ed]" (PHK 1; W2: 41). For the mind to barely represent an idea is simply for the mind to produce a copy of it, and the mental faculty responsible for this copying (or "imaging") function is the imagination (PHK 33; W2: 54–5). As Berkeley puts the point in the *Notebooks* (N):

Ideas of Sense are the Real things or Archetypes. Ideas of Imagination, Dreams etc are copies, images of these. (N 823; W1: 98)

Given that copies are usually less vivid and crisp than are the originals from which they derive, it is unsurprising to find Berkeley insisting that "[t]he ideas of sense are more strong, lively, and distinct than those of the imagination" (PHK 30; W2: 53—see also DHP 2; W2: 215 and DHP 3; W2: 235). But copying is not the sole function of the imagination. According to Berkeley, it is thanks to the imagination that the mind is capable of combining and separating ideas, including the "copies" formed via the function of bare representation. As Berkeley puts it in the very first section of PHK:

It is evident to any one who takes a survey of the objects of human knowledge, that they are either ideas actually imprinted on the senses, or else such as are perceived by attending to the passions and operations of the mind, or lastly ideas formed by help of memory and imagination, *either compounding, dividing, or barely representing* those originally perceived in the aforesaid ways. (PHK 1; W2: 41—emphasis added)

Berkeley accepts that the ideas originally acquired by sensation and reflection are simple. But the imagination can combine (i.e., "compound") complex ideas out of simple ideas, and then, if it so chooses, separate (i.e., "divide") them. Thus, it is the imagination that constructs the complex idea of an apple by putting together "a certain colour, taste, smell, figure and consistence" that have been "observed to go together" (PHK 1; W2: 41), and that constructs a complex idea of a cherry by putting together "the sensations of

softness, moisture, redness, tartness" that are "observed to attend each other"
(DHP 3; W2: 249). And it is the imagination that can divide these complex
ideas into their various components. As Berkeley puts it in PHK:

> I may indeed divide in my thoughts or conceive apart from each other those things
> which, perhaps, I never perceived by sense so divided. Thus I imagine the trunk of
> a human body without the limbs, or conceive the smell of a rose without thinking
> on the rose it self. (PHK 5; W2: 43)

Berkeley explicitly attributes both the compounding and dividing functions to the imagination in the Introduction to PHK:

> [F]or my self I find indeed I have a faculty of imagining, or representing to my self
> the ideas of those particular things I have perceived and of variously compounding
> and dividing them. I can imagine a man with two heads or the upper parts of a man
> joined to the body of a horse. [This is the operation of compounding.] I can
> consider the hand, the eye, the nose, each by it self abstracted or separated from the
> rest of the body. [This is the operation of dividing.] (I 10; W2: 29)

It is important to note that each of the operations of the imagination
discussed thus far (copying, compounding, and dividing) is performed as a
result of an act of will. In this way, the imagination differs from the senses,
in that ideas acquired through the senses, unlike the ideas acquired through
the imagination, are not dependent on the will.

Now bare representation, compounding, and dividing are not the only
functions of the imagination. In addition to performing these functions,
the imagination also associates ideas (even when it does not put them
together to form a new, complex idea). The association of ideas can occur
as a result of three different sorts of mental activities: stipulation, comparison, and deduction. Association of ideas by stipulation is based on a pure
act of will that is ungrounded in the perception of any connection
between them; association of ideas by comparison is based on a perceived
similarity between them; and association of ideas by deduction is based on
an inference (whether deductive or inductive) that leads from one idea to
the other. First, as to stipulation, it is thanks to the imagination that the
mind arbitrarily associates words with their referents ("apple" with apples,
and "cherry" with cherries). The fact that "apple" means apples rather than
cherries and that "cherry" means cherries rather than apples is completely
contingent: it is the product of brute, ungrounded stipulation. Similar
remarks apply to the imagination's arbitrary association of letters with
sounds (the letter "a" with the sound "ay," the letter "o" with the

sound "oh"—see NTV 143; W1: 229). Second, as to comparison, it is thanks to the imagination that the mind associates ideas that are perceived to be similar. Thus, if one perceived shade of blue is similar to another, I can find myself thinking of one when I think of the other, and this mental transition is effected by the imagination. Third, as to deduction, it is thanks to the imagination that I associate causes with the effects that I have inferred from them, that I associate effects with the causes I have inferred from them, and that I associate premises with the conclusions I have derived from them.

It is important to note that stipulation, comparison, and deduction are not themselves activities of the imagination. The imagination is responsible for the mental act of *associating* the ideas that are connected by virtue of stipulation, comparison, and deduction. For example, I might deduce proposition P from proposition Q. This is an act of reason, a faculty that Berkeley distinguishes from the faculty of imagination. But the deduction of Q from P grounds a mental association between P and Q, a mental association for which the imagination (and not reason) is responsible. Thus it can be (though it need not be) thanks to the imagination that I think of Q whenever I think of P. This happens when the thought of P simply triggers the thought of Q, without the employment of actual ratiocination.

Berkeley reserves a special name for the process by which an idea brings to mind another with which it is associated through the offices of the imagination (whether as the result of stipulation, comparison, or deduction). He calls this process, "suggestion." And Berkeley also reserves a special name for the relation between ideas that is facilitated by this process. He calls this relation, "signification." Berkeley's clearest account of the relationship between imagination, suggestion, and signification appears in TVV:

Ideas which are observed to be connected with other ideas come to be considered as signs, by means whereof things not actually perceived by sense are signified or suggested to the imagination, whose objects they are, and which alone perceives them. And as sounds suggest other things, so characters suggest those sounds; and, in general, all signs suggest the things signified, there being no idea which may not offer to the mind another idea which hath been frequently joined with it. In certain cases a sign may suggest its correlate as an image, in others as an effect, in others as a cause. But where there is no such relation of similitude or causality, nor any necessary connexion whatsoever, two things, by their mere coexistence, or two ideas, merely by being perceived together, may suggest or signify one the other, their connexion being all the while arbitrary; for it is the connexion only, as such, that causeth this effect. (TVV 39; W1: 264)

Notice, first, that in this passage Berkeley speaks of ideas that are connected with others as being suggested to the imagination. Such ideas are, in fact, perceived by the imagination, and not by any other faculty. Second, Berkeley emphasizes three different ways in which an idea may suggest its correlate: (i) "as an image," (ii) "as an effect [or] cause," and (iii) "merely by being perceived together, . . . their connexion being all the while arbitrary." These three forms of suggestion correspond to the relations between ideas that obtain through the operations of comparison, deduction, and stipulation: namely, similarity, entailment, and brute association.

On the view suggested by TVV 39, a cause can suggest its effect, and an effect can suggest its cause. Thus there is no incompatibility between deduction (or inference) and suggestion. Rather than thinking that ideas that are inferred one from the other cannot suggest each other, Berkeley thinks just the opposite. This compatibility is reinforced in the following passage:

> In treating of vision, it was my purpose to consider the effects and appearances, the objects perceived by my senses, the ideas of sight as connected with those of touch; to inquire how one idea comes to suggest another belonging to a different sense, how things visible suggest things tangible, how present things suggest things remote and future, *whether by likeness, by necessary connexion, by geometrical inference, or by arbitrary institution*. (TVV 14; W1: 257—emphasis added)

Again, Berkeley's point here is that ideas can come to suggest others in three different ways: (i) by likeness, (ii) by inference (or some other form of necessary connection), or (iii) by arbitrary fiat.

When one idea suggests another because of some arbitrarily instituted connection between them (but not when there is suggestion via likeness or inference), Berkeley emphasizes, as in the following passage from ALC, that the relevant mental association is the result of mere custom or habit:

> Alciphron [speaking to Euphranor, Berkeley's spokesman]:
> You would have us think, then, that light, shades, and colours, variously combined, answer to the several articulations of sound in language; and that, by means thereof, all sorts of objects are suggested to the mind through the eye, in the same manner as they are suggested by words or sounds through the ear, that is, *neither from necessary deduction to the judgment, nor from similitude to the fancy, but purely and solely from experience, custom, and habit*. (ALC 4:10; W3: 154—emphasis added)

This sort of suggestion, grounded in custom and habit, is the kind of suggestion upon which Berkeley builds his theory of perception of distance by sight in NTV. As we have seen, he makes it clear that distance is suggested to the imagination by virtue of the arbitrarily instituted and frequently perceived connections between the idea of distance and various sorts of sensations perceived in the act of vision. But, as we have also seen, in saying this Berkeley does not mean to exclude, by definitional necessity, the possibility that distance be suggested by ideas from which it might be inferred. Suggestion, after all, is compatible with inference. Were the geometric theory of distance perception correct, the idea of distance would also be suggested to the imagination; but instead of being suggested by means of ideas that are *arbitrarily* (and so contingently) connected with it, the idea of distance would be suggested by means of ideas that are *necessarily* connected with it.

What, then, on Berkeley's view, is the connection between mediate perception, perception with suggestion, and perception with inference? In the first place, as I have argued, mediate perception is primarily and definitionally perception with intermediary. To perceive O mediately via sense S is to perceive O by perceiving something numerically distinct from O (say, M) by sense S that is in some way related to O (by, say, R). As Berkeley sees it, mediate perception can occur only when the relevant relation between M and O (that is, R) consists in a relation of mental association performed by the imagination, that is, when R is the relation of suggestion. M suggests O when the imagination barely represents O (by producing a copy of O) immediately upon the mind's perceiving M. The fact that the mind is so constituted that M suggests O to the imagination is sufficient for M to signify (that is, to be a sign of) O. Suggestion itself is underwritten by three different kinds of mental processes: stipulation, comparison, and deduction. M can come to suggest O as a result of the mind's having arbitrarily chosen that M and O should be associated, as a result of the mind's having noticed that M and O are similar, or as a result of the mind's having inferred O from M or M from O.

On this picture, it is strictly speaking true, but somewhat misleading, to say (as Winkler and Atherton do) that mediate perception consists in perception with inference or suggestion. The statement is true because every mediate perception is a perception with inference or suggestion. The statement is misleading because it wrongly suggests that there are two fundamentally different, mutually exclusive kinds of mediate perception. In fact, perception with suggestion is in some sense the genus of which perception with inference (along with perception with stipulation and perception with comparison) is a species. There is no form of mediate perception that is not a form of perception with suggestion, and there is no form of perception with inference that is not a form of mediate perception (or perception with suggestion), but there are several kinds of mediate perception (and so several kinds of perception with suggestion) that do not count as perception with inference.

On balance, I think this picture makes the best sense of Berkeley's views on mediate perception, in large part because it is both moored in a large number of texts and grounded in Berkeley's overall theory of mind. The picture explains why Berkeley identifies mediate perception as perception with intermediary in the "Two Questions" passage, why he speaks of mediate perception via inference in passages from DHP and ALC, and also why he speaks of mediate perception via suggestion throughout NTV and TVV. It is even consistent with much of TVV 42, inasmuch as it does not require that suggestion be identified with inference. What it does not explain is why Berkeley implies, as he does in the "Once For All," "Perception of Matter," and "Sense or Reason" passages, that there is no form of mediate perception other than perception with inference.

I am not convinced that it is possible to integrate these passages seamlessly into the picture of mediate perception that I have been painting. But I think that a second look at these passages reveals that they *need not* be read as implying that perception with inference is the only possible form of mediate perception. Consider the "Perception of Matter" passage again:

Either you perceive the being of Matter immediately or mediately. If immediately, pray inform me by which of the senses you perceive it. If mediately, let me know by what reasoning it is inferred from those things which you perceive immediately.

At first glance, Philonous seems to be saying that anything that is perceived immediately is perceived by the senses and anything that is perceived mediately is perceived by reason (via inference). But it is important to read this passage in the overall argumentative context in which it is embedded. The relevant passage is extracted from DHP 2, at the beginning of which Philonous provides Hylas with a proof of God's existence grounded in the claim that the ideas of sense perceived by finite minds do not depend for their existence on those minds, and so (given that they are essentially dependent entities) must depend for their existence on the existence of an infinite mind (DHP 2; W2: 212). Hylas accepts Philonous's proof (DHP 2; W2: 215), but wonders whether inference might be able to establish the existence of material substance just as much as it establishes the existence of a Deity. The inference is from effect to cause:

Phil: The matter therefore which you still insist on, is something intelligible, I suppose; something that may be discovered by reason, and not by sense.

Hyl: You are in the right.

Phil: Pray let me know what reasoning your belief of matter is grounded on; and what this matter is in your present sense of it.

Hyl: I find myself affected with various ideas, whereof I know I am not the cause; neither are they the cause of themselves, or of one another, or capable of subsisting by themselves, as being altogether inactive, fleeting, dependent beings. They have therefore some cause distinct from me and them: of which I pretend to know no more, than that it is *the cause of my ideas*. And this thing, whatever it be, I call matter. (DHP 2; W2: 215–16)

So Hylas infers the existence of matter by inferring the existence of a cause of his ideas, a cause that he knows must be distinct from his mind and from the ideas his mind perceives. Philonous then criticizes this inference by pointing out that, in its "current proper signification" (DHP 2; W2: 216), the term "matter" signifies an unthinking, inactive substance, and that it is impossible for an unthinking thing to be the cause of thought and also impossible for an inactive thing to be a cause of any kind. Hylas then, acknowledging that only God could be the cause of his ideas, retreats, first to the view that matter might be "an *instrument* subservient to the supreme agent in the production of our ideas" (DHP 2; W2: 217), and second to the view that matter might be an occasional cause "at the presence whereof God excites ideas in our minds" (DHP 2; W2: 220). The "Perception of Matter" passage occurs immediately following Philonous's dismissal of both of Hylas's suggestions.

The function of the "Perception of Matter" passage is to reinforce the main challenge that Hylas faces in establishing the existence of matter. Hylas claims that sensible objects are material substances, that sensible objects are perceivable, and that he perceives them. In the passage, Philonous points out that the perception of matter must be either immediate or mediate, and that immediate perception is perception by means of the senses. Having been brought to accept in DHP 1 that matter is not immediately perceived, Hylas's only alternative is to claim that matter is mediately perceived. This he does at DHP 2 (W2: 215–16), insisting *not* that matter is mediately perceived through suggestion based on stipulation or comparison, but that matter is mediately perceived through inference. When Philonous then asks, as he does in the "Perception of Matter" passage, that Hylas provide him with a convincing piece of reasoning to ground the mediate perception of *matter*, he does not presuppose that perception via inference is the only possible form of mediate perception: he merely challenges Hylas to produce the inference that Hylas himself sees as underwriting his own claim that *matter* is mediately perceived.

Very similar remarks apply to the "Sense or Reason" passage:

> Whatever we perceive, is perceived either immediately or mediately: by sense, or by reason and reflexion.

Like the "Perception of Matter" passage, the "Sense or Reason" passage suggests that Berkeley conceives of only one kind of mediate perception, namely, perception with inference (and reflection). But first impressions can be misleading. Consider the "Sense or Reason" passage in its immediate context. Hylas and Philonous have been discussing the case of Julius Caesar's picture, which Hylas has used to illustrate the claim that some things that are perceived by sense (such as Caesar himself) are mediately perceived (in this case, via his picture). Philonous then demurs, arguing that Hylas does not perceive Caesar by sense, but by "reason and memory" (DHP 1; W2: 204). At this point, Philonous issues the very same challenge he raises later in the "Perception of Matter" passage, with his focus squarely on Hylas's reasons for thinking that matter exists:

*The Expanded "Sense or Reason" Passage*
Phil: I would therefore fain know, what arguments you can draw from reason for the existence of what you call *real things* or *material objects*. Or whether you remember to have seen them formerly as they are in themselves? or if you have heard or read of any one that did.
Hyl: I see, Philonous, you are disposed to raillery; but that will never convince me.
Phil: My aim is only to learn from you, the way to come at the knowledge of *material beings*. **Whatever we perceive, is perceived either immediately or mediately: by sense, or by reason and reflexion.** But as you have excluded sense, pray shew me what reason you have to believe their existence; or what *medium* you can possibly make use of, to prove it either to mine or your own understanding. (DHP 1; W2: 204–5; D5 in bold)

Again, the dialectical context shows that Philonous is focusing on Hylas's own proposal, according to which material substances are either immediately perceived by sense or mediately perceived by inference. Having previously excluded the possibility that material substances are immediately perceived by sense, Philonous now (in the Expanded "Sense or Reason" Passage) wants Hylas to tell him exactly *how* to infer the existence of matter. So Philonous need not be read as presupposing that there is no form of mediate perception other than perception with inference. He is simply working with Hylas's own hypothesis, which is that *matter* in particular is perceived by inference, rather than by suggestion based on comparison or stipulation.

Finally, let us reconsider the "Once For All" passage in its immediate context. Having brought Hylas to agree that sensible things are objects of immediate, rather than mediate, perception, Philonous concludes in the "No Sensing of Causes" passage that the causes of our ideas are not sensible things. The "Once For All" passage then appears immediately after the "No Sensing of Causes" passage as Hylas's summary of Philonous's reasoning:

Phil: It seems then, that by *sensible things* you mean those only which can be perceived immediately by sense.

Hyl: Right.

Phil: Doth it not follow from this, that though I see one part of the sky red, and another blue, and that my reason doth thence evidently conclude there must be some cause of that diversity of colours, yet that cause cannot be said to be a sensible thing, or perceived by the sense of seeing?

Hyl: It doth.

Phil: In like manner, though I hear a variety of sounds, yet I cannot be said to hear the causes of those sounds.

Hyl: You cannot.

Phil: And when by my touch I perceive a thing to be hot and heavy, I cannot say with any truth or propriety, that I feel the cause of its heat or weight.

Hyl: To prevent any more questions of this kind, I tell you once for all, that by *sensible things* I mean those only which are perceived by sense, and that in truth the senses perceive nothing which they do not perceive immediately: for they make no inferences. (DHP 1; W2: 174)

What this exchange reveals is that while Philonous's reasoning is impeccable, Hylas's summary leaves something to be desired. Philonous argues, validly, as follows:

(1) Sensible things are perceived immediately by sense.[39]

(2) The causes of our ideas of sense are perceived by inference.

(3) Anything that is perceived by inference is mediately perceived.

(4) Whatever is mediately perceived is not immediately perceived.

So, (5) The causes of our ideas of sense are not sensible things. [from 1, 2, 3, 4]

---

[39] At the beginning of the "No Sensing of Causes" passage, Philonous states a modal version of (1), namely "Sensible things *can be* immediately perceived by sense." And at the beginning of the second *Dialogue*, Hylas accepts that he has "long since" agreed to the proposition that "sensible things are all immediately perceivable" (DHP 2; W2: 209). That

Hylas, on the other hand, attempting to recapitulate Philonous's reasoning, argues, invalidly, as follows:

(6)   The senses make no inferences.

So, (7)   The senses perceive nothing which they do not perceive immediately.

This seems odd. Berkeley is clearly trying to use the "Once For All" passage to recapture the reasoning of the "No Sensing of Causes" passage, and yet his way of doing so is both inaccurate and misleading. There are three propositions in the "Once For All" passage:

(P1)   Sensible things are those only which are perceived by sense.

(P2)   The senses perceive nothing which they do not perceive immediately.

(P3)   The senses make no inferences.

How are these propositions related? And what is their connection with the argument of the "No Sensing of Causes" passage? First, notice that the conjunction of (P1) and (P2) entails (1), which is the first premise of the argument of the "No Sensing of Causes" passage:

(P1)   Sensible things are those only which are perceived by sense.

(P2)   The senses perceive nothing which they do not perceive immediately.

So, (1)   Sensible things are perceived immediately by sense.

---

this is *not* the version of (1) on which Philonous relies is clear from the many passages in which he endorses (1) itself, rather than its weaker modal version. For example, immediately after the "Once For All" passage, Philonous tells Hylas: "This point then is agreed between us, that *sensible things are those only which are immediately perceived by sense*" (DHP 1; W2: 174–5). Later, Philonous tells Hylas: "Our discourse proceeded altogether concerning sensible things, which you defined to be the things we *immediately perceive by our senses*" (DHP 1; W2: 180). And in the third *Dialogue*, Philonous (very much in his own voice) states that "things perceived by the senses are immediately perceived" (DHP 3; W2: 230). More importantly, when Philonous summarizes the very argument in the "No Sensing of Causes" and "Once For All" passages later in the first *Dialogue*, he says: "But the causes of our sensations are not things immediately perceived, and therefore not sensible. This point I thought had been already determined" (DHP 1; W2: 191). It is clear from this passage that the piece of reasoning that Philonous takes the two interlocutors to have previously endorsed proceeded, not on the assumption that sensible things *can be* immediately perceived, but rather on the assumption that sensible things *are* immediately perceived.

Presumably, then, (P3) is somehow meant to capture, albeit in a severely truncated form, premises (2)–(3), both of which concern inference. But, strictly understood, (P3) does not capture either (2) or (3). Moreover, while (P3) is represented in the "Once For All" passage as a premise from which (P2) (and possibly also (P1)) is supposed to follow, in the "No Sensing of Causes" passage both (2) and (3) are represented as premises that, when conjoined with (P1), (P2), and (4), are supposed to entail a further conclusion.

In light of these facts, the most reasonable interpretive hypothesis is that Hylas, and hence Berkeley, is simply confused. There is no way around two important facts: first, that the "Once For All" passage makes little sense conceived of as an argument that stands on its own, and second, that the "Once For All" passage fails miserably as a summary of the "No Sensing of Causes" passage. I conclude that Berkeley has miswritten the "Once For All" passage. Instead of the "Once For All" passage, he should have placed something like the following in Hylas's mouth:

> To prevent any more questions of this kind, I tell you once for all, that by *sensible things* I mean those only which are perceived by sense, and that in truth the senses perceive nothing which they do not perceive immediately. Hence, sensible things are immediately perceived, and given that the causes of our ideas of sense are perceived by inference, and that perception by inference is a form of mediate perception, it follows that the causes of our ideas of sense are not sensible things.

I conclude, on grounds of charity, that the "Once For All" passage should be discounted as an indication of Berkeley's considered views on the nature of mediate perception. In general, if passage P makes little sense when read on its own and when read in its immediate argumentative context, and if, in addition, P fits poorly with a host of other passages in which the very same author articulates views that are diametrically opposed to the view stated in P (with all indications that the author has not changed his or her mind on the relevant issues), then P should be taken to have little or no probative value with regard to the proper discernment of the author's intentions. On balance, then, the "Once For All," "Sense or Reason," and "Perception of Matter" passages do not establish that Berkeley's considered view is that perception with inference is the only possible kind of mediate perception. The interpretation that makes the best sense of all relevant texts considered as a whole supposes, rather, that for Berkeley perception by suggestion based on inference is one of three kinds of mediate perception by suggestion, the other two being (i) perception by suggestion based on comparison and (ii) perception by suggestion based on stipulation.

Before turning to the question of whether or not Berkeley thinks that sensible objects (as opposed to simple ideas or qualities) are objects of (immediate or mediate) perception, I want to consider the question, raised in section 1 above, as to whether immediate perception is necessary and/or sufficient for proper perception. As should now be clear, to say that X is immediately perceived by sense S is not to say that X is properly perceived by S. As I have been arguing, for X to be *immediately* perceived by S is simply for X to be perceived by S without intermediary (and so without suggestion of any kind). For X to be *properly* perceived by S is for X to be perceived by S and for X to be unperceivable by any sense other than S. So it does not follow solely from the nature or definition of immediate perception and proper perception that everything that is immediately perceived by S is properly perceived by S; nor does it follow that everything that is properly perceived by S is immediately perceived by S. However, it *is* Berkeley's view that the objects of immediate perception by S coincide with the objects of proper perception by S. Consider, as a mere sampling, the following passages:

[W]hat we immediately and properly see are only lights and colours in sundry situations and shades and degrees of faintness and clearness, confusion and distinctness. (NTV 77; W1: 202)

And as for figure and extension, I leave it to anyone to decide whether he has any idea intromitted immediately and properly by sight save only light and colours. (NTV 130; W1: 224)

All that is properly perceived by the visive faculty amounts to no more than colours, with their variations and different proportions of light and shade: But the perpetual mutability and fleetingness of those immediate objects of sight render them incapable of being managed after the manner of geometrical figures. (NTV 156; W1: 234)

[L]ight and colours . . . alone are the proper and immediate objects of sight. (PHK 46; W2: 59–60)

Here Berkeley claims that what is properly perceived by sight is identical to what is immediately perceived by sight, namely light and colors. And, although he doesn't often speak of the proper and immediate objects of the other senses, it is clear that he would identify them too. Thus, for instance, it is clear that he holds that sounds are both the only things properly perceived by hearing and the only things immediately perceived thereby.

And consider the following passage from NTV:

No sooner do we hear the words of a familiar language pronounced in our ears, but the ideas corresponding thereto present themselves to our minds . . . We even act in all respects as if we heard the very thoughts themselves. So likewise the secondary objects, or those which are only suggested by sight, do often more strongly affect us, and are more regarded than the proper objects of that sense; along with which they enter into the mind, and with which they have a far more strict connexion, than ideas have with words. Hence it is we find it so difficult to discriminate between the immediate and mediate objects of sight. (NTV 51; W1: 190)

Here Berkeley contrasts the "secondary objects" of a sense, namely those that are only "suggested by" it, with the sense's "proper objects." But his point is that because the secondary objects oftentimes "more strongly affect us" than do the primary or proper objects that suggest them, we are left with the erroneous sense that the secondary objects are primary. Berkeley concludes that this phenomenon explains our frequent inability "to discriminate the immediate and mediate objects of sight." Clearly, then, Berkeley is simply taking for granted that all primary and proper objects of a sense are immediately perceived thereby, and all secondary objects of a sense are mediately perceived thereby.

But if it is not *definitionally true* that all proper objects of a sense are immediately perceived and vice versa, then Berkeley must accept this proposition on the basis of a proof. And indeed he does. In the first place, Berkeley thinks that mere reflection should be sufficient to recognize the truth of the claim that all objects properly perceived by S are immediately perceived by S. By vision, we properly perceive "light and colours"; by touch, "hard and soft, heat and cold, motion and resistance"; by smell, "odours"; by taste, "tastes"; and by hearing, "sounds" (PHK 1; W2: 41). In each of these cases, the items that are properly perceived are perceived without intermediary and without suggestion, and hence are immediately perceived.

In the second place, to say that all objects immediately perceived by S are properly perceived by S is to say that no immediately perceived objects are perceived by more than one sense. This is Berkeley's famous Heterogeneity Thesis. At NTV 128–37 (W1: 223–7), Berkeley provides three arguments for a specific instance of the Heterogeneity Thesis, namely the claim that none of the objects immediately perceived by sight is identical to any of the objects immediately perceived by touch. The first is that "a man born blind would not at first reception of his sight think the things he saw were of the same nature with the objects of touch, or had anything in common with them; but that they were a new set of ideas, perceived in a new manner, and intirely different from all he had ever perceived before" (NTV 128; W1: 223 and NTV 132–7; W1: 225–7). The second is that, because (i) "light and colours . . . constitute a sort or species intirely different from the ideas of touch" and (ii) "there is no other immediate object of sight besides light and colours," it follows that "there is no idea common to both senses" (NTV 129; W1: 223). And the third is that, from the fact that (i) "quantities of the same kind may be added together" and the fact that (ii) visible objects cannot be added to tangible objects, it follows that visible objects and tangible objects are "heterogeneous" (NTV 131; W1: 224). Berkeley then concludes, presumably by parity of reasoning, that the Heterogeneity Thesis must be true in all generality.

It is, then, the truth of the claim that the objects of proper perception necessarily coincide with the objects of immediate perception that explains why Berkeley uses the words "immediate" and "proper" interchangeably, and why, in particular, he does not bother to say in NTV and ALC that the same argument that establishes that distance is not immediately perceived by sight also establishes that distance is not properly perceived thereby.

# 2

# The Perception of Sensible Objects

Does Berkeley hold that finite minds perceive sensible objects immediately or mediately? This is a vexed question among Berkeley scholars, and the purpose of this chapter is to contribute something by way of an all-things-considered answer to it.

On some accounts, Berkeley's view is that human minds can and do perceive sensible objects immediately.[1] On other accounts, Berkeley's view is just the opposite.[2] For yet others, Berkeley adopts both views, and hence holds an inconsistent position on the issue.[3] Unsurprisingly, there is textual backing for each of these interpretations. As I will argue, it is Berkeley's understanding of the distinction between mediate and immediate perception, along with his rather generous ontology of the sensible world, that explains why he is committed to the perfectly consistent view that *some* sensible objects can be (and are) immediately perceived by sense, while *other* sensible objects can only be mediately perceived by sense.

## 1 Are Sensible Objects Immediately Perceived?

A good many Berkeley scholars believe that Berkeley holds that sensible objects are perceived by sense, and, indeed, immediately perceived. There are several passages that support such an interpretation. Pappas (2000, 174–6) divides them into two groups: passages in which Berkeley commits to the view that sensible objects are perceived by sense without saying whether such

---

[1] See Jessop (1952), Luce (1963; 1966), Ayers (1975, xiv; 1978, 680), Grayling (1986), Winkler (1989, 155–61), and Pappas (2000, 172–82).
[2] See Pitcher (1986) and Atherton (1995; 2007).
[3] See Stoneham (2002).

objects are *immediately* perceived, and passages in which Berkeley commits to the view that sensible objects are immediately perceived by sense.

Let us begin by considering the passages in the first group. In PHK, Berkeley considers the objection that, on the idealist picture that identifies sensible objects with collections of ideas, the world of sensible objects turns into nothing but "a chimerical scheme of ideas." He answers thus:

> What therefore becomes of the sun, moon, and stars? What must we think of houses, rivers, mountains, trees, stones; nay, even of our own bodies? Are all these but so many chimeras and illusions on the fancy? To all which . . . I answer, that by the principles premised, we are not deprived of any one thing in Nature. Whatever we see, feel, hear, or any wise conceive or understand, remains as secure as ever, and is as real as ever . . . I do not argue against the existence of any one thing that we can apprehend, either by sense or reflexion. That the things I see with mine eyes and touch with my hands do exist, really exist, I make not the least question. (PHK 34–5; W2: 55)

It is clear that Berkeley here assumes that sensible objects, both celestial and terrestrial, including human bodies, are perceived by sight, touch, and hearing. Similar remarks apply to the following passages:

> I shall only observe, that if at table all who were present should see, and smell, and taste, and drink wine, and find the effects of it, with me there could be no doubt of its reality. (PHK 84; W2: 77)

*The "Glove" Passage*
> But to fix on some particular thing; is it not a sufficient evidence to me of the existence of this *glove*, that I see it, and feel it, and wear it? (DHP 2; W2: 224)

*The "Cherry" Passage*
> I see this *cherry*, I feel it, I taste it: and I am sure *nothing* cannot be seen, or felt, or tasted: it is therefore *real*. Take away the sensations of softness, moisture, redness, tartness, and you take away the cherry. (DHP 3; W2: 249)

In these passages, Berkeley commits to the claim that sensible objects (including gloves and cherries) are perceived by sense, indeed that the same sensible object is perceived by different senses. Does it follow that he *also* commits to the claim that sensible objects are *immediately* perceived by sense? Pappas thinks so:

> [T]hough [Berkeley] does not use the term 'immediately perceives,' it is more than likely that is his meaning, as we would expect him to use a term like 'mediately perceive' or 'suggested' if that were his point. More generally, . . . immediate perception is the primary sort of perception for Berkeley. And when we find

him dropping the prefix 'immediately,' but without alerting us as to some special meaning, he indicates immediate perception.[4]

Pappas claims that "immediately perceives" is the *default* interpretation of Berkeley's use of "perceives," and that in the absence of an explicit indication to the contrary (for example, through the use of words such as "mediately" or "suggested"), we should understand PHK 34–5, PHK 84, the "Glove" passage, and the "Cherry" passage to be claiming that sensible objects are *immediately* perceived.

But this interpretation seems to me an over-reading of these texts. There are passages in which Berkeley clearly uses "perceives" to mean "mediately perceives" without *explicitly* indicating (by the use of such words as "mediately" or "suggested") that this is what he means. For example, in NTV, Berkeley writes:

My design is to shew the manner wherein we perceive by sight the distance, magnitude, and situation of objects. (NTV 1; W1: 171)

Here Berkeley says no more than that we perceive distance, magnitude, and situation by sight. In particular, he does not explicitly say that we perceive these qualities mediately, nor that these qualities are suggested to the mind. On Pappas's "default" principle, then, we should read NTV 1 as saying that we *immediately* see distance, magnitude, and situation. But, as we have seen, this is not Berkeley's view at all. As he will argue later in NTV, his view is that distance, magnitude, and situation are only the *mediate* objects of sight.

Moreover, Berkeley emphasizes that we should not in fact infer that a sensible object is immediately perceived from the fact that it is perceived by sense, as the following exchange from ALC 4:10 reveals:

Alc: How? Do we not, strictly speaking, perceive by sight such things as trees, houses, men, rivers, and the like?
Euph: We do indeed, perceive or apprehend those things by the faculty of sight. But will it follow from thence that they are the proper and immediate objects of sight, any more than that all those things are the proper and immediate objects of hearing which are signified by the help of words or sounds? (ALC 4:10; W3: 154)

[4] Pappas (2000, 174).

In ALC 4:10, Berkeley points out that the things suggested to the imagination by sounds are only mediately perceived by hearing, and that, similarly, the sensible objects (such as trees and houses) suggested to the imagination by patterns of light and color are only mediately perceived by sight. Given that it is perfectly correct to say that we see trees and houses, it follows that we cannot infer that sensible objects are immediately perceived from the fact that they are perceived by sight. On balance, then, PHK 34–5, PHK 84, the "Glove" passage, and the "Cherry" passage do not establish that Berkeley commits himself to the view that we *immediately* perceive sensible objects by means of the senses. These texts are perfectly consistent with the claim that we only perceive sensible objects mediately by sense.[5]

However, the second group of texts seems unequivocal:

> But, say you, it sounds very harsh to say we eat and drink ideas, and are clothed with ideas. I acknowledge it does so, the word *idea* not being used in common discourse to signify the several combinations of sensible qualities, which are called *things*: and it is certain that any expression which varies from the familiar use of language, will seem harsh and ridiculous. But this doth not concern the truth of the proposition, which in other words is no more than to say, we are fed and clothed with those things which we perceive immediately by our senses. (PHK 38; W2: 56)

*The "Wood and Stones" Passage*
> Wood, stones, fire, water, flesh, iron, and the like things, which I name and discourse of, are things that I know. And I should not have known them, but that I perceived them by my senses; and things perceived by the senses are immediately perceived. (DHP 3; W2: 230)

*The "Death" Passage*
> I see no difficulty in conceiving a change of state, such as is vulgarly called Death, as well without as with material substance. It is sufficient for that purpose that we allow sensible bodies, *i.e.* such as are immediately perceived by sight and touch. (*Letter to Johnson*; W2: 282)

In each of these passages, Berkeley says, quite plainly, that sensible objects are immediately perceived by sense, and it is largely on the strength of this

---

[5] Pappas (2000, 175) cites additional passages from DHP (DHP 3; W2: 236, 237, 246, 249) as evidence that Berkeley holds that we immediately perceive sensible objects. But, again, in these passages Berkeley says or implies no more than that sensible objects are perceived by sense. This leaves it open whether he holds that such objects are immediately or mediately perceived.

textual evidence that many Berkeley scholars take this to be Berkeley's considered view.

However, there are also passages that suggest otherwise, most notably ALC 4·10 and the "Coach" passage. There is also the following passage from ALC 4:11:

> Alc: I see, therefore, in strict philosophical truth, that rock only in the same sense
> that I may be said to hear it, when the word *rock* is pronounced.
> Euph: In the very same. (ALC 4:11; W3: 155)

In these passages, as we have seen, Berkeley suggests that sensible objects (such as coaches and rocks) are not *immediately*, but rather *mediately*, perceived. His point is that we hear the coach mediately, by perceiving a sound that suggests the coach as a result of the arbitrarily established connection between certain sorts of sounds and the immediate coach-constituting objects of sight and touch (and perhaps, smell) that are "wont to be connected with them" (the "Coach" passage). Similarly, just as we only mediately *hear* a rock by perceiving a sound that suggests it as a result of the arbitrarily established connection between utterances and their referents, so we only mediately *see* a rock by perceiving a pattern of colors that suggests the rest of the immediately perceived qualities that constitute it.

One reaction to these passages is to discount them. Here is Winkler:

> [In the "Coach" passage, ALC 4:10, and ALC 4:11], where Berkeley or his representative speaks in truth and strictness, he is speaking not about the immediate objects of perception in general, but about the *proper* and immediate objects of the various senses in particular. The objects he is talking about in [the "Coach" passage and ALC 4:11] are the ideas characteristic of the various senses. He is not talking about the objects these ideas compose when they are blended together, objects which are not the *proper* and immediate objects of any sense but which can, none the less, be immediately perceived. To put the point another way, there is an ambiguity in Berkeley's notion of an object. An object can be what *Principles* 25 calls 'an idea or object of thought', or it can be the kind of object that comes into being when, as *Principles* 3 and 38 explain, objects of the first kind are blended together. There is a related ambiguity in the notion of immediate perception. Both a sound and a coach are immediately perceived, but only sound is the *proper* and immediate object of a sense. The coach is not the proper and immediate object of *any* sense, though it is an immediate object of sight, touch, and hearing.[6]

---

[6] Winkler (1989, 156–7). See also Pappas (2000, 180).

Winkler's point, then, is that in the "Coach" passage, ALC 4:10, and ALC 4:11, Berkeley does not claim that sensible objects are not *immediate* objects of perception, but rather that sensible objects are not the *proper and immediate* objects of perception. The reason that sensible objects are not the *proper* objects of perception, even though they *are* immediately perceived, is that they can be apprehended by more than one sense.

Now it is true that Berkeley speaks of *proper* perception in the "Coach" passage and ALC 4:10. Thus, in the "Coach" passage, Philonous says that "the coach is then not properly perceived by sense." And in ALC 4:10, Euphranor suggests that "trees, houses, men, rivers, and the like" are not "the proper and immediate objects of sight." However, it would be a mistake to suppose that these two passages suggest *no more than* that sensible objects are not *properly*, and hence not both properly and immediately, perceived by sense. As we have seen, the "Coach" passage strongly suggests, not only that the coach is not *properly* perceived by hearing, but also that the coach is not *immediately* perceived by hearing either. As Philonous puts it: "[W]hen I hear a coach drive along the streets, immediately I perceive *only* the sound" (emphasis added). In saying that the *only* thing that is *immediately* perceived by hearing is sound, Philonous is *excluding* the coach as an immediate object of perception (at least under these circumstances).

Winkler claims that Philonous here trades on an ambiguity in Berkeley's notion of an *object*. As Winkler sees it, Philonous should be read as saying, not that the only immediately perceived *object of thought* is sound, but that the only immediately perceived *proper (or simple) object of thought* is sound. However, although it is true that Berkeley uses the word "object" to mean two different things, he does not use it to mean "object of thought" or "proper object of thought." As Winkler himself recognizes, he uses it to mean "object of thought" or "complex idea." So the fact that Berkeley uses the term "object" in two different ways does not suggest that Philonous's statement should be read to mean that it is only the sound of the coach that is *properly* and immediately perceived.

Winkler also claims that Philonous here trades on an ambiguity in Berkeley's notion of *immediate perception*. As Winkler sees it, Philonous should be read as saying, not that the sound is the only thing he perceives *without intermediary*, but that the sound is the only thing he perceives *properly without intermediary*. So Winkler must suppose that Berkeley's use of "immediately" is ambiguous as between "without intermediary" and "properly without intermediary." The problem with this supposition is not that it fails to make sense of Philonous's statement: the problem is that there is no *independent* evidence that Berkeley *ever* uses the word "immediately" to mean two different things. It may be that Berkeley uses the word "object" to mean one thing in PHK 25 and another thing in PHK 3 and PHK 38. But which are the texts that suggest that Berkeley uses "immediately" to mean anything other than "without intermediary"?

On balance, then, the available evidence indicates that the "Coach" passage should be read as saying that the coach is not immediately perceived by hearing, but rather mediately perceived thereby. Philonous's point, it seems, is that the sound of the coach functions as the mediating element in his perception of the coach by hearing: that is, Philonous hears the coach mediately, namely by immediately hearing a sound that suggests (via arbitrary divine stipulation) the other ideas that constitute the coach. But what of the passages from ALC? Should they not be read to say no more than that sensible objects are not *properly* perceived by sense?

Here it must be admitted that ALC 4:10 and ALC 4:11 are consistent with Winkler's reading. But these are not the only passages from ALC that bear on the relevant issue. Immediately after A3, Alciphron summarizes the result of his exchange with Euphranor in A2:

You would have us think, then, that light, shades, and colours, variously combined, answer to the several articulations of sound in language; and that, by means thereof, all sorts of objects are suggested to the mind through the eye, in the same manner as they are suggested by words or sounds through the ear, that is, neither from necessary deduction to the judgment, nor from similitude to the fancy, but purely and solely from experience, custom, and habit. [ALC 4:10; W3: 154]

Above (on pp. 48–9), we were concerned with the last part of this passage. But in this context it is the *first* part of the passage that has probative value. There Berkeley (speaking through Alciphron) makes three points: (i) that "the several articulations of sound in language" suggest various combinations of "light, shades, and colours," (ii) that such color-patterns and sensible objects are related "in the same manner" as are sounds and color-patterns, and hence (iii) that sensible objects "are suggested to the mind" by color-patterns. In saying (iii), Berkeley is clearly telling his reader that the very point of ALC 4:10, which immediately precedes this passage, is that sensible objects are mediately perceived by sight. Under the circumstances, then, it is highly unlikely that Berkeley intends ALC 4:10 to be read as saying *no more than* that sensible objects are not *proper* (and hence, not proper and immediate) objects of sight.

In defense of Winkler's claim that the "Coach" passage, ALC 4:10, and ALC 4:11 should be read in light of the claim that sensible objects are immediately perceived by sense, Pappas cites Berkeley's famous championing of common sense:

> One of the key elements of common sense, for Berkeley, is the claim that physical objects are immediately perceived. [Any position on which Berkeley would be read as saying that physical objects are not immediately perceived] would push one to the view that strictly speaking Berkeley does not really defend common sense at all . . . His real view, at least on perception and its objects, [would] actually [be] opposed to common sense . . . But this is a very hard consequence to accept. Berkeley says repeatedly that he is a champion of common sense, and indeed that his primary aim is to bring people back from metaphysical dead-ends and absurdities to common sense. This is *the* prominent theme in the *Dialogues*, but it also surfaces in the *Principles* and in the *Commentaries*.[7]

Now, as Pappas notes, there is clearly no gainsaying Berkeley's commitment to common sense. But the real question here is what Berkeley takes to be included in the commonsensical picture of perception and its objects. And there is good reason to think that, as Berkeley sees it, the commonsensical picture does *not*, in fact, include the claim that sensible objects are immediately perceived. Atherton puts the point rather nicely:

> Berkeley's views can be identified with common sense only if common sense has a position on the question whether we perceive physical objects immediately or mediately. But these terms are surely technical terms pertaining to Berkeley's theory and not matters on which common sense has any opinion.[8]

The point here is that you would not catch an ordinary person saying (or even agreeing to) the statement that sensible objects are *immediately* seen. The reason for this, as Atherton notes, is that the concept of immediate perception is entirely *theoretical*, in the sense that it plays no role in the folk conception of reality.[9] As we have seen, for S to perceive X immediately is

---

[7] Pappas (2000, 181).

[8] Atherton (2007, 109). See also Baxter (1991, 88): "[T]he vulgar do not use the phrase 'immediately perceives'. The vulgar use only 'perceives'. The modifiers 'immediately' and 'mediately' are used with 'perceives' only to construct technical terms to express a distinction made by philosophers, notably Berkeley."

[9] Berkeley does say at the very end of DHP that "the vulgar [are] of opinion, that *those things they immediately perceive are the real things*" (DHP 3; W2: 262). This might suggest that

for S to perceive X but not by perceiving something else that suggests X (in the technical sense of "suggests"). So if Berkeley were indeed to claim that sensible objects are not immediately perceived, his position would not clash with common sense in the slightest. If there is any statement in the general vicinity that common sense endorses, it is simply the proposition that sensible objects are perceived by sense. The proverbial woman on the Clapham omnibus insists on no more than that she can *see* and *touch* and *hear* and *smell* and (but only if forced to) *taste* the bus. In saying this, she leaves it open whether she perceives the bus mediately or immediately. The decision whether the bus is mediately or immediately perceived by sense rests entirely with the philosopher.

So the textual evidence suggests both that Berkeley thinks sensible objects are immediately perceived and that he thinks that sensible objects are only mediately perceived. Pappas and Winkler react to this interpretive conundrum by discounting the passages that suggest the latter. In a short but highly influential article, Pitcher reacts by discounting the passages that suggest the former. Pitcher notes Berkeley's "famous injunction [from PHK 51; W2: 62] '*to think with the learned, and speak with the vulgar*'."[10] The point of Berkeley's injunction, in the context of PHK 51, is that whereas he is willing to side with the vulgar (i.e., the common folk) in *saying* that "fire heats, or water cools," what is strictly and philosophically true is the *thought* that "spirit heats, and so forth." Berkeley is willing to agree with

Berkeley's conception of common sense includes the proposition *that the things we immediately perceive are real*. But the relevant quotation is ambiguous as between a *de re* and *de dicto* reading. On the *de dicto* reading, the quotation says that the vulgar believe the proposition that immediately perceived things are real. On the *de re* reading, the quotation says that the vulgar are of the opinion, *concerning those things they immediately perceive*, that they are real. On the latter reading (which I take to be the correct one), there is no reason to suppose that the concept of immediate perception plays any role in Berkeley's conception of common sense.

It might be suggested that if one takes an ordinary person and explains to her that to perceive a bus mediately is to perceive it by perceiving something numerically distinct from it, and if one explains that we perceive a bus mediately when we see its image in a rearview mirror, then she will say, when she is standing at the bus-stop and about to board, that she perceives the bus immediately. I agree. But we may also presume that, as Berkeley sees it, if one reads the Introduction to PHK to an ordinary person, she will come to deny the existence of abstract ideas. In both cases, what one has done is explain philosophical concepts (mediate perception, abstract idea) to an ordinary person, thereby turning her into a philosopher (even if only momentarily). The concept of mediate perception, no less than the concept of an abstract idea, is a *theoretical* concept, that is, a concept that is neither needed nor adverted to by those who do not reflect on their experience in the manner of philosophers.

[10]  Pitcher (1986, 103).

the common folk only insofar as what they say is taken as a *façon de parler*, in the same way that heliocentrists are willing to accept that "the sun rises, the sun sets, or comes to the meridian." Strictly speaking, the sun no more rises or sets than fire heats or water cools.

The nub of Pitcher's interpretation is that, in PHK 38, the "Wood and Stones" passage, and the "Death" passage, Berkeley is speaking with the vulgar, while in the "Coach" passage, ALC 4:10, and ALC 4:11, he is speaking (and thinking) with the learned. On Pitcher's view, Berkeley's claim that sensible objects are immediately perceived should be taken as a *façon de parler*, i.e., as a piece of pragmatically acceptable discourse that is strictly speaking false. By contrast, Berkeley's claim that sensible objects are mediately perceived should be taken as strictly and philosophically true.

Atherton takes issue with Pitcher's interpretation, claiming that Berkeley treats what on Pitcher's view is a mere *façon de parler* as strictly speaking true:

> I do want to differ, however, from Pitcher, in that I would reject his proposal that it is only when Berkeley is talking about immediate perception that he is telling the truth, "speaking with the learned," while when he talks in terms of mediate perception, this is just a *façon de parler*. This is because I think that, according to Berkeley, mediate perception is real perception.[11]

As Atherton sees it, Pitcher's mistake is to suppose (i) that Berkeley means us to take his claims about mediate perception as a mere *façon de parler*, and (ii) that Berkeley means us to take his claims about immediate perception as strictly speaking true.

Unfortunately, Atherton's criticism misses the mark. What Pitcher in fact supposes is not (i) and (ii), but the exact opposite. According to Pitcher, Berkeley means us to take his claims about *immediate* perception (such as the claim that we immediately perceive sensible objects) as a mere *façon de parler*, but also means us to take his claims about *mediate* perception (such as the claim that we mediately perceive sensible objects) as strictly speaking true. So it does no good to remind Pitcher, as Atherton does, that for Berkeley "mediate perception is real perception," for this is something that Pitcher already recognizes (and, indeed, emphasizes).

The main problem with Pitcher's interpretation lies elsewhere. According to Pitcher, Berkeley means us to treat the claim that we immediately perceive sensible objects as a piece of pragmatically acceptable discourse on a par with

---

[11]   Atherton (2007, 115).

the claim that the sun rises and sets. But in fact, as Berkeley well knows, there is nothing pragmatically acceptable about the claim that we immediately perceive sensible objects: this is not the sort of thing that common folk say (or would agree to), because, as we have seen, claims about immediate perception are paradigmatically philosophical. The folk would no more say that they *immediately* perceive the sun than they would say that they *mediately* perceive it. So, on balance, I am not inclined to treat PHK 38, the "Wood and Stones" passage, and the "Death" passage as texts in which Berkeley wants us to understand him as speaking with the vulgar: Berkeley clearly means us to understand the claim that sensible objects are immediately perceived as strictly speaking true.

We are therefore left exactly where we started, namely with passages that, if read together as Berkeley means us to read them, suggest both that sensible objects are immediately perceived by sense and that sensible objects are only mediately perceived by sense. The obvious conclusion is that Berkeley has unwittingly contradicted himself.[12] But, as most scholars agree, such an interpretation sits poorly with any principle of charity: surely Berkeley would not have been so unthinking or philosophically inept not to recognize that he had taken contradictory stances on the very same issue.

## 2  An Ontological Solution

There is a clear and simple way of solving our textual conundrum by finding "a plausible way of reconciling the passages in which Berkeley appears to be contradicting himself."[13] The key to unlocking the mystery, I suggest, lies with Berkeley's conception of a sensible object. As Berkeley sees it, *some* sensible objects can be immediately perceived by sense, while *other* sensible objects can only be mediately perceived by sense. The reason for this is that there are different sorts of sensible objects in Berkeley's universe, some composed of (simple) ideas all of which are immediately

---

[12]  I believe that this is Stoneham's view. Stoneham (2002, 274–82) claims on the one hand that Berkeley's considered view is that sensible objects are immediately perceived, but on the other hand that Berkeley actually and mistakenly argues for the opposite position in the "Coach" passage. Thus, as Stoneham sees it, Berkeley does commit himself to contradictory propositions regarding the question whether we perceive sensible objects mediately or immediately by sense.

[13]  Pitcher (1986, 105).

perceived at a single time, others composed of (simple) ideas some of which are not immediately perceived at a single time: the former are immediately, the latter only mediately, perceived by sense.

Let us begin by considering the sensible objects Berkeley thinks we perceive immediately by sight. In both NTV and ALC, Berkeley discusses circumstances in which continuous change in the position of one's body results in continuous change in what is immediately seen. The first of these cases concerns the visible moon at different times:

> Suppose, for example, that looking at the moon I should say it were fifty or sixty semidiameters of the earth distant from me. Let us see what moon this is spoken of: It is plain it cannot be the visible moon, or anything like the visible moon, or that which I see, which is only a round, luminous plain of about thirty visible points in diameter. For in case I am carried from the place where I stand directly toward the moon, it is manifest the object varies, still as I go on; and by the time that I am advanced fifty or sixty semidiameters of the earth, I shall be so far from being near a small, round, luminous flat that I shall perceive nothing like it; this object having long since disappeared. (NTV 44; W1: 187)

Berkeley's moon thought-experiment works like this. At time T1, subject S immediately sees only "a round luminous plain, of about thirty visible points in diameter." Call what S perceives at T1, "M1." As S travels forward in the direction of what he takes to be a distant moon, S immediately sees a succession of objects, each numerically distinct from M1. At the end of his travels, S (say, at T2000) immediately sees an object (call it "M2000") that is nothing like M1, perhaps something like the "vast opaque globe, with several unequal risings and valleys" mentioned at ALC 4:9 (W3: 153). The claim that M2000 is numerically distinct from M1 is justified by a simple application of Leibniz's Law:

1. M1 is a round luminous plane.
2. M2000 is not a round luminous plane.

So, 3. M1 is numerically distinct from M2000.

Notice now that the moon thought-experiment brings to light many more visible moons than just M1 and M2000. At successive moments along S's path, S immediately sees a whole host of moons (M1, M2, M3, . . . , M1998, M1999, M2000), each one numerically distinct from its predecessors thanks to Leibniz's law. So, for instance:

1. M1 is a round luminous plane, of thirty visible points in diameter.
2. M2 is a round luminous plane, of thirty one visible points in diameter.

So, 3. M1 is numerically distinct from M2.

1. M2 is a round luminous plane, of thirty-one visible points in diameter.
2. M3 is a round luminous plane, of thirty-two visible points in diameter.

So, 3. M2 is numerically distinct from M3.

1. M1 is a round luminous plane, of thirty visible points in diameter.
2. M3 is a round luminous plane, of thirty-two visible points in diameter.

So, 3. M1 is numerically distinct from M3.

Similar remarks apply to a similar thought-experiment discussed in both NTV 44 and ALC 4:9. Here is the sequel to the previous passage from NTV 44:

> Again, suppose I perceive by sight the faint and obscure idea of something which I doubt whether it be a man, or a tree, or a tower, but judge it to be at the distance of about a mile. It is plain I cannot mean that what I see is a mile off, or that it is the image or likeness of anything which is a mile off, since that every step I take toward it the appearance alters, and from being obscure, small, and faint, grows clear, large, and vigorous. And when I come to the mile's end, that which I saw first is quite lost, neither do I find anything in the likeness of it. (NTV 44; W1: 187)

In this thought-experiment, Berkeley imagines himself immediately seeing something (call it "C1") "obscure, small, and faint" at T1, and then, after walking one mile, immediately seeing something "clear, large, and vigorous" (call it "C50") at, say, T50. Again, Leibniz's Law establishes that C1 and C50 are numerically distinct. And Leibniz's Law also establishes that, as Berkeley walks from start to finish, he immediately sees a succession of different objects, each one clearer, larger, and more vigorous than its predecessor. Berkeley's reliance on Leibniz's Law is clearest in a similar example discussed in ALC 4:9:

> Alc: Can anyone question but yonder castle is at a great distance?
> Euph: Tell me, Alciphron, can you discern the doors, windows, and battlements of that same castle?

Alc: I cannot. At this distance it seems only a small round tower.

Euph: But I, who have been at it, know that it is no small round tower, but a large square building with battlements and turrets, which it seems you do not see.

Alc: What will you infer from thence?

Euph: I would infer that the very object which you strictly and properly perceive by sight is not that thing which is several miles distant.

Alc: Why so?

Euph: Because a little round object is one thing, and a great square object is another. Is it not?

Alc: I cannot deny it. (ALC 4:9; W3: 153)

Again, Berkeley argues that what he "strictly and properly" (and so immediately) sees from afar (call it "O1") is a "small round tower," but that what he immediately sees from up close (call it "O2") is "a large square building with battlements and turrets." Euphranor then appeals to Leibniz's Law to show that O1 is numerically distinct from O2:

> 1.    O1 is a "little round object."
> 2.    O2 is "a great square object," and so not a little round object.
> So, 3.    O1 is numerically distinct from O2.

It is also thanks to an implicit appeal to Leibniz's Law that Berkeley can tell us that "[a] microscope brings us, as it were, into a new world: It presents us with a new scene of visible objects quite different from what we behold with the naked eye" (NTV 85; W1: 206).

Repeated applications of Leibniz's Law therefore establish that what we take to be one object seen from different vantage points at different times is actually a large number of numerically distinct objects, each of which is immediately seen. Philonous puts the point rather well in the following passage from DHP 1:

Phil: Upon approaching a distant object, do the visible size and figure change perpetually, or do they appear the same at all distances?

Hyl: They are in a continual change.

Phil: Sight therefore doth not suggest or any way inform you, that the visible object you immediately perceive, exists at a distance, or will be perceived when you advance farther onward, *there being a continued series of visible objects succeeding each other, during the whole time of your approach.* (DHP 1; W2: 201—emphasis added)

According to Berkeley, then, there are, in strict and philosophical truth, many more sensible objects than are dreamed of in the ontology of common sense. According to the woman on the Clapham omnibus, the town hall looks small from a distance and appears ever larger as the bus travels down the high street. But if Berkeley is right, what the woman immediately perceives by sight is a "continued series of visible objects succeeding each other during the whole time of [her] approach." There are in fact hundreds, if not thousands, of immediately seen objects where the common folk think there is just one.

Berkeley appeals to his rather large ontology of immediately seen objects to respond to a question concerning the epistemological consequences of his idealistic metaphysics. As we have seen, Berkeley holds that it is impossible for us to be mistaken about the immediate objects of perception, for he holds both that immediate objects of perception are ideas and that ideas are wholly present to the mind. This doctrine of infallibilism, however, does not at first blush sit well with the existence of sensory illusions. Hylas makes the point in DHP 3, and Philonous provides a ready answer:

Hyl: What say you to this? Since, according to you, men judge of the reality of things by their senses, how can a man be mistaken in thinking the moon a plain lucid surface, about a foot in diameter; or a square tower, seen at a distance, round; or an oar, with one end in the water, crooked?

Phil: He is not mistaken with regard to the ideas he actually perceives; but in the inferences he makes from his present perceptions. Thus in the case of the oar, *what he immediately perceives by sight is certainly crooked*; and so far he is in the right. But if he thence conclude, that upon taking the oar out of the water he shall perceive the same crookedness; or that it would affect his touch, as crooked things are wont to do: in that he is mistaken. In like manner, if he shall conclude from what he perceives in one station, that in case he advances toward the moon or tower, he should still be affected with the like ideas, he is mistaken. (DHP 3; W2: 238—emphasis added)

As Hylas sees it, the very same oar that *appears* crooked in the water is *actually* straight. But as Philonous sees it, what Hylas treats as mere visual appearance is in fact an immediate object of sight; and where Hylas takes the relevant subject to see one stick at two different times, Philonous takes him to see two. As Berkeley would put it, at T1 the subject (call him "S") immediately sees a stick that is indeed crooked, while at T2 S immediately sees a stick that is straight. By Leibniz's Law, the crooked stick and the straight stick are numerically distinct. Strictly speaking, then, *there is no such thing as a visual illusion in the realm of the immediately seen.*[14] According to Hylas, S is mistaken about the nature of what he immediately sees at T1: what S judges to be crooked is really straight. According to Philonous, S is *not* mistaken about the nature of what he immediately sees at T1: what S judges to be crooked is really crooked. Berkeley concludes that the "crooked oar" example is no counterexample to his doctrine of infallibilism. And what allows him to parry this objection is his exceedingly generous ontology of immediately seen objects.

In addition to the immediate objects of sight, Berkeley's universe also contains a great many immediate objects of touch. As we have seen, Berkeley's Heterogeneity Thesis entails that the immediate objects of sight are numerically distinct from the immediate objects of touch. And this point applies not merely to the individual simple ideas that are immediately apprehended by sense: it also applies to the complex ideas (that is, to the sensible objects) that are constructed from them. Thus, for example, at NTV 55 (W1: 191), Berkeley distinguishes between "tangible magnitude" and "visible magnitude," claiming that "as you approach or recede" from a tree, the tangible magnitude remains fixed while the visible magnitude varies. But Berkeley also emphasizes that "the tangible and visible magnitude do in truth belong to two distinct objects," that is, that the tangible magnitude belongs to the tangible tree and that the visible magnitude belongs to the visible tree. Thus, again, where the common folk take it that there is one tree that is both seen and felt, Berkeley insists that there are two trees, one (immediately) seen, the other (immediately) felt.

---

[14] Lennon (1988, 235) makes a similar point, though without emphasizing the importance of immediate perception: "Berkeley shares with the materialist the view that all ideas have the character of physical things; that is, ideas really have the qualities they appear to have."

In saying that the realm of the immediately seen does not allow for the possibility of illusion, I do not mean to say that Berkeley denies that there is a distinction, within this realm, between the real and the chimerical. Berkeley quite clearly states that there is such a distinction (PHK 33–4; W2: 54–5), and analyzes it as the difference between ideas that are more, and ideas that are less, "regular, vivid and constant" (PHK 33; W2: 54). So in the metaphysical sense of "illusory" according to which it is synonymous with "chimerical" (as, e.g., at PHK 34; W2: 55), there are indeed illusions in the realm of the immediately seen. But the sense of "illusory" at issue in the main text here is epistemic, rather than metaphysical. When I say that, for Berkeley, there is no illusion in the realm of the immediately seen, I mean that we are *epistemically infallible* about the features of things that are immediately seen. Such infallibility is perfectly compatible with the metaphysical distinction between real and chimerical things.

There is therefore not merely an explosion of immediately seen objects in Berkeley's ontology: there is also an explosion of objects that are immediately felt. Thus, at NTV 102 (W1: 212), Berkeley distinguishes between the tangible earth and the tangible man on the one hand, and the visible earth and the visible man on the other, claiming that "the ideas which constitute the tangible earth and man are intirely different from those which constitute the visible earth and man." And at NTV 117 (W1: 218), Berkeley tells us that the visible man is constituted by a "certain variety and disposition of colours," while the tangible man is constituted by "that other combination of far different ideas, sensible by touch." More particularly, Berkeley writes in NTV 96 (W1: 210) of how, for a man born blind, "one combination of a certain tangible figure, bulk, and consistency of parts is called the [tangible] head, another the [tangible] hand, a third the [tangible] foot, and so of the rest: All which complex ideas could, in his understanding, be made up only of ideas perceivable by touch." And, by parity of reasoning, it would follow that, for a sighted man, one combination of a certain visible disposition of colors is called the visible head, another the visible hand, a third the visible foot, and so on; all which complex ideas are made up only of ideas perceivable by sight.

But Berkeley's ontology is even more generous than one that allows for visible objects and tangible objects. It can happen, of course, that the folk construct complex ideas out of simple ideas that belong to a *single* sense. But it is far more common for them to construct complex ideas out of simple ideas that belong to *different* senses. So, for example, for most folk an apple is constituted by "a certain colour, taste, smell, figure, and consistence having being observed to go together" (PHK 1; W2: 41), and a cherry, which is constituted by "the sensations of softness, moisture, redness, [and] tartness," is "nothing but a congeries of sensible impressions, or ideas perceived by various senses: which ideas are united into one thing (or have one name given them) by the mind; because they are observed to attend each other" (DHP 3; W2: 249). In truth, then, when I am doing what the folk would describe as looking at and feeling the apple in my hand, I am perceiving at least three things: (i) the visible apple, which is nothing but a disposition of colors, (ii) the tangible apple, which is nothing but a combination of tangible bulk, figure, and consistency, and (iii) the "folk" apple, which is a combination of qualities belonging to all five senses.

Berkeley is well aware that his exceedingly generous ontology of the sensible world will seem counterintuitive to common folk. But he has a ready explanation for why it (albeit mistakenly) appears to the folk that there is one sensible object where there are in fact many. It is one of the main theses of NTV that we perceive tangible qualities (such as tangible distance, tangible magnitude, and tangible situation) mediately by sight. What makes this possible is that immediately seen patterns of light and color suggest tangible qualities, where the existence of such a relation is underwritten by the natural laws that are purely the result of God's will. The mental transition from suggest*ing* to suggest*ed* qualities is, as Berkeley emphasizes, so quick as to be usually unnoticed:

> We cannot open our eyes but the ideas of distance, bodies, and tangible figures are suggested by them. So swift and sudden and unperceived is the transition from visible to tangible ideas that we can scarce forbear thinking them equally the immediate object of vision. (NTV 145; W1: 230)

According to Berkeley, it is the long-standing and constantly reinforced connection between visible and tangible ideas among the folk that explains, at least in part, why they come to adulthood having prejudged the issue in favor of a minimalist ontology. As Berkeley puts the point in TVV:

> There hath been a long and close connexion in our minds between the ideas of sight and touch. Hence they are considered as one thing: Which prejudice suiteth well enough with the purposes of life; and language is suited to this prejudice. (TVV 35; W1: 263)

So part of the reason why the folk fail to distinguish between visible objects and tangible objects is that, as a result of past experience, the perception of the former carries their minds almost effortlessly to the perception of the latter. But in addition to not paying attention to the mental transition that is suggestion, the folk also care hardly at all about the visible objects themselves. As Berkeley puts it in NTV, we folk only care about the objects we perceive insofar as they can damage or benefit our bodies:

> We regard the objects that environ us in proportion as they are adapted to benefit or injure our own bodies, and thereby produce in our minds the sensations of pleasure or pain. Now bodies operating on our organs, by an immediate application, and the hurt or advantage arising there-from, depending altogether on the tangible, and not at all on the visible, qualities of any object: This is a plain reason why those should be regarded by us much more than these . . . Hence it is that when we look at an object, the tangible figure and extension thereof are principally attended to; whilst there is small heed taken of the visible figure and magnitude,

which, though more immediately perceived, do less concern us, and are not fitted to produce any alteration in our bodies. (NTV 59; W1: 193)

So not only do the folk not pay attention to the mental transition from visible objects to tangible objects, it is also the case that they do not pay attention to the visible objects themselves. No wonder, then, that the folk grow up with the false prejudice that there are many fewer objects of perception than there actually are.

It does not help the cause of strict and philosophical truth that, as Berkeley puts it at TVV 35 (W1: 263), "language [is] accommodated to the praenotions of men and use of life." The prejudice of ontological minimalism having taken hold in the folk from a very early age is then enshrined in language. As Philonous puts it to Hylas in DHP 3:

Strictly speaking, Hylas, we do not see the same object that we feel; neither is the same object perceived by the microscope, which was by the naked eye. But in case every variation was thought sufficient to constitute a new kind or individual, the endless number or confusion of names would render language impracticable. Therefore to avoid this as well as other inconveniencies which are obvious upon a little thought, men combine together several ideas, apprehended by divers senses, or by the same sense at different times, or in different circumstances, but observed however to have some connexion in Nature, either with respect to co-existence or succession; all which they refer to one name, and consider as one thing. (DHP 3; W2: 245)

So purely practical considerations related to the end of effective linguistic communication require that there be one name where the cause of speculative truth would argue for many. But where there is one name, the folk will tend to think there is just one referent:

It is customary to call written words and the things they signify by the same name: For words not being regarded in their own nature, or otherwise than as they are marks of things, it had been superfluous, and beside the design of language, to have given them names distinct from those of the things marked by them. (NTV 140; W1: 228)

So, as Berkeley sees matters, it is easy to understand why the folk would mistakenly infer, from the fact that there is one name rather than many (say, "apple," rather than "visible apple" and "tangible apple"), that there is only one sensible object where there are many.

It should now be clear that Berkeley's sensible world is composed of a whole host of different sorts of sensible objects, some composed of ideas of one sense, others composed of ideas of different senses. The multiplicity of sensible objects now leaves room for the possibility that some of these objects are immediately, while others are only mediately, perceived by sense. Although Berkeley himself never discusses the issue directly, I think the available evidence strongly suggests (or, at least, makes room for the possibility) that he would endorse something like the following picture. *Some* sensible objects are composed of simple ideas, whether belonging to one sense or many, that are *all* immediately perceived by sense at a single time. These are the sensible objects we *immediately* perceive by sense. *Other* sensible objects are composed of simple ideas, whether belonging to one sense or many, *not* all of which are immediately perceived by sense at a single time. These are the sensible objects we *mediately* perceive by sense. So, for example, the pattern of light and color that constitutes the visible moon is immediately perceived by sight inasmuch as all of its constituent ideas are seen without intermediary. Similarly for the patterns of light and color that constitute a visible man, a visible head, a visible foot, a visible tower, and so on. It is for the same reason that the pattern of immediately perceived tangible ideas that constitutes a small tangible pebble wholly enclosed in my palm is immediately perceived by touch. By contrast, because *some* of the simple ideas that constitute a "folk" apple or cherry are not immediately perceived at the relevant time, "folk" apples and cherries are only *mediately* perceived by sense. Thus, if I immediately see an apple-shaped color pattern that suggests the other ideas that constitute my complex idea of an apple (ideas such as sweetness and crunchiness), then I mediately see the apple by virtue of the fact that I mediately perceive some of its constituent ideas by sight. And if I immediately taste a familiar tartness that suggests the other ideas that constitute my complex idea of a cherry (ideas such as softness, moisture, and redness), then I mediately taste the cherry by virtue of the fact that I mediately perceive some of its constituent ideas by the palate. In fact, it can even happen that *all* of the ideas that constitute a sensible object are mediately perceived. So, for example, if the immediate perception of a visible apple by sight reminds me of (and so suggests) a tangible cherry I am not presently immediately perceiving, then I count as mediately perceiving the tangible cherry by sight.

On the whole, then, we should not be surprised to find (as we do) passages that suggest that Berkeley takes sensible objects to be immediately perceived by sense, as well as passages that suggest that Berkeley takes sensible objects to be mediately perceived by sense. What Berkeley leaves unsaid is that the sensible objects that are immediately perceived are numerically distinct from the sensible objects that are mediately perceived. Given Berkeley's rather generous ontology of sensible objects, there is no need to discount the passages that favor the Pappas interpretation and no need to discount the passages that favor the Pitcher interpretation. And there is also no need to read Berkeley as committing to a contradiction. All of the relevant passages, read as whole and in the most reasonably charitable way, are mutually consistent.

## 3  Can the Same Sensible Object be Perceived by Different Senses?

So far we have been considering the question whether, on Berkeley's view, sensible objects are immediately and/or mediately perceived by means of the senses. There are two further questions in the vicinity of the first that have exercised commentators: first, whether Berkeley holds that the same sensible object can be perceived (whether mediately or immediately) by means of different senses, and, second, whether Berkeley holds that the same sensible object can be perceived (whether mediately or immediately) by different minds. As I will now argue, a proper conception of Berkeley's ontology of sensible objects, coupled with a proper understanding of Berkeley's conception of immediate perception, helps us answer both of these questions.

Let us begin with the first. As Berkeley sees it, can sensible objects be immediately perceived by means of different senses? Some scholars, including most notably Pappas, answer this question in the affirmative. Pappas writes that there are "a number of passages in which Berkeley claims that the same object is immediately seen and felt."[15] The passages to which Pappas refers here are identical to the passages that support his claim that Berkeley takes sensible objects to be objects of immediate perception, namely PHK 34–5, PHK 84, the "Glove" passage, the "Cherry" passage, PHK 38, the "Wood and Stones" passage, and the "Death" passage.

My view is that these passages do not establish what Pappas thinks they do. Berkeley does speak of "the things I see with mine eyes and touch with mine hands" (PHK 34–5; W2: 55), of "see[ing], and smell[ing], and tast[ing] . . . wine" (PHK 84; W2: 77), of seeing and feeling the same glove (in

---

[15] Pappas (2000, 181).

the "Glove" passage), and of seeing, feeling, and tasting the same cherry (in the "Cherry" passage). So it is clear that Berkeley holds that the same sensible object may be perceived by more than one sense. But does it follow that the same sensible object may be *immediately* perceived by more than one sense? Indeed not. For all Berkeley tells us in PHK 34–5, PHK 84, the "Glove" passage, and the "Cherry" passage, it may be that the same sensible object can only be *mediately* perceived by more than one sense. And, indeed, on the interpretation I have been defending, this is exactly what Berkeley holds.

On Berkeley's view, there are different sorts of sensible objects. Some sensible objects are collections of ideas of a *single* sense *all of which are* immediately perceived by a single subject at a single time (call these "sensible objects of type 1"); other sensible objects are collections of ideas of *different* senses *all of which are* immediately perceived by a single subject at a single time (call these "sensible objects of type 2"); and yet other sensible objects are collections of ideas (whether of the same sense or of different senses) *some of which are not* immediately perceived by a single subject at a single time (call these "sensible objects of type 3"). On my reading of Berkeley, his view is that it is only possible for a subject to immediately perceive a collection of ideas by means of a particular sense by immediately perceiving *all* of the members of the collection by means of that sense. And according to Berkeley's Heterogeneity Thesis, the immediate objects of one sense are numerically (and specifically) distinct from the immediate objects of another. It follows directly that sensible objects of type 1 cannot be immediately perceived by more than one sense.

Suppose, for example, that I am looking at a visible apple composed of a particular pattern of colors. By virtue of the fact that I immediately perceive all the colors in the pattern by sight, I immediately see the visible apple. But the visible apple is not something that I can immediately feel (or taste, or smell, or hear). For in order to immediately feel the visible apple, I would have to immediately feel all of its constituent ideas, that is, I would have to feel all of the colors in the color pattern. But by the Heterogeneity Thesis, this is impossible: colors are the proper objects of sight, and cannot be immediately perceived by touch. The result is no different when it comes to sensible objects of type 2. Suppose, for example, that the pebble in my hand is a collection of ideas, some of which I immediately perceive by sight (say, S1, S2, and S3), others of which I immediately perceive by touch (say, T1, T2, and T3). On Berkeley's view, can I immediately perceive the pebble (that is, the collection {S1, S2, S3, T1, T2, T3}) by sight? On my view, the answer is "no," for, as Berkeley sees it, I cannot immediately perceive the pebble by sight without immediately perceiving all of its constituent ideas by sight. Now it is true that I immediately see S1, S2, and S3. But, by the Heterogeneity Thesis, I do not immediately see T1, T2, or T3. Similar reasoning shows that I cannot immediately perceive the pebble by touch. For I cannot immediately perceive the pebble by touch without immediately perceiving all of its constituent ideas by touch. And, although I do immediately touch T1, T2, and T3, the Heterogeneity Thesis entails that I cannot immediately touch S1, S2, or S3. By extrapolation, then, on Berkeley's view it is impossible for the same sensible object of type 2 to be immediately perceived by more than one sense.[16] And the situation is no different in the case of sensible objects of type 3. Suppose, for example, that the cherry on the table is a collection of ideas, some of which (say, its red color) I immediately perceive by sight, but the rest of which (including its tart taste and soft feel) I only mediately perceive by sight. Again, given that I cannot immediately perceive *all* of the cherry's constituents by sight, I cannot immediately see the cherry itself.

As Berkeley sees matters, then, no sensible object can be immediately perceived by more than one sense. Does the same thesis hold true for *mediately* perceived sensible objects? Surely not. Mediate perception, as we have seen, operates through the relation of suggestion. On Berkeley's view, it is possible for any idea (or group of ideas) to suggest any other idea (or group of ideas), as long as the two ideas (or groups) are connected (whether by resemblance, deduction, or regular association) in our experience. So imagine a sensible object O (of any one of the three types). If I immediately perceive an idea I1 by sense S1, and idea I1 suggests O, then I count as mediately perceiving O by sense S1. And if I immediately perceive an idea I2 by sense S2, and idea I2 suggests O, then I count as mediately perceiving O by sense S2. So Berkeley's conception of mediate

---

[16] Some qualifications are in order here. First, it is possible to perceive *part* of a sensible object of type 2 by means of a single sense. If such an object O is a collection of sensible ideas, say {S1, S2, S3, T1, T2, T3}, then, assuming that {S1, S2, S3} constitutes a part of O, then, because it is possible to perceive all of S1, S2, and S3 by sight, it follows that it is possible to perceive a part of O by sight. Similarly for the part of O constituted by {T1, T2, T3}. Second, if all the ideas constituting O are perceived at the same time, then O counts as perceived by sense, even if not by a *single* sense. In this sort of case, O is perceived by the faculties of sight and touch taken together (even if not by these faculties taken individually).

perception allows for the mediate perception of the same sensible object by more than one sense.

On the view that I am defending, Berkeley holds that sensible objects cannot be immediately perceived, though they can be mediately perceived, by more than one sense. We have seen that this view is perfectly consistent with PHK 34–5, PHK 84, the "Glove" passage, and the "Cherry" passage. Is the view contradicted by the rest of the passages Pappas cites (namely, PHK 38, the "Wodd and Stones" passage, and the "Death" passage)? In PHK 38 (W2: 56), Berkeley commits to the claim that "we eat and drink ideas, and are clothed with ideas," that "we are fed and clothed with those things we perceive immediately by our senses." And in the "Wood and Stones" passage, he says that he immediately perceives such things as wood, stones, fire, flesh, and iron "by the senses." But none of these statements need be read to imply that it is possible to immediately perceive the same sensible object by means of different senses. Perhaps Berkeley is imagining that he is clothed with items he immediately feels but cannot immediately see (or taste, or smell, or hear), that he is fed with items he immediately tastes but cannot immediately see (or feel, or smell, or hear), that he immediately sees (but cannot immediately perceive by any other sense) visible stones, and that he immediately touches (but cannot immediately perceive by any other sense) tangible stones. It is true that in the "Death" passage Berkeley says that there are "sensible bodies [that] are immediately perceived by sight and touch." But this statement is ambiguous as between two claims: (i) that some sensible bodies are immediately perceived by both sight and touch, and (ii) that some sensible bodies are immediately perceived by sight, while *other* bodies are immediately perceived by touch. Nothing in the language Berkeley uses requires us to read him as being committed to the view that sensible objects can be immediately perceived by more than one sense.

Baxter (1991, 86) cites another passage that supports Pappas's claims:

> Take away this *material substance*, about the identity whereof all the dispute is, and mean by *body* what every plain ordinary person means by that word, to wit, that which is immediately seen and felt, which is only a combination of sensible qualities, or ideas: and then their most unanswerable objections come to nothing. (PHK 95; W2: 82)

Here Berkeley appears to commit quite plainly to the view that bodies are both immediately seen and immediately felt. But there are two problems with this passage. The first is that the conception of body that Berkeley describes in PHK 95 is supposed to belong to "every plain ordinary person." But, as we have seen, "plain ordinary people" do not use the concept of immediate perception, and so would not characterize bodies as things that are both immediately seen and immediately felt. The second is that this passage has a twin in DHP 3, a passage in which, interestingly, the reference to immediate perception is removed:

But if by *material substance* is meant only sensible body, that which is seen and felt (and the unphilosophical part of the world, I dare say, mean no more) then I am more certain of matter's existence than you, or any other philosopher, pretend to be. (DHP 3; W2: 237)

Given that the folk do not work with the concepts of mediate and immediate perception, it is no surprise that Berkeley describes them as conceiving of bodies as things that are seen and felt, rather than as things that are *immediately* seen and felt. And I suspect that Berkeley penned this passage as he did precisely because he saw that what he had previously written in PHK 95 was erroneous. On balance, then, PHK 95 provides little or no reason to believe that it is Berkeley's considered view that sensible objects can be immediately perceived by more than one sense.

Interestingly, Berkeley is well aware of the counterintuitive nature of his position on this issue. As Hylas puts the objection to Philonous in DHP:

Why is not the same figure, and other sensible qualities, perceived all manner of ways? And why should we use a microscope, the better to discover the true nature of a body, if it were discoverable to the naked eye? (DHP 3; W2: 245)

In a passage, with part of which we are already familiar, Philonous answers thus:

Strictly speaking, Hylas, we do not see the same object that we feel; neither is the same object perceived by the microscope, which was by the naked eye . . . [W]hen I examine by my other senses a thing I have seen, it is not in order to understand better the same object which I had perceived by sight, the object of one sense not being perceived by the other senses. And when I look through a microscope, it is not that I may perceive more clearly what I perceived already with my bare eyes, the object perceived by the glass being quite different from the former. (DHP 3; W2: 245)

The objects under discussion in this passage are fairly clearly objects of immediate, rather than mediate, perception. This is the import of Philonous's use of the expression, "strictly speaking." To see this, consider NTV

45 (W1: 188), where Berkeley states that "in truth and strictness of speech I neither see distance it self, nor anything that I take to be at a distance." Berkeley cannot mean that he does not literally see distance, for, as we have seen, it is a major thesis of NTV that distance is literally seen, albeit only mediately. So, in saying that distance is not seen *strictly speaking*, Berkeley must simply mean that distance is not *immediately* seen. Similarly, in the passage from DHP 3 (W2: 245), in saying that we do not see the same object that we feel *strictly speaking*, Berkeley must simply mean that the same object is not both an *immediate* object of sight and an *immediate* object of touch. And in saying that the object of one sense is not perceived by the other senses, he must mean that the *immediate* object of one sense is not *immediately* perceived by the other senses. Thus Berkeley *embraces* what may seem like a counterintuitive consequence to the common folk.

My argument that, on Berkeley's view, the same sensible object cannot be immediately perceived by more than one sense rests in part on the Heterogeneity Thesis. As I read it, this thesis says that anything that is immediately perceived by one sense is necessarily numerically (and specifically) distinct from anything that is immediately perceived by another sense. According to Pappas, this is a mistake. Pappas distinguishes between two statements:

(1)   No idea which is immediately perceived by sight is numerically or specifically identical to an idea which is immediately perceived by touch.

(2)   Nothing which is immediately seen is also immediately touched.[17]

Pappas then claims that (1), but not (2), expresses the Heterogeneity Thesis, and that (1) does not entail (2) because the scope of (2) is much broader than the scope of (1). Pappas concludes that although the Heterogeneity Thesis, properly understood, commits Berkeley to the view that no *idea* that is immediately perceived by one sense is immediately perceived by another, it does *not* commit Berkeley to the view that no *sensible object* that is immediately perceived by one sense is immediately perceived by another.

Now it is surely true, as Pappas notes, that (1) does not entail (2). But it does not follow from this that Berkeley is not committed to (2). In defense

---

[17]   Pappas (2000, 182).

of the claim that Berkeley holds no more than (1), Pappas cites the following passage:

> The extension, figures, and motions perceived by sight are specifically distinct from the ideas of touch called by the same names, nor is there any such thing as one idea or kind of idea common to both senses. (NTV 127; W1: 222–3)

Clearly Berkeley commits to (1), but not to (2), in NTV 127. But elsewhere in NTV, Berkeley also commits to (2). Consider, for example, the following passage:

> But if we take a close and accurate view of things, it must be acknowledged that we never see and feel one and the same object. That which is seen is one thing, and that which is felt is another. If the visible figure and extension be not the same with the tangible figure and extension, we are not to infer that one and the same thing has divers extensions. The true consequence is that the objects of sight and touch are two distinct things. It may perhaps require some thought rightly to conceive this distinction. And the difficulty seems not a little increased, because the combination of visible ideas hath constantly the same name as the combination of tangible ideas wherewith it is connected: Which doth of necessity arise from the use and end of language. (NTV 49; W1: 189)

Here Berkeley says that "visible figure and extension" differs from "tangible figure and extension." This claim is no more than an instance of (1). But Berkeley also says that from this claim "we are not to infer that one and the same thing has divers extensions." What he means by this is that we are not to infer that visible extension and tangible extension are qualities of the same sensible object. Rather, what we should infer, he says, is that "the objects of sight and touch are distinct things," by which he means that the sensible objects immediately perceived by sight and the sensible objects immediately perceived by touch are numerically distinct. This is clearly (2), and not just (1). That this reading is accurate is confirmed by what Berkeley goes on to say at the end of the passage. There he writes that what makes it difficult for common folk to recognize that the immediate objects of sight are numerically distinct from the immediate objects of touch is that "the combination of visible ideas hath constantly the same name as the combination of tangible ideas wherewith it is connected." This explanation would be beside the point if Berkeley were trying to explain why the folk mistakenly believe that (1) is false. It only makes sense on the supposition that Berkeley is trying to explain why the folk mistakenly believe that (2) is false.

This way of reading NTV 49 is confirmed by the following passage:

It hath been shewn there are two sorts of objects apprehended by sight; each whereof hath its distinct magnitude, or extension. The one, properly tangible, *i.e.* to be perceived and measured by touch, and not immediately falling under the sense of seeing: The other, properly and immediately visible, by mediation of which the former is brought into view. (NTV 54; W1: 191)

Berkeley's point here is that there are two different sorts of objects, tangible objects and visible objects. The former, which *have* tangible magnitude or extension, are immediately perceived by touch, but not immediately perceived by sight. The latter, which *have* visible magnitude or extension, are immediately perceived by sight, but not immediately perceived by touch. This claim is clearly an instance of (2), rather than merely an instance of (1). On balance, then, it seems that the Heterogeneity Thesis to which Berkeley commits in NTV does indeed entail (with the help of further assumptions) that the same sensible object cannot be immediately perceived by more than one sense.

## 4  Can the Same Sensible Object be Perceived by Different Minds?

Let us now move on to the second question. As Berkeley sees it, can sensible objects be immediately perceived by different *minds*? Are Berkeley's sensible objects, as it were, public or private? According to Pitcher (1977, 146–50; 1986, 103 ff.), the answer is clear. As Berkeley sees matters, the immediate objects of perception are ideas. But ideas are private to the minds that perceive them: I cannot immediately perceive the ideas you immediately perceive, nor can you immediately perceive the ideas I immediately perceive. Given that sensible objects are nothing but collections of ideas, so Pitcher argues, it follows that no two minds can immediately perceive the same sensible object. The claim that Berkeley's sensible objects are private therefore follows logically from other claims to which he is antecedently committed.

Pappas questions this claim of Pitcher's. Pappas claims that even if we restrict our attention to *finite* perceivers, it does not follow from the claim that *ideas* are private and that sensible objects are collections of ideas that *sensible objects* are private too. Focusing on "a case of [two generals] on the reviewing stand as the troop marches past," Pappas argues as follows:

[T]wo generals on different sections of the reviewing stand may see different members of the troop, but still each would see the troop. Two people can see the same object even though they do not see the same parts or constituent elements of the object.[18]

I think we should agree with Pappas that Berkeley is not logically committed to the view that sensible objects are private merely on the grounds that sensible objects are collections of private elements. But it does not follow that Berkeley is not in fact committed to the view that Pitcher attributes to him. For Berkeley could be committed to the view on different grounds.

Indeed, on the interpretation I have been defending, Berkeley *is* committed to the claim that sensible objects are private. Pappas's "troop review" example works only because the troop consists of elements that are immediately perceived by different minds. But, on Berkeley's conception of sensible objects, every immediately perceived sensible object (that is, every sensible object of type 1 or type 2) is composed of ideas that are immediately perceived by a single (finite) mind. The cherry *I* see on the table is composed entirely of *my* ideas; the cherry *you* see on the table is composed entirely of *your* ideas. If I cannot immediately perceive your ideas and you cannot immediately perceive mine, then I have no hope of immediately perceiving the cherry you see on the table, and you have no hope of immediately perceiving the cherry I see there. Pappas assumes that Berkeley's immediately perceived sensible objects are composed of ideas that belong to different minds. But this assumption is not moored in the text.

Berkeley considers the question of the publicity of sensible objects explicitly in DHP 3. Hylas raises the following objection:

But the same idea which is in my mind, cannot be in yours, or in any other mind. Doth it not therefore follow from your principles, that no two can see the same thing? And is not this highly absurd? (DHP 3; W2: 247)

Philonous's response seems altogether rather coy. He distinguishes between two senses of the word "same." According to the "vulgar acceptation," to say that X is the same as Y is to say that "no distinction or variety [between X and Y] is perceived." But according to "the acceptation of philosophers," to say that X is the same as Y is to say that X bears the (abstracted) relation of "philosophic identity" to Y. If the word "same" is

---

[18]   Pappas (2000, 198 and 200–1).

taken in the vulgar sense, then, given the qualitative similarity of ideas belonging to different finite minds, it can be perfectly true to say that you and I both immediately perceive the same ideas, and hence that you and I both immediately perceive the same sensible object. But if the word "same" is taken in the "philosophic" sense, then, depending on how one conceives of the nature of philosophic identity, "it may or may not be possible for divers persons to perceive the same thing."

As Pitcher sees it, Philonous's response indicates that, for Berkeley, the claim that two or more people cannot immediately perceive the numerically same sensible object is "the sober philosophical truth."[19] Although my sympathies are with Pitcher here, I believe that we need a more nuanced interpretation. Pitcher takes for granted that there is a single, clear, and unequivocal *philosophical* sense of "same," namely the concept of numerical identity. There is no doubt that Berkeley sometimes helps himself to this concept, as when he argues that no idea immediately perceived by sight is the same as any idea immediately perceived by touch (the Heterogeneity Thesis). For here his point is not that no idea immediately perceived by sight *resembles* any idea immediately perceived by touch; after all, every idea resembles every other idea in some way or other. His point, rather, is that no idea immediately perceived by sight is *numerically identical* to any idea immediately perceived by touch. But in responding to Hylas's objection in DHP 3, Berkeley does not explicitly and self-consciously recognize that "same" can be used to mean numerical, as opposed to qualitative, identity. Instead, he claims, first, that philosophers have tried to define sameness in many different ways, that these different definitions have engendered disputes, and that those disputes are merely verbal, in the sense that it is entirely arbitrary whether X counts as the same as Y; and, second, that philosophers have wrongly thought that there is such a thing as an *abstract* idea of identity. This may all be true, but it leaves open the possibility that philosophers (and the vulgar!) often use the word "same" to mean numerical identity, and that, *in this sense*, the idea that I immediately perceive is not the same as the idea that you immediately perceive, no matter how qualitatively similar those ideas may be. The reason we read Philonous's response as coy is that he doesn't answer Hylas's question head on. His official view is that if we speak with the vulgar, then we are

---

[19]   Pitcher (1986, 104).

entitled to say that two finite minds can immediately perceive the same ideas, whereas if we speak with the learned, then there is no fact of the matter whether two finite minds can immediately perceive the same ideas. whether they can depends on which of the many philosophical senses of "same" one is choosing to work with. What this answer leaves open is the answer to the question Hylas has in mind, namely whether it is possible for the idea that you immediately perceive to be numerically identical to the idea that I immediately perceive. Given that we know that Berkeley sometimes uses the word "same" to mean numerical identity, it makes sense to say, as Pitcher does on Berkeley's behalf, that Berkeley is committed to the view that, *in that sense*, the idea that you immediately perceive is *not* numerically identical to the idea that I immediately perceive. But this is not something to which Berkeley unequivocally commits himself in penning Philonous's reply to Hylas's objection.

None of this excludes the possibility that different finite minds might *mediately* perceive the same sensible object. It is true that the sensible objects perceived by a finite mind are (at least, typically) constituted by ideas that are immediately or mediately perceived by that very same mind. But, in Berkeley's scheme, there is no bar to one finite mind mediately perceiving ideas that belong to another. Berkeley himself provides an interesting instance of this phenomenon at NTV 9 (W1: 173): "[T]he passions which are in the mind of another are of themselves to me invisible. I may nevertheless perceive them by sight, though not immediately, yet by means of the colours they produce in the countenance. We often see shame or fear in the looks of a man, by perceiving the changes of his countenance to red or pale." In this sort of (rather commonplace) situation, one mind mediately perceives ideas that belong to another. And if one mind's *passions* can be mediately perceived by another, surely the sensible objects constituted by that mind's immediately and/or mediately perceived ideas can also be mediately perceived by another.[20]

In sum, Berkeley's picture of the perceptual relation between minds and sensible objects is this. Some sensible objects (namely, those all of whose constituents are immediately perceived at a single time) can be

---

[20] McKim (1992, 220) claims that Berkeley holds "that each perceiver perceives only her own ideas." As I argue in the text, this is not strictly true, given Berkeley's insistence that perceivers sometimes *mediately* perceive ideas in others' minds. But I agree with McKim that the principle holds in the realm of *immediate* perception.

immediately perceived. Other sensible objects (namely, those not all of whose constituents are immediately perceived at a single time) can only be mediately perceived. Strictly and philosophically, it is impossible for the same sensible object to be immediately perceived by different senses. Also strictly and philosophically, there may be a sense in which the same sensible object can be immediately perceived by different finite minds, though there may also be a sense (perhaps, upon reflection, the sense of numerical identity) in which the same sensible object *cannot* be immediately perceived by different finite minds. But it can (and does) happen that the same sensible object is mediately perceived by means of different senses, and it can (and does) happen that the same sensible object is mediately perceived by different minds. If I am right, this picture follows naturally from Berkeley's generous ontology of sensible objects, coupled with his conception of mediate and immediate perception by sense and his account of the possibilities of suggestion.

# 3

# The Argument for Idealism in the *Principles*

NTV does not contain an argument for idealism. It does endorse the claim that "colours, which are the proper and immediate object of sight, are not without the mind," and argues that *visible* extension, *visible* figure, and *visible* motion, being exactly where colors are, must also be mind-dependent (NTV 43; W1: 186–7). It follows directly that *visible* objects (such as the "visible moon" discussed in NTV 44; W1: 187 and the "visible feet" discussed in NTV 107; W1: 213–14), being nothing but collections of visible qualities (NTV 107; W1: 213–14 and NTV 110; W1: 215), have no mind-independent existence either. But NTV is silent on the question of the ontological status of *tangible* objects, as well as the more general question of the ontological status of any sensible object that consists of more than merely visible qualities. In PHK, Berkeley explains that his silence was no accidental omission, claiming that "it was beside [his] purpose to examine and refute [the supposition that tangible objects exist without the mind] in a discourse concerning *vision*" (PHK 44; W2: 59).

It is in PHK that Berkeley first announces a completely general denial of the mind-independent existence of sensible objects. In fact, the announcement of idealism arrives as early as sections 3 and 4. For in PHK 3 (W2: 42), Berkeley claims that the being (*esse*) of all unthinking things (including sensible qualities, such as color and shape, as well as sensible objects, such as tables and chairs) is to be perceived (*percipi*); and in PHK 4 (W2: 42), Berkeley explicitly denies the "strangely prevailing" (i.e., the widely accepted) opinion that "houses, mountains, rivers, and in a word all sensible objects have an existence natural or real, distinct from their being perceived by the understanding."

On Berkeley's embrace of idealism in the early sections of PHK scholars of his work are almost universally agreed. But there is serious disagreement regarding Berkeley's *reasons* for holding that sensible objects cannot exist unperceived. According to some, Berkeley treats the mind-dependence of sensible objects as self-evident, a fact that may be apprehended by intuition and needs no demonstration.[1] According to others, Berkeley actually *argues* that tables and chairs cannot exist unperceived. But even among the latter, there is no agreement as to the nature of the argument itself. Some find evidence that Berkeley rests idealism on his denial of materialism.[2] Others take the argument to depend on Berkeley's denial of the possibility of abstraction.[3] And yet others read into the argument implicit reliance on the likeness principle (the claim that an idea can be like nothing but an idea).[4] As I will argue, though some of these interpretations are nearer the truth than others, all are mistaken.

The truth, as it happens, is much simpler than it is commonly taken to be. Although Berkeley offers semantic reasons in PHK 3 for thinking that idealism is self-evident, the cogency of these reasons depends on an assumption that remains undefended in PHK and requires further support. Berkeley provides an *explicit* non-semantic argument for idealism in PHK 4: he argues that sensible objects are perceived by the senses, that the only objects perceived by the senses are ideas, and hence that sensible objects are ideas. In addition, Berkeley offers an *implicit* non-semantic argument in PHK 1: he argues that sensible objects are collections of sensible qualities, that sensible qualities are ideas, and hence that sensible objects are collections of ideas. It is on the basis of these three arguments *and no others* that Berkeley argues for idealism in PHK.[5] As will become evident, these

---

[1]  See Fogelin (2001).

[2]  See Allaire (1963; 1982; 1995), Cummins (1963), Watson (1963), Hausman (1984), and Wilson (1995).

[3]  See Pappas (1985), Atherton (1987), and Bolton (1987).

[4]  See Winkler (1989).

[5]  In saying that Berkeley uses no other arguments to establish the truth of idealism in PHK, I am using the term "argument" as analytic philosophers commonly use the term, namely as referring to a piece of deductive (or perhaps inductive) reasoning leading from a number of premises to a single conclusion. There is a looser sense of "argument" according to which an argument is nothing more than a set of "considerations...capable of determining the intellect either to give or withhold its assent to [a] doctrine" (Mill 1861/1979, 5). Such considerations might include reasons to reject alternative or competing doctrines or responses to objections to one's conclusion. If "argument" is used in this looser, Millian sense, then I do not mean to suggest that the two Simple Arguments of PHK are the only arguments Berkeley employs in the service of idealism. Still, the stricter use of "argument," from the logical point of view, is the more important of the two. For even if one provides excellent reasons to reject alternatives to idealism and excellent responses to objections to idealism, it does not follow from such "considerations" that idealism is *true*.

arguments too, such as they are, beg the question against Berkeley's materialist opponents. As I argue in chapter 4, it is largely to correct this problem (in particular, by filling out the arguments of PHK 3, PHK 1, and PHK 4) that Berkeley pens DHP 1.

## 1 The Semantic Argument

In the early sections of PHK Berkeley says very little in defense of idealism. But some of what Berkeley *does* say strongly suggests that he finds idealism to be self-evident. For example, Berkeley writes:

Some truths there are so near and obvious to the mind, that a man need only open his eyes to see them. Such I take this important one to be, to wit, that all the choir of heaven and furniture of the earth, in a word all those bodies which compose the mighty frame of the world, have not any subsistence without a mind, that their being is to be perceived or known. (PHK 6; W2: 43)

Here Berkeley characterizes idealism as "near and obvious to the mind." This is, as Berkeley must himself have realized, a surprising claim. If Berkeley is right, then not merely *some*, but *virtually all* of his philosophical predecessors and contemporaries are committed to an obvious untruth, the falsity of which they "need only open their eyes to see."[6] How could so many gifted, reflective philosophers (including Descartes, Locke, and Malebranche) have missed so obvious a truth?

The answer lies in the fact that Berkeley's opponents, reflective though they may be, have an inadequate grasp of the semantics of existence claims. The importance of semantics as a grounding for Berkeley's idealism is already evident in the following entries from the *Notebooks*:

---

[6] Burnyeat (1982, 3–4) claims that "idealism . . . is one of the very few major philosophical positions that did *not* receive its first formulation in antiquity." See also Williams (1981). Others counter that idealism or proto-idealism is to be found in the Neoplatonic tradition, including Gregory of Nyssa (see Sorabji (1983)—but see Hibbs (2005)), Proclus (see Beierwaltes (1985)), Plotinus (see Emilsson (1996)), and Eriugena (see Beierwaltes (1972; 1994) and Moran (1989; 1999)). Arthur Collier embraces idealism in *Clavis Universalis* (1713), probably without having been influenced by Berkeley (see Stoneham (2006; 2007)). Leibniz holds that sensible objects are mind-dependent aggregates of mental substances. So although he is an idealist in some sense, he is not a Berkeleian idealist. For discussion of Leibniz's idealism, see Adams (1994, chapters 9 and 10), Lodge (2001), and Rutherford (2008).

['T]is on the Discovering of the nature & meaning & import of Existence that
I chiefly insist. This puts a wide difference betwixt the Sceptics & me. This I think
wholly new. I am sure 'tis new to me (N 491; W1: 61–2)

Let it not be said that I take away Existence. I onely declare the meaning of the
Word so far as I can comprehend it. (N 593; W1: 74)

I am persuaded would Men but examine w$^t$ they mean by the Word Existence
they wou'd agree with me. (N 604; W1: 75)

Berkeley's point appears to be that idealism follows from the semantics of
"exists," and hence that the best explanation for the hostility to idealism
displayed by his predecessors and contemporaries is the implicit or explicit
adoption of an erroneous semantics for existence claims.

Berkeley provides what he takes to be the correct semantics in PHK 3:

[I]t seems . . . evident that the various sensations or ideas imprinted on the
sense, however blended or combined together (that is, whatever objects they
compose) cannot exist otherwise than in a mind perceiving them. I think an
intuitive knowledge may be obtained of this, by any one that shall attend to
what is meant by the term *exist* when applied to sensible things. The table
I write on, I say, exists, that is, I see and feel it; and if I were out of my study
I should say it existed, meaning thereby that if I was in my study I might perceive it,
or that some other spirit actually does perceive it. There was an odour, that is, it was
smelled; there was a sound, that is to say, it was heard; a colour or figure, and it
was perceived by sight or touch. This is all that I can understand by these and the
like expressions. (PHK 3; W2: 42)

Berkeley's semantics for "exists" is complicated. In the first place, PHK 3
offers only a *partial* semantics of "exists," namely a semantics for the word
only "*when applied to sensible things.*" Berkeley offers to explicate statements to
the effect that such-and-such *unthinking* thing (i.e., sensible quality or sensible
object) exists. What he does not here explicate are statements to the effect
that such-and-such *thinking* thing (i.e., mind) exists. For the latter sort of
claims, Berkeley offers us a different semantics. As he tells us in the *Notebooks*:

Existere is percipi or percipere. (N 429; W1: 53)

Cogito ergo sum, Tautology, no mental Proposition, answering thereto. (N 738;
W1: 90)

For unthinking things, to be is to be perceived (*existere* is *percipi*). For
thinking things, to be is to perceive (*existere* is *percipere*). Indeed, the reason
why the cogito is a tautology is that, for any mind M, the proposition that
M exists is identical to the proposition that M perceives.

Even with regard to the attribution of existence to *unthinking* things, Berkeley's semantic theory is far from simple. In PHK 3, Berkeley distinguishes between two kinds of circumstances: (i) situations in which the subject S who claims that such-and-such unthinking thing T exists is in the same location as T, and (ii) situations in which the relevant subject S is *not* in the same location as T. In circumstances of type (i), the proposition that T exists is identical to the proposition that S perceives T. But in circumstances of type (ii), the proposition that T exists is to be assimilated *either* to the proposition that if S were in the same location as T, S might perceive T *or* to the proposition that some other subject perceives T.

It is on the strength of this semantic theory of "exists" that Berkeley suggests in PHK 6 that idealism is intuitively, rather than demonstratively, known. Berkeley seems to be saying that mere understanding of what is meant by the term "exists" when it is applied to sensible things is sufficient for recognizing the truth of the claim that such things cannot exist unperceived. Put simply, the proposition that the *esse* of sensible things is *percipi* is analytic.

Berkeley's move from the semantics of "exists" to the idealist conclusion that sensible objects cannot exist unperceived works well in two of the three possible ways of understanding the claim of some sensible object that it exists. When I am in the presence of a table T, Berkeley's view is that my claim that T exists reduces to the claim that I perceive T. Under these circumstances, the claim that T exists entails that T is perceived, and it follows from this that T cannot exist unperceived. Something similar is true when I am *not* in the presence of T but mean by "T exists" that some other subject perceives T. For in this case too the claim that T exists entails that T is perceived, from which it follows that T cannot exist unperceived. But there is a problem with the third way of understanding "T exists." Berkeley tells us that when I am not in the room where T is located, when I say that T exists I might mean that if I were in the room I might perceive T. But if this is indeed what I mean, then idealism does not follow, at least not directly. For it is compatible with the claim that I might perceive T if I were in the room that T is something other than an idea or collection of ideas, something that can exist unperceived. To see this, suppose that T is a material substance (an unthinking support of sensible qualities, such as rectangularity and brownness) that God has a standing disposition to place in the room whenever I enter it. In such a hypothetical scenario, it would be true that if I were in the room I might perceive T, even though T is a material substance that could in principle exist unperceived. So Berkeley's semantic theory of "exists," if unsupplemented by further reasoning, does not entail that sensible objects (such as tables) cannot exist unperceived.

To what sort of reasoning might Berkeley appeal to bolster his claim that the proposition that if I were in the room I might perceive T entails that T cannot exist unperceived? Consider what it means to say that under such-and-such circumstances I *might* perceive T. To say that under such-and-such circumstances I might perceive T is to say that T is perceiv*able* by me, and this entails that T is perceiv*able*. Interestingly, Berkeley *argues* that the perceiv*ability* of sensible things entails that they can't exist unperceived. Consider the following passages:

Phil: Sensible things are all immediately perceivable; and those things which are immediately perceivable, are ideas; and these exist only in the mind. Thus much you have, if I mistake not, long since agreed to.
Hyl: I do not deny it. (DHP 2; W2: 209)

Hyl: Yes, Philonous, I grant the existence of a sensible thing consists in being perceivable, but not in being actually perceived.
Phil: And what is perceivable but an idea? And can an idea exist without being actually perceived? These are points long since agreed between us. (DHP 3; W2: 234)

In the second of these passages, Philonous runs a *reductio* of Hylas's claim that the existence of a sensible thing consists in being perceivable, not in being perceived. The reasoning runs as follows:

(AR)   The existence of a sensible thing consists in being perceivable, not in being perceived.

(1)   Anything that is perceivable is an idea.
So, (2)   If the existence of Y consists in being perceivable, then Y is an idea. (From [1])
So, (3)   Sensible things are ideas. (From [AR] and [2])
(4)   The existence of an idea consists in being perceived.
So, (5)   The existence of a sensible thing consists in being perceived. (From [3] and [4])
So, (6)   It is not the case that the existence of a sensible thing consists in being perceived. (From [AR])

Given that (5) and (6) constitute a contradiction, Berkeley infers from the truth of (1) and (4) that the assumption for *reductio* is false.

Notice now that (1) and (4) together entail (7):

(7)   The existence of anything perceivable consists in being perceived.

And suppose that sometimes, when I say that table T exists, I mean that T is perceivable. It follows from (7), then, that if what I say is true, the existence of T consists in being perceived, and thus T cannot exist unperceived.

Berkeley's Semantic Argument in PHK 3 for the claim that the existence of sensible objects consists in being perceived, when appropriately supplemented, is therefore far from a non-starter. But it does implicitly rely on two claims: (i) that perceivable things (and so, sensible things) are ideas, and (ii) that ideas cannot exist unperceived. If it turns out that sensible things are not ideas, then the Semantic Argument fails. Moreover, the claim that sensible things are ideas is not self-evident, and requires support that is independent of the Semantic Argument. There is therefore no easy road from the semantics of existence claims to idealism.

## 2 The Argument from Immaterialism and Inherence

Some scholars claim that Berkeley's argument for idealism in PHK rests, at bottom, on his denial of materialism and his commitment to the Aristotelian Dictum that accidents necessarily inhere in a substance.[7] The argument is admirably simple:

    1.   Sensible objects are collections of qualities.
    2.   Qualities must inhere in substances. [Aristotelian Dictum]
So, 3.   Sensible objects must inhere in substances. [From 1, 2]
    4.   There is no such thing as material substance. [Immaterialism]
    5.   Every substance is either material or mental.
So, 6.   Sensible objects must inhere in mental substances (i.e., minds). [From 3, 4, 5]
    7.   To inhere in a mind is to be perceived by it.
So, 8.   Sensible objects must be perceived by minds (i.e., sensible objects cannot exist unperceived). [From 6, 7]

The attribution of this way of reasoning to Berkeley has come to be known as the Inherence Interpretation, and there is a great deal to

---

[7] These scholars include Allaire (1963; 1982; 1995), Cummins (1963), Watson (1963), Hausman (1984), and Wilson (1995). Critics of this approach include Bracken (1964), Cummins (1975), Oaklander (1977), Muehlmann (1978; 1992, 170–89), and Pappas (1980; 2000, 128–31).

be said in its favor. In the first place, there are texts that strongly suggest that Berkeley accepts every independent premise of the argument. At PHK 1 (W2: 41), Berkeley tells us that sensible objects (such as apples, stones, trees, and books) are "collections of ideas," where the relevant ideas are clearly identified as sensible qualities (such as "colour, taste, smell, figure, and consistence"). This text supports (1). At PHK 91 (W2: 80), Berkeley writes that "[i]t is acknowledged on the received principles, that extension, motion, and in a word all sensible qualities, have need of a support, as not being able to subsist by themselves." This text supports (2). At PHK 9 (W2: 44–5), Berkeley tells us that materialists define matter as "an inert, senseless substance, in which extension, figure, and motion, do actually subsist." But he points out at PHK 7 (W2: 44) that "there can be no unthinking substance or *substratum* of" such qualities as extension, figure, and motion, and concludes at PHK 9 (W2: 45) that "the very notion of what is called *matter* or *corporeal substance*, involves a contradiction in it." This text supports (4). The fact that Berkeley reasons at PHK 7 from the non-existence of material substance to the claim that "there is not any other substance than *spirit* [i.e., mental substance]" indicates that he accepts (5). And finally, at PHK 2 (W2: 42) Berkeley claims that it is the "same thing" to say that X exists in (i.e., inheres in) mind M and to say that M perceives X.[8] Thus there is strong textual support for (7).

However, the Inherence Interpretation has been attacked from many angles.[9] Several scholars point to the following difficulty. If, as the Inherence Interpretation holds, Berkeley is committed to the Aristotelian Dictum (namely, that qualities must inhere in substances) and to the claim that minds are the only substances, then he is committed to the view that all sensible qualities inhere in minds. But the Aristotelian concept of inherence is bound up with the concept of predication: according to the Aristotelian world view, from the fact that X inheres in Y it follows that X may be predicated of Y. But in that case it would follow from the fact that sensible qualities (including colors and shapes) inhere in

---

[8] In DHP, Philonous says: "Farther, I know what I mean, when I affirm that there is a spiritual substance or support of ideas, that is, that a spirit knows and perceives ideas" (DHP 3; W2: 234). So Berkeley identifies M's serving as support for X (i.e., X's inhering in M) with M's perceiving X. This too supports (7).

[9] See, in particular, Oaklander (1977), Muehlmann (1978), and Pappas (1980; 2000, 128–31). For a defense of the Inherence Interpretation in the face of some of these objections, see Hausman (1984).

minds that sensible qualities may be predicated of minds, and hence that minds possess both color and shape. Thus it would seem that acceptance of the Aristotelian Dictum would commit Berkeley to what he himself would consider a metaphysical impossibility.

To this criticism, proponents of the Inherence Interpretation have a ready response. As they see it, Berkeley decouples the concept of inherence from the concept of predication. Their evidence for this derives from the following passage:

> [T]o me a die seems to be nothing distinct from those things which are termed its modes or accidents. And to say a die is hard, extended and square, is not to attribute those qualities to a subject distinct from and supporting them, but only an explication of the meaning of the word *die*. (PHK 49; W2: 62)

Berkeley's point here, as they see it, is that to *predicate* a quality F of an object O is not to *attribute* F to O, but rather to say that F is a part or constituent of O. Given that sensible qualities (such as color and shape) are not parts or constituents of minds, it follows that sensible qualities may not be *predicated* of minds even though they *inhere in* minds. Thus, as proponents of the Inherence Interpretation have it, it is possible for Berkeley to commit to the Aristotelian Dictum without thereby committing to the claim that minds are blue and square.[10]

To this line of reasoning in defense of the Inherence Interpretation, Pappas (1980, 190) objects that "the relation of sensible qualities to the objects which 'have' them is that of member to group, and not that of part to whole." Although what Pappas says is true, his objection fails. For let us suppose, along with Pappas, that Berkeley holds that sensible objects are not wholes composed of sensible qualities, but rather groups (or collections) of sensible qualities. Would this topple the reading of PHK 49 adopted by proponents of the Inherence Interpretation? No. For, taking Pappas's point, these theorists would simply claim that part of the point of PHK 49 is to claim that predicating F of O amounts to saying that F is a member (rather than a part) of O. And this claim yields the kind of result they are looking for. For, just as they claim that, for Berkeley, sensible qualities are not *parts* of minds, so they can also claim that, for Berkeley, sensible qualities are not *members* of minds. So whether sensible objects are conceived of as wholes of parts or as groups of members, it still follows

---

[10] See Allaire (1963, 237–9) and Cummins (1963, 213).

that Berkeley can commit to the Aristotelian Dictum without thereby committing to the claim that sensible qualities are *predicable* of minds.

More radically, Pappas claims that PHK 49 does not offer an alternative theory of predication at all. He writes:

[Berkeley] is, to be sure, rejecting one theory of predication, *viz.*, the one which requires substances with accidents inherent in them. But he concludes *not* with an alternative view of predication based on part to whole or on member to group, but rather with the claim that in asserting 'A die is hard, extended and square' we are just giving an explication of the meaning of the word 'die'. Thus, Berkeley's point seems to be that in asserting 'A die is hard, extended and square' no predication is involved at all, for in fact the statement is about 'die' and not about (a) die. (Pappas 1980, 190)

But this is a misreading of the relevant portion of PHK 49. Berkeley writes there, not that "to say a die is hard, extended and square, is not to attribute those qualities to a subject," but rather that "to say a die is hard, extended and square, is not to attribute those qualities to a subject *distinct from and supporting them*." Were Berkeley to have written the former, then Pappas would be justified in claiming that, for Berkeley, "no predication is involved at all" in statements such as "A die is hard, extended and square." But Berkeley wrote the latter. And the latter allows us to say that, for Berkeley, such statements *do* involve predication; it is only that the kind of predication involved does not involve the attribution of qualities to a subject that is distinct from them.

Pappas (2000, 130) argues that the Inherence Interpretation fails because "Berkeley is sharply critical of the notion of inherence, even to the point of ridiculing that concept in connection with material substance." Now it is true, as Pappas says, that Berkeley makes fun of those who would explicate the concept of inherence through the concept of *supporting* or *standing under*. For, as he explains, it could only be in an as yet unexplicated metaphorical sense that a material substance supports or stands under a sensible quality (see DHP 1; W2: 199). But it doesn't follow from this that Berkeley ridicules the concept of inherence itself, particularly when it comes to the application of the concept to mental substances. As Pappas (2000, 130) himself recognizes, Berkeley holds that for a sensible quality to inhere or be supported by a mind M is for it to be perceived by M. And with this proponents of the Inherence Interpretation wholeheartedly agree.

As I see it, there are in fact two main problems for the Inherence Interpretation. The first is that, upon reflection, Berkeley does not in fact endorse the Aristotelian Dictum, i.e., (2). The second is that Berkeley's opposition to materialism is founded on a premise that would make it unnecessary for him to argue from immaterialism to idealism. Consider the first point. The main textual evidence favoring the attribution of (2) to Berkeley is the following passage:

It were a mistake to think, that what is here said derogates in the least from the reality of things. It is acknowledged on the received principles, that extension, motion, and in a word all sensible qualities, have need of a support, as not being able to subsist by themselves. But the objects perceived by sense, are allowed to be nothing but combinations of those qualities, and consequently cannot subsist by themselves. Thus far it is agreed on all hands. So that in denying the things perceived by sense, an existence independent of a substance, or support wherein they may exist, we detract nothing from the received opinion of their *reality*, and are guilty of no innovation in that respect. All the difference is, that according to us the unthinking beings perceived by sense, have no existence distinct from being perceived, and cannot therefore exist in any other substance, than [*spirits*]: whereas philosophers vulgarly hold, that the sensible qualities exist in an inert, extended, unperceiving substance, which they call *matter*. (PHK 91; W2: 80–1)

The question is whether PHK 91 supports attributing the Aristotelian Dictum to Berkeley, and it should be clear that the answer is that it does not. The purpose of PHK 91 is to compare Berkeley's own views about the *reality* of sensible things with the "received principles." Berkeley claims that, on *his* principles, sensible things are *real* (PHK 33–6; W2: 54–6 and PHK 90–1; W2: 80–1) and have no "existence independent of a substance" (PHK 91; W2: 80). As he sees it, the same conclusion follows from the "received principles." The only difference is that whereas Berkeley holds that sensible things have no existence independent of an *immaterial* substance, the received view holds that sensible things have no existence independent of *material* substance. So Berkeley is not *endorsing* the "received" Aristotelian Dictum that all qualities need a support. His point is merely that his own theory of sensible things, according to which the existence of sensible things depends on their being perceived, no less than the Aristotelian Dictum, allows for the reality of sensible things.

Now Berkeley does say that "it is agreed on all hands" that *sensible* qualities have need of a support. But PHK 91 does not make it clear whether Berkeley takes this to be true because he accepts the Aristotelian

Dictum that *all* qualities inhere in a substance, or whether he takes this to be true because he accepts that *sensible* qualities are ideas and ideas in particular cannot exist unperceived. If the latter, then we do not find Berkeley arguing for idealism on the strength of the Aristotelian Dictum; rather, we find Berkeley arguing for one aspect of the Aristotelian Dictum (namely, the claim that *sensible* qualities must inhere in a substance) on the strength of idealism.

This brings us to the second main problem for the Inherence Interpretation. According to the Inherence Interpretation, Berkeley argues from immaterialism (the claim that there is no such thing as material substance) to the idealistic claim that sensible objects cannot exist unperceived. But Berkeley's procedure in PHK makes it clear that he means to argue for immaterialism in a way that would make it unnecessary for him to base his idealism on his immaterialism were he to accept at the outset, as the Inherence Interpretation has it, that sensible objects are collections of sensible qualities.

To see this it is sufficient to look at Berkeley's argument against the very coherence of the concept of matter in the early sections of PHK. Consider the following texts:

> [T]he sensible qualities are colour, figure, motion, smell, taste, and such like, that is, the ideas perceived by sense. Now for an idea to exist in an unperceiving thing, is a manifest contradiction; for to have an idea is all one as to perceive: that therefore wherein colour, figure, and the like qualities exist, must perceive them; hence it is clear there can be no unthinking substance or *substratum* of those ideas. (PHK 7; W2: 43–4)

> By matter . . . we are to understand an inert, senseless substance, in which extension, figure, and motion, do actually subsist. But it is evident from what we have already shewn, that extension, figure and motion are only ideas existing in the mind, and that an idea can be like nothing but another idea, and that consequently neither they nor their archetypes can exist in an unperceiving substance. Hence it is plain, that the very notion of what is called *matter* or *corporeal substance*, involves a contradiction in it. (PHK 9; W2: 44–5)

In these passages Berkeley's argument is clear. Matter is defined to be an unperceiving support of sensible qualities (such as extension, figure, and motion). But sensible qualities, as has already been established (or so Berkeley claims), are "only ideas existing in the mind." Therefore matter is an unperceiving support of sensible ideas. But to support (or have) an idea is just to perceive it. Therefore matter is an unperceiving perceiver of sensible ideas. So the very concept of matter is self-contradictory.

It is a crucial premise of this argument that sensible *qualities* are ideas. This is not exactly the position I have described as idealism, namely the position that sensible *objects* are ideas or collections thereof. But it is clear that if Berkeley takes himself to be entitled at the outset to the claim that sensible *qualities* are ideas, then he needs nothing like an argument from immaterialism to establish that sensible *objects* are ideas or collections thereof. All he needs is the first premise of the argument foisted on Berkeley by proponents of the Inherence Interpretation, namely the claim that sensible objects are collections of sensible qualities. For if sensible objects are collections of sensible qualities and sensible qualities are ideas, it follows directly that sensible objects are collections of ideas. And given that ideas cannot exist unperceived, it would follow directly that sensible objects cannot exist unperceived. The upshot is that if, as PHK 7 and PHK 9 show, Berkeley argues from the claim that sensible qualities are ideas to the claim that materialism is incoherent, then it would be completely otiose for Berkeley to argue from immaterialism to idealism were he to accept at the outset that sensible objects are collections of sensible qualities.[11,12]

---

[11] Pappas (1980, 191) mounts a similar objection to the Inherence Interpretation: "The first mistake in [the Inherence Interpretation] is that Berkeley is made to argue from the non-existence of matter to the conclusion that for ideas, *esse est percipi*. However, Berkeley argues in exactly the reverse fashion: having first established that *esse est percipi* holds for sensible qualities, he then goes on to argue that the non-existence of matter follows." However, Pappas's claim that Berkeley argues "in exactly the reverse fashion" is not strictly speaking accurate. As Pappas describes it, the Inherence Interpretation finds Berkeley arguing from immaterialism to the claim that the being of an *idea* is to be perceived. But this is not quite right. Proponents of the Inherence Interpretation claim that Berkeley argues from immaterialism to the claim that the being of a *sensible object* is to be perceived. (Even if, as Berkeley accepts, all sensible objects are collections of ideas, it would not follow from the claim that the being of a *sensible object* is to be perceived that the being of an *idea* is to be perceived.) Furthermore, were Berkeley actually to argue "in exactly the reverse fashion," he would reason from the claim that the being of an idea is to be perceived to immaterialism. But, as Pappas rightly describes him, Berkeley's argument for the incoherence of materialism rests on the claim that sensible qualities are ideas, not on the claim that the being of an idea is to be perceived.

[12] It might be claimed, against the position for which I have argued, (i) that Berkeley argues not only for the incoherence of *matter conceived as substratum of sensible qualities*, but also for the incoherence of matter conceived in a myriad of other ways (as object, cause, instrument, occasion, or something-in-general—DHP 2; W2; 221, 223), and (ii) that Berkeley infers from the fact that matter *conceived in all these ways* is incoherent, that the only reasonable alternative to materialism, namely idealism, is true. I do not believe that there is

## 3  The Argument from Anti-Abstractionism

One of the more interesting and puzzling aspects of PHK is that Berkeley spends the entirety of the Introduction disparaging the doctrine of abstract ideas. Most commentators agree that Berkeley frames his fundamental metaphysical views by rejecting abstractionism at least in part because he finds this doctrine implicated in a variety of pernicious philosophical errors. But a number of scholars, proponents of what I will call the "Nominalist Interpretation," go further. As they argue, Berkeley uses the denial of the possibility of abstract ideas as a premise in his argument for idealism in PHK.[13] My purpose in this section is to establish that this Nominalist Interpretation is mistaken.[14]

According to the doctrine of abstraction, as Berkeley understands it, the mind has the power to form, both from the simple ideas derived from sensation and reflection and from the complex ideas derived from the combination of simple ideas in the imagination, a new and different kind of idea by a process of mental separation. Berkeley distinguishes between two forms of mental separation that the proponents of the doctrine claim are possible. Following Bolton (1987), let us call the first kind of mental separation, "singling abstraction." And following Thomas Reid (1785: Essay 5, Chapter 3), let us call the second kind of mental separation, "generalizing abstraction." Singling abstraction is the subject of Introduction 7:

[W]e are told, the mind being able to consider each quality singly, or abstracted from those other qualities with which it is united, does by that means frame to it

---

any probative textual evidence indicating that Berkeley's argument *for* idealism (as opposed to his arguments against noted alternatives to idealism) relies on this kind of reasoning. And this is no surprise. For if Berkeley attempted to argue for idealism on the basis of (i) and (ii), then, for reasons already pointed out above, his reasoning would be otiose. This is because, in order to establish (i), Berkeley must establish that *matter conceived as substratum of sensible qualities* is incoherent; and, as I have already argued, his argument for *this* claim rests on an assumption (namely, that sensible qualities are ideas) that, together with the assumption that sensible objects are collections of sensible qualities, provides him with a quick argument for idealism that does not rest on immaterialism.

[13]  These scholars include Pappas (1985), Atherton (1987), and Bolton (1987). Muehlmann (1978; 1992) argues that anti-abstractionism is an important premise in Berkeley's argument for idealism in DHP.

[14]  As I argue in chapter 4, anti-abstractionism *does* figure as a premise in Berkeley's argument for idealism in DHP. (In this I agree with Muehlmann (1978; 1992).) But Berkeley scholars (including Muehlmann) have not accurately characterized the role that Berkeley's hostility to abstractionism plays there.

self abstract ideas. For example, there is perceived by sight an object extended, coloured, and moved: this mixed or compound idea the mind resolving into its simple, constituent parts, and viewing each by it self, exclusive of the rest, does frame the abstract ideas of extension, colour, and motion. (I 7; W2: 27–8)

Singling abstraction, then, involves the mental separation of one particular idea from another. Sometimes the ideas that are separated signify generally (i.e., serve as signs for other particular ideas), sometimes not: according to abstractionists, just as it is possible to abstract (i.e., mentally separate) the general idea of color from the general idea of extension, so it is possible to abstract the very particular shade of brownness of the table on which my computer sits from the table's very particular rectangular shape.[15] Moreover, as Berkeley emphasizes, although we experience qualities as blended together (so that, for example, the table's rectangular shape, felt degree of hardness, and particular shade of brown are experienced as a whole, rather than experienced individually), abstractionists believe that ideas of these qualities can be separated by the mind even if the qualities themselves cannot exist apart in reality.

Generalizing abstraction is the subject of the next two sections of the Introduction. In section 8 we find the following description of the process of abstraction:

[T]he mind having observed that in the particular extensions perceived by sense, there is something common and alike in all, and some other things peculiar, as this or that figure or magnitude, which distinguish them one from another; it considers apart or singles out by it self that which is common, making thereof a most abstract idea of extension, which is neither line, surface, nor solid, nor has any figure or magnitude but is an idea entirely prescinded from all these. So likewise the mind by leaving out of the particular colours perceived by sense, that which distinguishes them one from another, and retaining that only which is common to all, makes an idea of colour in abstract which is neither red, nor blue, nor white, nor any other determinate colour. And in like manner by considering motion abstractedly not only from the body moved, but likewise from the figure it describes, and all particular directions and velocities, the abstract idea of motion is framed; which equally corresponds to all particular motions whatsoever that may be perceived by sense. (I 8; W2: 28)

Generalizing abstraction, then, involves the mental separation of a general quality from its particular determinations. Thus, I might perceive a baseball, a basketball, and a soccer ball, consider the circular shape they share, mentally

---

[15] Here I agree with Ott (2004, 409): "Under [singling] abstraction, Berkeley classes both the separation of determinates from determinates and determinables from determinables."

separating it from the particular ways in which they manifest circularity, and thereby construct an abstract idea of roundness. Or I might perceive a tomato, a Toreador's cape, and a fire engine, consider the color they share, mentally separating it from the particular shades of redness they manifest, and thereby construct an abstract idea of red. In each case, the idea produced by this process of abstraction is taken to be general, rather than particular; an idea of roundness that applies to all round things, no matter the ways in which they differ; an idea of red that applies to all red things, no matter the ways in which *they* differ. So, unlike the process of singling abstraction, the process of generalizing abstraction *necessarily* yields ideas of general signification.[16]

The thesis that Berkeley distinguishes between two purported ways of forming abstract ideas is confirmed by a passage from Introduction 10 in which he attempts to prove that all abstract ideas are impossible:

> To be plain, I own my self able to abstract in one sense, as when I consider some particular parts or qualities separated from others, with which though they are united in some object, yet, it is possible they may really exist without them. But I deny that I can abstract one from another, or conceive separately, those qualities which it is impossible should exist so separated; or that I can frame a general notion by abstracting from particulars in the manner aforesaid. Which two last are the proper acceptations of *abstraction*. (I 10; W2: 29–30)

Here, Berkeley runs two separate arguments, one against ideas formed by singling abstraction, the other against ideas formed by generalizing abstraction. Winkler ably summarizes the argument against the former as follows:

> What an abstract idea purports to represent is impossible. But what is impossible is inconsistent, and what is inconsistent cannot be conceived. It follows that there can be no abstract ideas.[17]

---

[16] Ott (2004, 411) claims, rightly, that in the second edition of PHK (published in 1734), Berkeley treats selective attention as a third kind of abstraction. For Berkeley there adds to the Introduction the following passage: "And here it must be acknowledged that a man may consider a figure merely as triangular, without attending to the particular qualities of the angles, or relations of the sides. So far he may abstract" (I 16; W2: 35). But, as Ott also notes, "it is not clear that Berkeley held the selective attention model of abstraction" at the time of the first edition of PHK, for "he saw no need to include it explicitly" in that edition (Ott 2004, 410–11).

[17] Winkler (1989, 33). As Winkler rightly points out, a similar argument may also be found in the First Draft of the Introduction to PHK, where Berkeley writes: "It is, I think, a receiv'd axiom that an impossibility cannot be conceiv'd. For what created intelligence will pretend to conceive, that which God cannot cause to be? Now it is on all hands agreed, that nothing abstract or general can be made really to exist, whence it should seem to follow, that it cannot have so much as an ideal existence in the understanding" (W2: 125). See also ALC 7:6; W3: 333–4 (in the first and second editions).

The problem with singling abstraction articulated here is that the use of such a faculty would make it possible to conceive or imagine impossible states of affairs. The crucial premise in this attack on the possibility of singling abstraction, as Winkler rightly emphasizes, is the principle that impossibility entails inconceivability.

Winkler claims that Berkeley's attack on *generalizing* abstraction also rests on this kind of argument. But I think that this is a mistake.[18] The problem with generalizing abstraction, as Berkeley sees it, is that the mind's powers are simply inadequate to the purported task.[19] For example, Berkeley writes in Introduction 10:

[W]hatever hand or eye I imagine, it must have some particular shape and colour. Likewise the idea of man that I frame to my self, must be either of a white, or a black, or a tawny, a straight, or a crooked, a tall, or a low, or a middle-sized

---

Ott claims that Berkeley does not argue from impossibility to inconsistency because "there is no hint at all of what the inconsistency is supposed to be" (Ott 2004, 412). Ott also claims, paradoxically, that "the inference runs the other way: *from* impossibility to inconsistency" (Ott 2004, 412). But Winkler does not claim that the inference runs the wrong way. Indeed, Winkler emphasizes that Berkeley infers inconsistency from impossibility, not that Berkeley infers impossibility from inconsistency.

[18] Berkeley does apply Winkler's version of the argument to ideas putatively obtained by generalizing abstraction in the first two (1732) editions of ALC (at ALC 7:6; W3: 333–4). However, in the third and definitive (1752) edition, the relevant passage has been removed. Luce and Jessop (1950, 291) hypothesize that the removal is no more than an "artistic improvement," but this is pure speculation. My own hypothesis is that by 1752 Berkeley realized that he could not, on reflection, endorse the form of reasoning encapsulated in the excised passage.

Berkeley also applies Winkler's version of the argument to purported abstract ideas of objects possessing mutually contradictory properties. In *A Defence of Free-Thinking in Mathematics* (1735), Berkeley targets Locke's description of an idea of a triangle formed by generalizing abstraction as being an idea of something that possesses inconsistent properties. He writes: "[W]hatsoever . . . is said to be somewhat which cannot exist, the idea thereof must be inconsistent" (DFM 45; W4: 134). And given that what is inconsistent is impossible, Berkeley is clearly deriving the impossibility of the general idea of a triangle Locke describes from the impossibility of there *being* such a triangle. But it does not follow from this that Berkeley takes his attack on Locke's description of an abstract idea of a triangle to generalize to general ideas *not so described*. And, to be sure, he should not: Locke's description is in many ways unfortunate, and hardly representative. Indeed, it would even be possible for Locke himself to describe the general idea of a triangle as having *none* (rather than *all*) of the properties (scalene, obtuse, isosceles, equilateral, etc.) possessed by particular triangles without falling foul of Berkeley's argument. It would be too much to believe that Berkeley did not see this.

[19] Doney (1983) makes a similar point, but over-generalizes in claiming that Berkeley appeals to the mind's inability to perform the requisite task to argue against all forms of abstraction. As Winkler rightly emphasizes, this is a mistake: Berkeley's hostility to at least some forms of abstraction relies on the principle that impossibility entails inconceivability.

man. *I cannot by any effort of thought conceive the abstract idea above described.* (I 10; W2: 29—emphasis added)

Or consider the following exchange from DHP 1:

> Phil: Without doubt you can tell, whether you are able to frame this or that idea. Now I am content to put our dispute on this issue. If you can frame in your thoughts a distinct abstract idea of motion or extension, divested of all those sensible modes, as swift and slow, great and small, round and square, and the like, which are acknowledged to exist only in the mind, I will then yield the point you contend for. But if you cannot, it will be unreasonable on your side to insist any longer upon what you have no notion of.
>
> Hyl: To confess ingenuously, I cannot. (DHP 1; W2: 193)

Berkeley's point in these passages is that the mind simply cannot meet the challenge of mentally separating an idea from all its particular determinations. Try as hard as we might, we simply cannot frame an idea of a red ball that is of no particular shade of red and of no particular size, or an idea of a man that is of no particular height or color.[20]

Whatever the grounds, Berkeley's rejection of the possibility of abstraction is abundantly clear. And the fact that Berkeley introduces the entirety of PHK with this rejection strongly suggests that he means it to play a central role in his argument for idealism. This suggestion is seemingly reinforced by passages from the early sections of PHK. In

---

[20] Why does Winkler think that Berkeley bases his opposition to generalizing abstraction on the claim that ideas formed by this putative process would represent impossible things? Berkeley's fundamental assumption, as Winkler sees it, is that all things—i.e., all entities that are capable of independent existence—are particular, and consequently that universals (i.e., non-particular properties that are capable of existing in many different places at the same time) are unable to exist by themselves, i.e., independently of the particulars that exemplify them. But ideas formed by generalizing abstraction are supposed to be ideas of separately existing universals. It then follows directly from the principle that impossibility entails inconceivability that it is impossible to frame ideas *via* generalizing abstraction.

The problem with Winkler's reconstruction here is that there is no reason to suppose that Berkeley assumes that ideas formed by generalizing abstraction would have to be ideas of universals that are capable of existing independently of the particulars that exemplify them. Berkeley assumes no more than that generalizing abstraction purportedly produces ideas of X that are not ideas of any particular X, such as ideas of shape that are not ideas of any particular shape, or ideas of human being that are not ideas of any particular human being. All that generalizing abstraction purportedly accomplishes is the mental separation of an idea from its particular determinations. Importantly, it is not necessary for Berkeley to assume that every idea thereby produced would have to represent a separately existing universal. It is certainly consistent with the process of generalizing abstraction as Berkeley describes it that it should issue in ideas of universals that cannot exist independently of the particulars that exemplify them. The problem with the purported process of generalizing abstraction, as I say, is that our minds simply cannot undertake it.

PHK 4 (W2: 42), Berkeley claims that sensible objects are nothing but "ideas and sensations," that ideas and sensations cannot exist unperceived, and hence that sensible objects cannot exist unperceived. Then, in the next section, explaining how it came to pass that the contrary opinion should have become so prevalent (at least among philosophers), Berkeley writes:

If we thoroughly examine this tenet [i.e., that sensible objects can exist unperceived], it will, perhaps, be found at bottom to depend on the doctrine of *abstract ideas*. For can there be a nicer strain of abstraction than to distinguish the existence of sensible objects from their being perceived, so as to conceive them existing unperceived?[21] (PHK 5; W2: 42)

Later Berkeley makes a similar point:

Thus we see how much the tenet of extended, moveable substances existing without the mind, depends on that strange doctrine of *abstract ideas*. (PHK 11; W2: 45–6)

A number of scholars have been moved by these passages to suggest that Berkeley means to argue from the falsity of abstractionism to the truth of idealism. For example, Pappas claims that the second sentence of the PHK 5 passage asserts P1:

(P1)   To conceive a sensible object existing unperceived *is* to conceive an abstract general idea.

But P1 entails P2:

(P2)   One can conceive of a sensible object existing unperceived only if one can conceive of an abstract general idea (of the right sort).

And P2 entails P3:

(P3)   One can conceive of a sensible object existing unperceived only if there are abstract general ideas.

Using P3 as a premise, Pappas then constructs the following argument for idealism on Berkeley's behalf:

---

[21]  Here, "nice" is being used in the sense of "finely discriminative."

(P3)   One can conceive of a sensible object existing unperceived only if there are abstract general ideas.

(P4)   If one cannot conceive of a sensible object existing unperceived, then sensible objects cannot exist unperceived.[22]

(P5)   There are no abstract general ideas. [Anti-Abstractionism]

So, (C)   Sensible objects cannot exist unperceived. [Idealism][23]

Now I agree with Pappas that Berkeley accepts P4 and P5. But, *contra* Pappas, I deny that the second sentence of PHK 5 encapsulates P1, or, for that matter, any claim that entails P3. In that sentence, Berkeley suggests that, if the doctrine of abstraction were true, then one might be able to "distinguish the existence of sensible objects from their being perceived, *so as to* conceive them existing unperceived" (emphasis added). That is to say, if the doctrine of abstraction were true (and one could, in particular, abstract the idea of existence from the idea of being perceived), then one could conceive of sensible objects existing unperceived. But this is the *converse* of P3, not P3 itself. And if P3 were replaced by its converse in Pappas's reconstruction, then the reconstructed argument would be straightforwardly invalid. Assuming that Berkeley does not intend to provide a straightforwardly invalid argument for idealism, I conclude that PHK 5 provides us with no reason to suppose that Berkeley's argument for idealism runs through his rejection of the doctrine of abstraction.

It might be argued in response that the two sentences from PHK 5 say, not merely that the truth of the doctrine of abstraction is *sufficient*, but also that the truth of the doctrine is *necessary*, for the ability to conceive sensible objects existing unperceived. For the claim that tenet T *depends on* doctrine D suggests that the falsity of D entails the falsity of T, and hence that the truth of T *requires* the truth of D. If this were so, then P3 would be true and Pappas's reconstruction would fit the text. But this is not the only way, and indeed in the relevant context it is not the best way, to understand the claim that T depends on D. At the beginning of PHK 4, Berkeley notices that the opinion (in this case, tenet T) that sensible objects *can* exist unperceived is "strangely prevailing amongst men." Having argued in the rest of PHK 4 that T is false, Berkeley employs PHK 5, *not to provide*

---

[22] This assumption is supposed to follow from the claim that inconceivability entails impossibility, a claim that Pappas extracts from the Master Argument at PHK 22–3 (W2: 50–1). I discuss the Master Argument later in this chapter.

[23] Pappas (1985, 58–9).

*yet another argument for the falsity of T* (for, after all, he does not need such an argument), but rather to explain why belief in T is so widespread, and, importantly, why it is so entrenched. The reason it is so entrenched is that it depends on (that is, it is grounded in and supported by) the doctrine of abstraction (in this case, D). It is *because* of a commitment to D that belief in T is so prevalent amongst men. In the second sentence of PHK 5, Berkeley points out that acceptance of D makes it reasonable to suppose that it is possible to mentally separate the existence of sensible objects from their being perceived, and thereby makes it reasonable to suppose (on the basis of the assumption that conceivability entails possibility) that it is possible for sensible objects to exist without being perceived. *This* is the function of the "so as" clause in the second sentence of the passage. On balance, it makes far better sense of the passage to read Berkeley as providing an explanation for the prevalence of T based on the widespread and entrenched belief in D than as providing a supplementary and otiose argument for the falsity of T based on the falsity of D.[24]

Convinced that Berkeley's opposition to abstract ideas is more important than is commonly thought, Atherton (1987) tries to explain how his "central principle, that the being of a sensible thing lies in its being perceived, . . . depends on anti-abstractionism."[25] On her picture, Berkeley claims that abstract ideas are inconceivable. Abstraction, as Atherton thinks Berkeley understands it, is either the mental separation of one quality from another or the mental separation of one quality from its sensory determinates. This mental separation involves the mental removal (the "peeling off," as she puts it) of one quality from another. Atherton's Berkeley claims that, e.g., extension cannot be abstracted from color, because (i) an abstract idea of extension would be an idea of colorless

---

[24] It might be suggested that in the first two sentences of PHK 5, Berkeley is saying that any materialist worth his or her salt—any materialist willing to say that he or she can conceive of an unperceived object—is mired in illegitimate abstraction. But Berkeley does not here say, nor is he committed to saying, that those who claim to be able to conceive sensible objects existing unperceived *must* be committed to the doctrine of abstraction. A materialist worth her salt might simply rest her belief that it is possible to conceive a sensible object's existing unperceived on an exercise of imagination similar to the exercise that Berkeley describes in the passage that has come to be known as the Master Argument. As Hylas, the arch-materialist, says: "As I was thinking of a tree in a solitary place where no one was present to see it, methought that was to conceive a tree as existing unperceived or unthought of" (DHP 1; W2: 200). This perfectly ordinary purported imaginative exercise does not require prior commitment to the doctrine of abstraction. For more on the Master Argument, see below.

[25] Atherton (1987, 46).

extension, and (ii) the impossibility of conceiving such an idea follows directly from the fact that "the way to take up visual space is by being colored."[26] Similarly (and this is the claim that is crucial for Atherton's reconstruction of Berkeley's argument for idealism), the existence of sensible qualities cannot be abstracted from their being perceived, because (i) an abstract idea of a sensible quality would be an idea of an unperceived quality, and (ii) the impossibility of conceiving such an idea follows directly from the fact that "sensible qualities occur only as determinants of perception or as ways of being perceived."[27] She summarizes her point thus:

> When Berkeley says that sensible qualities can't exist unperceived, this is a special case of [his claim] that it is impossible to conceive separately what isn't experienced in separation.[28]

As I see matters, this way of putting the point is a little unfortunate. Robert McKim, for one, rightly points out that although he has "never had the experience of finding the roof of [his] house detached from the rest of the house, [he] can easily conceive of that occurrence."[29] Thus it cannot be that Berkeley derives idealism from the claim that it is *impossible* to conceive separately what *is not* experienced in separation, because, even for Berkeley, it is in fact *possible* to conceive separately what *is not* experienced in separation.

But I take it that Atherton's point goes a little deeper. What she should emphasize is (i) that, thanks to the fact that inconceivability entails impossibility, the conclusion that sensible qualities cannot exist unperceived follows from the impossibility of conceiving an idea of a sensible quality abstracted from its being perceived, and (ii) that the impossibility of conceiving an idea of a sensible quality abstracted from its being perceived follows from the fact that the way for a sensible quality to be is by being perceived.

Unfortunately, even if Atherton's reconstruction can avoid McKim's criticism, it still faces the following problem. Atherton supposes that Berkeley takes idealism (that is, the claim that sensible things, including sensible qualities, cannot exist unperceived) to follow from the impossibility of conceiving an idea of a sensible quality abstracted from its being perceived. But she takes Berkeley to infer the impossibility of conceiving this abstract idea from the claim that the way for a sensible quality to be is by being perceived. This is perilously close to a circular argument. It seems,

---

[26] Atherton (1987, 50).     [27] Atherton (1987, 51).
[28] Atherton (1987, 51).     [29] McKim (1997–8, 6).

at the very least, that there is no more reason for an opponent of idealism to accept that the way for a sensible quality to be is by being perceived than there already is to accept the claim that sensible qualities cannot exist unperceived. Moreover, if Atherton's reconstruction is accurate, the logic of the situation would allow Berkeley to argue for idealism directly from the claim that the way for a sensible quality to be is by being perceived: for it seems self-evident that if the way for a sensible quality to be is by being perceived, then sensible qualities cannot exist unperceived. Appeal to the impossibility of abstraction would amount to an unnecessary detour in the road to idealism.

According to Bolton (1987), Berkeley does not argue directly from anti-abstractionism to idealism. Rather, as she sees it, Berkeley embraces as axiomatic a thesis from which both anti-abstractionism and idealism follow. This thesis is the "theory of idea-objects," according to which, as Bolton argues, "an idea is its own object; if there is an idea of x, then x itself is that idea."[30] She writes:

Berkeley . . . uses the expression "idea of," but whereas other idea theorists mean by it "idea that represents," he typically means "idea, namely." When Berkeley writes that someone who perceives something triangular has an idea *of* a triangle, he means the person perceives an idea that *is* a triangle.[31]

The nice thing about the theory of idea-objects is that anti-abstractionism falls out of it. As Bolton argues:

An abstract idea is its own object and thus has all the properties its object does; but it must also lack some of these properties, because it is supposed to omit some properties of its object(s). Thus all abstract ideas are logically impossible.[32]

So, for example, the abstract idea of a triangle has angles of no particular size. But the triangle that is the object of the idea has angles of some particular size. Given that every idea is its own object, it follows that the relevant abstract idea must also have angles of some particular size. Hence the abstract idea does and does not have angles of some particular size. So, given the theory of idea-objects, abstract ideas are by their very nature self-contradictory and impossible.

The main problem with Bolton's reconstruction is that the argument for idealism that falls out of the theory of idea-objects is just too easy. As

---

[30] Bolton (1987, 68).  [31] Bolton (1987, 68).  [32] Bolton (1987, 70).

McKim (1997–8, 10–11) points out, anyone who takes the theory of idea-objects for granted is in no better dialectical position than someone who takes idealism itself for granted.[33] For consider a situation in which I am looking at, and so have an idea of, a table T. It is an immediate consequence of the claim that my idea of T is identical to T that T is itself an idea. But this is too quick of an argument for idealism: the claim that ideas are their own objects surely requires as much defense as the claim that all sensible objects are mind-dependent. Yet on Bolton's view Berkeley's theory of idea-objects is "fundamental."[34]

One might ask, on behalf of those who insist that Berkeley's argument for idealism rests on his anti-abstractionism, why Berkeley relates idealism and anti-abstractionism as he does at PHK 5 and PHK 11. The answer is that the aim of these passages is to point out how a philosopher's commitment to abstractionism might lead him to think (wrongly, as it happens) that idealism is false. When Berkeley says, as he does in PHK 5 (W2: 42), that "this tenet [namely, the thesis that "sensible objects have an existence natural or real, distinct from their being perceived by the understanding" (PHK 4; W2: 42)] . . . will, perhaps, be found at bottom to depend on the doctrine of *abstract ideas*," and when he says, as he does in PHK 11 (W2: 45–6), that "we see how much the tenet of extended, moveable substances existing without the mind, depends on that strange doctrine of *abstract ideas*," he means no more than that there is an easy road from abstractionism to the denial of the idealism, a road that might explain why so many philosophers refuse to accept idealism despite its self-evidence.[35] In PHK 5 (W2: 42), Berkeley explains that an abstractionist might well think it possible "to distinguish the existence of sensible things from their being perceived, so as to conceive them existing unperceived." That is, an abstractionist might well think it possible to mentally separate the idea of a chair's existence from the idea of the chair's being perceived. Were such mental separation possible, then it would be possible to conceive a chair existing unperceived. And if it were possible to conceive a chair existing unperceived, then, by the principle that conceivability entails possibility, it

---

[33] McKim (1997–8, 10–11).

[34] Bolton (1987, 68). McKim (1997–8, 10) also points out, rightly in my view, that for Berkeley not all ideas could be their own objects. In particular, in imagining or remembering X, the idea of X that I form is not identical to X itself.

[35] Newman (2002, 314–15) makes a similar point in a review of Pappas (2000).

would be possible for a chair to exist unperceived, and thus idealism would be false. Of course, as Berkeley sees matters, abstractionism is false. But it doesn't follow from this that idealism is true. Rather, what follows is that there is one less reason to think that idealism is false.

# 4 The Argument from the Likeness Principle

Up to this point, we have seen that in PHK Berkeley does not argue for idealism from immaterialism and inherence, nor does he argue for the same conclusion directly from anti-abstractionism. Perhaps, then, there is nothing more to Berkeley's argument for idealism in PHK than the semantic argument for the self-evidence of the claim that sensible objects cannot exist unperceived.

One scholar who finds more of an argument for idealism than this is Winkler (1989). Winkler (rightly, in my view) focuses on the following passage:

For what are [sensible objects] but the things we perceive by sense? And what do we perceive besides our own ideas or sensations? (PHK 4; W2: 42)

Replacing Berkeley's questions with statements, we arrive at the following piece of reasoning:

(1)   Sensible objects are perceived by means of the senses.
(2)   Ideas are the only things perceived by means of the senses.
So, (C)   Sensible objects are ideas. [From 1, 2][36]

---

[36] Flage (2004, 38) provides an epistemic reading of the argument of PHK 4. The argument, as he reads it, is roughly this: (1F) Sensible objects, *as known*, are objects known by sense; (2F) All objects known by sense are ideas; so, (CF) Sensible objects, *as known*, are ideas. Flage emphasizes that the argument of PHK 4 is much tamer than it is taken to be by those who provide an ontological reading of it: "[My] reconstruction of Berkeley's argument does *not* entail that ordinary objects themselves are identical with collections of ideas; it claims such an identity *only as they are known*" (Flage 2004, 38). As Flage sees it, (CF) is not merely endorsed by Berkeley; it is also endorsed by "Locke and other proponents of the 'way of ideas'" (Flage 2004, 37).

Flage's main motivation for reading the argument of PHK 4 epistemically, rather than ontologically, is that, so read, the argument is not open to the objections that bedevil it when it is given the standard ontological reading. But the price of reading the argument epistemic- ally is too high. First, the epistemic reading trivializes Berkeley's conclusion. The point of PHK 4 is to contest the "strangely prevailing" view that sensible objects are not merely ideas in minds. But on the epistemic reading, the view that Berkeley ends up contesting in PHK 4 is the claim that sensible objects, *as known*, are not merely ideas. This view is not only not

On its own, however, this argument is hardly persuasive. Although Berkeley's realist opponents will grant him the truth of (1), they will hardly grant him the truth of (2). For they will insist that mind-independent unthinking things are (or at least can be) perceived by means of the senses. The trick, then, is to find a way of cleaning up the argument on Berkeley's behalf without straying from the relevant texts. Winkler's (clever) strategy is to base Berkeley's justification for (2) in his acceptance of the likeness principle in PHK 8.

Winkler begins his discussion of the argument of PHK 4 with the claim that there is a "structural" cause for concern, for (as he puts it) "the argument appears to turn on an ambiguity in the notion of perception."[37] As we have seen, there is an important difference between *mediate* perception and *immediate* perception. As Winkler understands the distinction, for X to *mediately* perceive Y is for X to perceive Y by virtue of perceiving an idea that *represents* Y, and for X to *immediately* perceive Y is for X to perceive Y, but not mediately. According to Winkler, Berkeley is "vividly aware" of an equivocation objection that turns on this distinction. A Lockean materialist, for instance, could easily object that the argument from PHK 4 begs the question against her unless the word "perceived" is read one way in (1) and another way in (2). In particular, since the Lockean materialist insists both that sensible objects are not ideas and that they are *mediately* perceived (namely, by immediately perceiving

"strangely prevailing"; it is (obviously) necessarily false. Second, there is nothing in the text to suggest the "as known" qualifications that Flage adds to (1) and (C). And third, given that, as even Flage acknowledges, Berkeley ends up as an idealist, and given that the conclusion of PHK 4 *can* be read as the thesis of idealism, there is already very strong *prima facie* reason to read the argument of PHK 4 as an argument for (C), rather than as an argument for (CF).

It is true, of course, as Flage rightly emphasizes, that PHK, as its full title indicates, is an epistemic treatise. But this shows only where Berkeley is heading, not how he proposes to get there. Flage supposes that Berkeley argues from epistemic premises to epistemic conclusions (e.g., the falsity of skepticism). On the standard view, Berkeley argues from ontological premises to epistemic conclusions. Both interpretations have a ready explanation for Berkeley's focus on epistemic matters.

As I argue below, commentators are well within their rights to criticize the argument of PHK 4. As an argument designed to convince Berkeley's materialist opponents, it ranks as a failure. But in chapter 4 I argue that Berkeley probably became aware of this failure shortly after the publication of PHK. For there is overwhelming evidence that DHP 1 is designed to fill in, and thereby eliminate the defective aspects of, the argument of PHK 4.

[37] Winkler (1989, 138).

ideas that represent them), she will not grant the truth of (1) and (2) unless they are read as follows:

(1ᴬ)  Sensible objects are *mediately* perceived by means of the senses.

(2⋆)  Ideas are the only things *immediately* perceived by means of the senses.

But in that case the argument of PHK 4 becomes:

(1⋆)  Sensible objects are *mediately* perceived by means of the senses.

(2⋆)  Ideas are the only things *immediately* perceived by means of the senses.

So, (C)  Sensible objects are ideas.

And this argument is plainly invalid.

As Winkler sees it, Berkeley's reply to this objection relies on the likeness principle. According to the likeness principle, "an idea can be like nothing but an idea," that is, an idea cannot resemble anything that is not itself an idea (PHK 8; W2: 44). Winkler imagines Berkeley's opponent insisting that (1) is true only if it is read as saying (1⋆), i.e., that sensible objects are *mediately* perceived by means of the senses. But on Winkler's account of the nature of mediate perception, X mediately perceives Y only if X perceives Y by virtue of perceiving an idea that *represents* Y. The objector must then accept that we perceive sensible objects by virtue of perceiving ideas that represent them, and must therefore accept that sensible objects are represented by ideas. However, as Winkler argues, "Berkeley believes that representation can only be a matter of resemblance."[38] For example, in the First Draft of the Introduction to PHK, Berkeley writes that ideas "are suppos'd to be the copies & images" of things, and that "they are not thought to represent them any otherwise, than as they resemble them" (W2: 129). But then if the objector accepts that sensible objects are represented by ideas, then she must also accept that ideas resemble the sensible objects they represent. Thus the likeness principle entails that sensible objects, which resemble the ideas that represent them, must themselves be ideas. And this is simply to grant Berkeley's idealist conclusion.

If we put this all together on Winkler's behalf, we arrive at the following completion of the argument for (2):

---

[38]  Winkler (1989, 138).

(P1)    All perception is either mediate or immediate.

(P2)    Ideas are the only things immediately perceived by means of the senses.

So, (L1)    If sensible objects are immediately perceived by means of the senses, then  they are ideas. [From P2]

(P3)    For X to perceive Y mediately is for X to perceive Y by perceiving an idea that represents Y. [Definition of Mediate Perception]

(P4)    For an idea X to represent Y is for X to be like Y.

(P5)    An idea can be like nothing but an idea. [Likeness Principle]

So, (L2)    If sensible objects are mediately perceived by means of the senses, then they are ideas. [From P3, P4, P5]

So, (2)    If sensible objects are perceived by means of the senses, then they are ideas. [From P1, L1, L2]

Clever as this interpretation is, I do not believe that it is accurate to Berkeley's intentions. The main problem here is that there is considerable textual evidence against the claim that Berkeley embraces the definition of mediate perception Winkler attributes to him (in the shape of P3). As Winkler sees it, Berkeley allows for mediate perception of Y only when there is intervention of something other than Y that either *suggests* or *entails* Y.[39] (As I argued in chapter 1, this is strictly accurate, even if misleading.) For Berkeley, suggestion and inference are two very different mental operations belonging to separate mental faculties, the one to imagination and memory, the other to reason (or understanding). It is sufficient for suggestion that there be memory of past association.[40] This sort of relation obtains between, e.g., words and their meanings. To use an example of Berkeley's own, I might, by means of my imagination, arbitrarily associate the word "God" with a certain notion (the notion of God).[41] The next time I meet up with the word "God," I think of the

---

[39]  Winkler (1989, 149).

[40]  See, for example, NTV 25 (W1: 176): "That one idea may suggest another to the mind it will suffice that they have been observed to go together."

[41]  Berkeley distinguishes explicitly between ideas and notions in the 1734 edition of PHK (PHK 142; W2: 106). (It should be noted that even in the 1713 edition of DHP, Berkeley tells us that while he has "no idea . . . of God," he does have "a notion of Him" (DHP 3; W2: 231–2). This suggests that, at least by 1713, Berkeley had recognized the need to distinguish between two kinds of representations.) Ideas are passive, whereas notions, which Berkeley

right notion by virtue of the fact that I remember the relevant association. It is in this sense that the word "God" now *suggests* the notion of God. And my perception of the notion is here *mediated* by my perception of the word that suggests it. By contrast, memory of past association is not sufficient for inference. Rather, inference requires passing from one idea to another idea that is logically (and so necessarily) connected with it. To use one of Berkeley's own examples, given the self-evidence of the principle that everything has a cause, I might think of the cause of my sensations by inferring that something must be producing them (DHP 1; W2: 174–5). In that case, my thinking of the cause of my sensations is *mediated* by my perception of the sensations from which I infer the existence of their cause.

Now the important point here is that the relata of the only relations that make mediate perception possible, namely suggestion and inference, need not be (and often are not) similar to each other. Consider suggestion. At PHK 27 (W2: 52), Berkeley points out that ideas cannot resemble minds because, whereas ideas are passive, minds are active, and nothing passive can resemble anything active. By the same token, the word "God" cannot resemble the notion of God it suggests because, whereas the word "God" is a passive idea (as is entailed by Berkeley's idealism), notions are active. And consider inference. Berkeley claims that the mental process of inference may lead me from perception of my sensations to thinking of their cause. But, as Berkeley argues at PHK 29–33 (W2: 53–5), the cause of our sensations is God. And my sensations, which are passive ideas, do not resemble God, who is an active mental substance. Yet the relevant relata would have to be similar to each other if Winkler's account of Berkeley's definition of mediate perception were accurate. This is because, as Winkler sees it, for Berkeley mediate perception of Y requires perception of an intervening idea that represents, and so resembles, Y. I conclude that there is sufficient textual evidence to deny that Berkeley accepts P3. It follows that Winkler's supplementation of the argument of PHK 4 with material extracted from PHK 8, clever as it may be as a defense of idealism, should not be attributed to Berkeley.[42]

---

identifies with the meanings of words denoting minds and their operations (as well as relations) are "active thinking image[s]" (DHP 3; W2: 232). See also *Siris* 308 (W5: 142): "Some, perhaps, may think the truth to be this—that there are properly no ideas, or passive objects, in the mind but what are derived from sense: but that there are also besides these her own acts or operations; such are notions."

[42] Further evidence that Berkeley does not automatically suppose that the mediately perceived thing resembles the mediator appears in ALC, where Euphranor (Berkeley's

One might ask, on Winkler's behalf, what the point of the likeness principle is if Berkeley does not mean to rely on it in his argument for idealism. The answer requires a closer look at the context in which Berkeley appeals to the principle, namely the first part of PHK 8:

> But say you, though the ideas themselves do not exist without the mind, yet there may be things like them whereof they are copies or resemblances, which things exist without the mind, in an unthinking substance. I answer, an idea can be like nothing but an idea; a colour or figure can be like nothing but another colour or figure. If we look but ever so little into our thoughts, we shall find it impossible for us to conceive a likeness except only between our ideas. (PHK 8; W2: 44)

As the passage makes plain, Berkeley appeals to the likeness principle to answer an objection to the claim of PHK 7 (W2: 43) that "there is not any other substance than *spirit*, or that which perceives." The objection is that there *may be* a kind of substance other than spirit, namely an unthinking substance that supports things (i.e., qualities) that resemble our sensory ideas. Berkeley answers that the likeness principle makes it impossible for such a substance to exist. For let us suppose the existence of an unthinking substance S that supports a quality Q that resembles a sensory idea I. If the likeness principle is true, then anything that resembles an idea must itself *be* an idea. So Q, which, by hypothesis, resembles I, must be an idea. Now, again by hypothesis, S supports Q. But the only way for a substance to *support* an idea is by perceiving it. So S perceives Q. But, yet again by hypothesis, S is an unthinking, and hence unperceiving, substance. So S both perceives and does not perceive. Contradiction. There is no reason to suppose that Berkeley appeals to the likeness principle for any other purpose than to defeat this particular objection.

## 5  The Two Simple Arguments

Even if it is a mistake to think that Berkeley rests his argument for idealism in PHK on the likeness principle of PHK 8, it is not, I think, a mistake to

---

mouthpiece) says: "To me it seems that a man may know whether he perceives a thing or no; and, if he perceives it, whether it be immediately or mediately; and, *if mediately, whether by means of something like or unlike*, necessarily or arbitrarily connected with it" (ALC 4:9; W3: 152—emphasis added). Here Euphranor explicitly countenances the possibility of mediately perceiving something by perceiving something else that is *unlike* it, a possibility that Winkler's interpretation of Berkeley's account of the relation of mediate perception automatically precludes.

think that there is more to Berkeley's argument than the simple semantic argument of PHK 3.

Let us return to the argument from PHK 1 (call it the "First Simple Argument" for idealism):

*The First Simple Argument*
Sensible objects are perceived by means of the senses.
Anything perceived by means of the senses is an idea.
So, Sensible objects are ideas.

As I see it, Berkeley offers his readers not much more than this as a defense of idealism in PHK. As we have seen, Berkeley takes idealism to have been established as early as PHK 6 (W2: 43), where he writes that "all the choir of heaven and furniture of the earth, in a word all those bodies which compose the mighty frame of the world, have not any subsistence without a mind." So the argument for idealism, such as it is, simply *must* occur before PHK 6. Apart from PHK 3, which contains the weak semantic argument already discussed, and PHK 5, the purpose of which is to explain how the doctrine of abstraction might lead one to believe that idealism is false, there is no *explicit* argument for idealism except the First Simple Argument.

However, there is a second argument for idealism that is *implicit* in the very first section of PHK. For ease of reference, I will discuss the section in four parts:

(PHK 1A) It is evident to any one who takes a survey of the objects of human knowledge, that they are either ideas actually imprinted on the senses, or else such as are perceived by attending to the passions and operations of the mind, or lastly ideas formed by help of memory and imagination, either compounding, dividing, or barely representing those originally perceived in the aforesaid ways. (W2: 41)

In PHK 1A, Berkeley divides the objects of human knowledge into three mutually exclusive and exhaustive categories: ideas of sense, ideas of reflection, and ideas of memory and imagination. Berkeley then turns his attention to the ideas of sense:

(PHK 1B) By sight I have the ideas of light and colours with their several degrees and variations. By touch I perceive, for example, hard and soft, heat and cold, motion and resistance, and of all these more and less either as to quantity or degree. Smelling furnishes me with odours;

the palate with tastes, and hearing conveys sounds to the mind in all their variety of tone and composition. (W2: 41)

PHK 1B appears to be a standard inventory of the qualities that even Berkeley's staunchest opponents would recognize as being perceived by sense. But the fact that Berkeley places this passage immediately following his claim that the objects of knowledge comprise ideas of three different kinds, including ideas of sense, strongly suggests that he takes for granted (without explicitly saying) that all sensible qualities (including light and colors, hard and soft, heat and cold, motion and resistance, odors, tastes, and sounds) are ideas.

The passage continues:

(PHK 1C) And as several of these [qualities] are observed to accompany each other, they come to be marked by one name, and so to be reputed as one thing. Thus, for example, a certain colour, taste, smell, figure and consistence having been observed to go together, are accounted one distinct thing, signified by the name *apple*. (W2: 41)

In PHK 1C Berkeley introduces two new theses, one metaphysical, the other semantic. The metaphysical claim is that sensible objects (such as apples) are collections of *sensible qualities* (such as color, taste, smell, figure and consistency). The semantic claim is that these collections of qualities are signified by the names we use to talk about them.

The section then ends thus:

(PHK 1D) Other collections of ideas constitute a stone, a tree, a book, and the like sensible things; which, as they are pleasing or disagreeable, excite the passions of love, hatred, joy, grief, and so forth. (W2: 41)

In PHK 1D Berkeley claims that sensible objects are collections of ideas. This claim follows directly from the claim we extracted from PHK 1B (i.e., that sensible qualities are ideas) and the metaphysical claim we extracted from PHK 1C (i.e., that sensible objects are collections of sensible qualities). This, then, is the Second Simple Argument for idealism:

*The Second Simple Argument*
    Sensible objects are collections of sensible qualities.
    Sensible qualities are ideas.
  So, Sensible objects are collections of ideas.

There is an apparent discrepancy between the First and Second Simple Arguments. In the First, Berkeley argues for the conclusion that sensible objects are ideas. In the Second, Berkeley argues for the conclusion that sensible objects are collections of ideas. But there is really no inconsistency here, for Berkeley thinks that collections of ideas are no more than complex ideas. Recall that in NTV 96 (W1: 210) Berkeley writes that tangible heads (hands, feet) are "complex ideas...made up only of [simple] ideas perceivable by touch." By parity of reasoning, then, it follows that visible heads (hands, feet) are complex ideas made up only of simple ideas perceivable by sight. And if we extend the claim to cover heads (not just tangible heads or visible heads), it follows that heads (and hence, all sensible objects) are complex ideas made up of simple ideas perceivable by all five senses. In addition, Berkeley tells us in DHP 3 that "men combine together several ideas, apprehended by divers senses, or by the same sense at different times, or in different circumstances...all which they...consider as one thing" (DHP 3; W2: 245). Similarly, a few pages later, Berkeley writes that "a *cherry*...is nothing but a congeries of sensible impressions, or ideas perceived by various senses: which ideas are united into one thing...by the mind" (DHP 3; W2: 249). So, as Berkeley sees it, the result of collecting or combining simple ideas of sensation is *one thing*, presumably a complex idea that has each of the simple ideas as its components. Thus, given that collections of ideas are themselves ideas (namely, complex ideas), it follows from the claim that sensible objects are collections of ideas that sensible objects are ideas.

Is the Second Simple Argument for idealism, considered on its own, any more persuasive than the First Simple Argument? The answer must be no, twice over. In the first place, Lockeans and Cartesians would deny the premise that sensible objects (such as tables and chairs) are collections of sensible qualities. As they see matters, sensible objects are things that *possess* sensible qualities, substances in which sensible qualities inhere. Given that nothing inheres in itself, it follows that sensible objects are not to be identified with the qualities that inhere in them. In the second place, Lockeans and Cartesians would also deny the premise that sensible qualities are ideas. According to Locke, primary qualities (such as shape and motion) are properties that exist in unthinking substances independently of being perceived to be in those substances, while secondary qualities (such as color and taste) are powers to produce sensations in our minds, powers in unthinking substances whose existence in those substances *does* depend on being perceived to be there.[43] So Locke denies that primary or secondary qualities are ideas. According to Descartes, primary qualities are mind-independent features of unthinking substances, while secondary qualities are ideas. So even for Descartes, not all sensible qualities are ideas. In the absence of any reason to accept its first or second premise, Berkeley's adversaries are therefore perfectly justified in standing their ground in the face of the Second Simple Argument.

It might be thought that Berkeley argues at least for the premise that sensible qualities are ideas in the early sections of PHK. For example, at PHK 10 he appears to infer the mind-dependence of primary qualities from the mind-dependence of secondary qualities, from which it would follow that all sensible qualities are mind-dependent ideas. But the function of PHK 10 is clearly *ad hominem*. The section begins:

> They who assert that figure, motion, and the rest of the primary or original qualities do exist without the mind, in unthinking substances, do at the same time acknowledge that colours, sounds, heat, cold, and such like secondary qualities, do not, which they tell us are sensations existing in the mind alone. (PHK 10; W2: 45)

Here Berkeley is referring to the Cartesians (and possibly also, albeit erroneously, to the Lockeans) who, at least as he sees it, claim that secondary qualities are ideas while primary qualities are not. The point of PHK 10 is to show that this position is metaphysically absurd. Berkeley's argument is simple:

> Now if it be certain, that those original qualities are inseparably united with the other sensible qualities, and not, even in thought, capable of being abstracted from them, it plainly follows that they exist only in the mind. (PHK 10; W2: 45)

Berkeley's main claim is that primary qualities are inseparable from secondary qualities, both in thought and in reality. But if two qualities are inseparable in reality, then where the one is, then other must also be. Thus, if secondary qualities are ideas in the mind (as the Cartesians insist), then primary qualities must also be ideas in the mind.[44] So Berkeley does not use PHK 10 to establish that sensible qualities are ideas. His sole aim in that

---

[43] For a detailed defense of this claim, see Rickless (1997).

[44] Notice that this argument does not work against Locke, who actually denies that secondary qualities are ideas. For Locke, secondary qualities are in bodies, even if their existence in bodies depends on being perceived to be there.

section is to establish that his Cartesian adversaries have an incoherent position on the nature of primary and secondary qualities.

Similar remarks apply to PHK 14, a section in which Berkeley appears to argue that the same arguments that are used to establish the mind-dependence of secondary qualities also establish the mind-dependence of primary qualities. Thus, Berkeley writes:

> I shall farther add, that after the same manner, as modern philosophers prove certain sensible qualities to have no existence in matter, or without the mind, the same thing may be likewise proved of all other sensible qualities whatsoever. (PHK 14; W2: 46)

The arguments to which Berkeley refers are arguments from perceptual relativity:

> Thus, for instance, it is said that heat and cold are affections only of the mind, and not at all patterns of real beings, existing in the corporeal substances which excite them, for that the same body which appears cold to one hand, seems warm to another. (PHK 14; W2: 46)

And Berkeley's claim, it appears, is that if this sort of argument is acceptable, then, by parity of reasoning, so are parallel arguments purporting to establish the mind-dependence of primary qualities:

> Now why may we not as well argue that figure and extension are not patterns or resemblances of qualities existing in matter, because to the same eye at different stations, or eyes of a different texture at the same station, they appear various, and cannot therefore be the images of any thing settled and determinate without the mind? (PHK 14; W2: 46–7)

But, again, Berkeley's point is entirely *ad hominem*. As Berkeley himself makes clear in PHK 15, the arguments from perceptual relativity do not even establish the mind-dependence of *secondary* qualities. Berkeley puts the point thus:

> Though it must be confessed this method of arguing doth not so much prove that there is no extension or colour in an outward object, as that we do not know by sense which is the true extension or colour of the object. (PHK 15; W2: 47)

Consider, for example, the example of the two hands placed in the same bucket of water. To the one hand the water seems hot; to the other hand the water seems cold. Does it follow that heat and cold are not in the water, but are rather in the perceiver's mind? Certainly not. As Berkeley makes clear, it could be that the water is cold (hot) but the perceiver mistakenly holds that it is hot (cold) because his senses are not detecting the water's temperature accurately. In sum, then, Berkeley thinks the arguments from perceptual relativity do not work. His point, then, is simply that those who (albeit erroneously) *believe* that arguments from perceptual relativity establish the mind-dependence of *secondary qualities* should also *believe*, by parity of reasoning, that the same sorts of arguments establish the mind-dependence of *primary qualities*. The aim of PHK 14 is to emphasize the internal inconsistency of the position adopted by those of his opponents who think both that arguments from perceptual relativity establish the mind-dependence of secondary qualities and that primary qualities are mind-independent features of unthinking substances.[45]

On the basis of the textual evidence, we are left to conclude that (aside from the semantic argument of PHK 3) Berkeley provides two Simple Arguments for idealism in PHK (explicitly in PHK 4 and implicitly in PHK 1), arguments that ultimately rest on undefended assumptions that beg the question against the vast majority of his contemporary philosophical opponents. It is therefore no surprise to learn that Berkeley's contemporaries, philosophers and non-philosophers alike, remained unconvinced after reading PHK. On August 26, 1710, Berkeley's close friend, John Percival (to whom NTV is dedicated), writes:

A physician of my acquaintance undertook to describe your person, and argued you must needs be mad, and that you ought to take remedies. A bishop pitied you that a desire and vanity of starting something new should put you on such an undertaking... Another told me an ingenious man ought not to be discouraged from exercising his wit, and said Erasmus was not the worse thought of for writing in praise of folly, but that you are not gone so far as a gentleman in town who asserts not only that there is no such thing as matter but that we have no being at all. (W9: 10)

---

[45]  It is therefore strange to find Berkeley saying, as he does in PHK 78, that "[q]ualities, *as hath been shewn*, are nothing else but *sensations* or *ideas*, which exist only in a *mind* perceiving them" (PHK 78; W2: 74—emphasis added). The strangeness derives from the fact that in none of the preceding seventy-seven sections has Berkeley actually *argued* for the mind-dependence of sensible qualities. He seems rather to have taken the premise that sensible qualities are ideas entirely for granted. As I will argue in the next chapter, a proper understanding of DHP 1 helps to remove at least some of the strangeness. For it may be that, even as he was writing PHK, Berkeley knew how he would argue for the relevant premise if he were asked. The argument he would have given may be the argument he ends up giving in DHP 1.

A few months later, on October 30, Percival writes again, reporting that William Whiston (a Newtonian physicist) and Samuel Clarke (a friend of Whiston's and a highly regarded philosopher in his own right) have formed their own opinions of PHK:

> They [Whiston and Clarke] think you are a fair arguer and a clear writer, but they say the first principles you lay down are false. (W9: 11–12)

The problem, as both Whiston and Clarke are quick to see, is not that Berkeley's arguments are invalid; it is that the premises of the arguments are false. It is not clear, of course, that Whiston and Clarke would have been able to pinpoint the premises with which they disagreed. (This might explain why Clarke refused to be drawn into correspondence with Berkeley (W8: 43–4).) But they certainly had the right philosophical instincts. Berkeley's arguments rest on three controversial claims: that everything that is perceived by sense is an idea, that sensible objects are collections of sensible qualities, and that sensible qualities are ideas. Without defending these principles Berkeley could not reasonably expect his readers to be persuaded of the truth of idealism.[46]

## 6 The Master Argument

At PHK 23 (W2: 50–1) and in DHP 1 (W2: 200), Berkeley provides what appears to be an all-purpose argument for idealism that does not depend on any previously stated premises or reasoning. Following Gallois (1974), let us call this "the Master Argument." Berkeley scholars are almost all agreed that the Master Argument fails, indeed that it commits a spectacularly shameful blunder.[47] But there is some disagreement about the nature of the blunder and about the proper explanation for why Berkeley

---

[46] It is true that, having taken himself to have established the truth of idealism in the early sections of PHK, Berkeley then attacks various materialist proposals that are inconsistent with idealism. There is therefore a sense in which Berkeley provides some indirect support for idealism by defeating some of its main adversaries. But as long as the premises of the two Simple Arguments are not self-evident (and they most definitely are *not*), the two Simple Arguments will not persuade. And this is particularly important inasmuch as the Berkeley of PHK actually relies on idealism in order to establish the incoherence of materialism! See note 11 above.

[47] Hacking (1975, 41) claims that the Master Argument is "widely regarded as the most preposterous argument ever to achieve lasting fame among philosophers." Hacking also insists that, but without explaining why, the argument is "impressive."

commits it. As I will now argue, the existing reconstructions of the Master Argument, particularly those on which it turns out to be invalid, are all mistaken. Properly understood, the Master Argument is valid and would be persuasive if only Berkeley could give us reason to accept one premise in particular. Unfortunately, this premise, to the effect that the objects of perception (or conception) are all ideas, is left undefended in PHK. As we will see in chapter 4, Berkeley does not attempt a defense of it until DHP 1.

Berkeley introduces the Master Argument by issuing the following challenge to his materialist reader:

> I am content to put the whole upon this issue; if you can but conceive it possible for one extended moveable substance, or in general, for any one idea or any thing like an idea, to exist otherwise than in a mind perceiving it, I shall readily give up the cause: And as for that *compages* of external bodies which you contend for, I shall grant you its existence, though you cannot give me any reason why you believe it exists, or assign any use to it when it is supposed to exist. I say, the bare possibility of your opinion's being true, shall pass for an argument that it is so. (PHK 22; W2: 50)

The opinion that Berkeley is willing to accept if his challenge is met is the materialist claim that there are extended moveable substances existing outside of all minds whatever. In order to accept this opinion, Berkeley says that his materialist opponent need not actually establish its truth; all that is needed is that the materialist establish the opinion's *possible* truth. That is, it is sufficient for Berkeley to give up the cause that the materialist prove that it is possible for sensible objects (such as tables and chairs) to exist unperceived.

In the very next section, Berkeley imagines his materialist opponent attempting to meet this challenge by means of a simple argument:

> But say you, surely there is nothing easier than to imagine trees, for instance, in a park, or books existing in a closet, and no body by to perceive them. (PHK 23; W2: 50)

The argument for the *possibility* of sensible objects existing unperceived that Berkeley here puts in the mouth of his materialist opponent rests on the *possibility of imagining* such objects existing unperceived. If this argument is to be valid, Berkeley's materialist opponent must also assume that the possibility that $p$ follows from the possibility of imagining that $p$, that is, that imaginability entails possibility. Here, then, is the kind of simple argument that, so Berkeley imagines, a materialist would rely on if challenged to prove that it is possible for a sensible object (say, a particular tree, T) to exist unperceived. Let us call it "the Materialist's Argument":

(M1)   It is possible to imagine that T exists unperceived.

(M2)   If it is possible to imagine that $p$, then it is possible that $p$.

So, (M3)   It is possible that T exists unperceived.

Berkeley's reaction to the Materialist's Argument falls somewhat short of complete perspicuity. I have divided the relevant passage into sections:

(A)   I answer, you may so [i.e., you may imagine trees in a park or books in a closet with nobody by to perceive them], there is no difficulty in it: but what is all this, I beseech you, more than framing in your mind certain ideas which you call *books* and *trees*, and at the same time omitting to frame the idea of any one that may perceive them?

(B)   But do not you your self perceive or think of them all the while?

(C)   This therefore is nothing to the purpose: it only shows you have the power of imagining or forming ideas in your mind;

(D)   but it doth not shew that you can conceive it possible, the objects of your thought may exist without the mind: to make out this, it is necessary that you conceive them existing unconceived or unthought of, which is a manifest repugnancy.

(E)   When we do our utmost to conceive the existence of external bodies, we are all the while only contemplating our own ideas. But the mind taking no notice of itself, is deluded to think it can and doth conceive bodies existing unthought of or without the mind; though at the same time they are apprehended by or exist in it self. (PHK 23; W2: 50–1)

As the division of the passage into sections makes plain, the structure of Berkeley's objection to the Materialist's Argument is contained in section (D). Berkeley's main claim is that the Materialist's Argument fails because premise (M1), according to which it is possible to imagine (or conceive) sensible objects such as T existing unperceived (or unconceived), is not merely false but self-contradictory.

But why, on Berkeley's view, is it self-contradictory ("a manifest repugnancy") to suppose that it is possible to conceive that T exists unconceived? It is tempting to suppose that the answer to this question lies in the following section of the corresponding passage in DHP 1:

Phil: How say you, Hylas, can you see a thing which is at the same time unseen?
Hyl: No, that were a contradiction.
Phil: Is it not as great a contradiction to talk of *conceiving* a thing which is *unconceived*?
Hyl: It is. (DHP 1; W2: 200)

Here Berkeley compares the thought of conceiving something that is unconceived with the thought of seeing something that is unseen, holding that both thoughts are self-contradictory for the same reason. It might then be thought that Berkeley infers that it is self-contradictory to suppose that it is possible to conceive that something exists unconceived from the fact that it is self-contradictory to suppose that it is possible to conceive something that is unconceived. The reasoning would rely on the following premise: To conceive that something exists unconceived is just to conceive something that exists unconceived.

If this is indeed how Berkeley argues for (M1), then, as Prior (1955) and Mackie (1976, 53–4) show, he is in a heap of trouble. For it simply does not follow from the fact that Fred conceives something's existing unconceived that there is something unconceived that Fred conceives. The error here, well known to philosophers of language and logic, involves the illegitimate exportation of an existential quantifier from an intensional context. In slightly more formal terms, the following inference rests on illegitimate scope confusion:

Fred conceives $(\exists x)$ (x is unconceived)
So, $(\exists x)$ (Fred conceives x & x is unconceived).[48]

Luckily, Berkeley does not commit this fallacy, as is evident from the continuation of the relevant passage from DHP 1:

Phil: The tree or house therefore which you think of, is conceived by you.
Hyl: How should it be otherwise? (DHP 1; W2: 200)

From the fact that it is self-contradictory to conceive something unconceived Berkeley infers, not that it is impossible to conceive that something exists unconceived, but rather that anything that is conceived to be

---

[48] For more on the criticism of scope confusion, see Szabó (2005, 467).

unconceived is not itself unconceived; for if it were unconceived, then, given that it is conceived to be unconceived, it would also be conceived; and thus the same thing would be both conceived and unconceived. The operative premise here is that anything that is conceived to be F is *ipso facto* conceived. Following Priest (1995, 68), let us call this the "Conception Schema":

(Conception Schema) If X conceives that T is F, then X conceives T.

That Berkeley wields the Conception Schema to infer that the books and trees that his opponent is attempting to conceive existing unconceived are themselves conceived is evident from section (B) of PHK 23:

(B)    But do not you your self perceive or think of them [i.e., the books and trees that you are trying to imagine existing unperceived] all the while?

So Berkeley does not infer that it is self-contradictory to suppose that it is possible to conceive that something exists unconceived on the basis of a fallacious inference that involves the exportation of an existential quantifier out of an intensional context. Rather, Berkeley's first step towards establishing the self-contradictoriness of (M1) involves using the Conception Schema to infer that X conceives T from the claim that X conceives that T exists unconceived.

But where, then, is the "manifest repugnancy"? Thus far, Berkeley has shown (at best) that anyone who conceives that T exists unconceived must thereby conceive T. It would appear that the only way to generate a contradiction would be to suppose that, as Winkler puts it, a proposition's being entertained (or conceived) spills over into its content.[49] That is, it might be thought that if X conceives the proposition [that T is F], then X conceives the proposition [that T is F and X conceives T]. In that case, it would follow from the fact that X conceives the proposition [that T exists unconceived] that X conceives the proposition [that X conceives T and T exists unconceived]. And thus it would follow from the fact that X conceives that T exists unconceived that X conceives a self-contradictory proposition. Assuming, then, that it is impossible for anyone to conceive a self-contradiction, it would follow that it is impossible for anyone to conceive a sensible object's existing unconceived.

---

[49] Winkler (1989, 185).

However, as Winkler himself emphasizes, Berkeley does not endorse the "spill-over" principle. Were he to do so, he would be forced to admit that it is impossible for anyone to conceive the existence of something that is unconceived *by herself*. Contrary to what Winkler suggests, this is not solipsism per se, but it is certainly a thesis in the theoretical vicinity and one that Berkeley denies. For if it is inconceivable that there should be something that is unconceived by me, then, given that inconceivability entails impossibility, it is impossible that there should be something that is unconceived by me, and hence necessarily everything that exists is conceived by me. Given that Berkeley himself accepts the principle that inconceivability entails impossibility, he would indeed be forced to accept a thesis to which he is implacably opposed.[50]

The standard view, then, is that Berkeley simply commits an egregious blunder, the fallacy of supposing that from the fact that any sensible object that is conceived to exist unconceived is itself conceived that it is self-contradictory (or even false) to suppose it possible to conceive a sensible object's existing unconceived. The error has been diagnosed as resulting from confusing the object of conception (what is conceived *of*) with the manner of conception (what is conceived *with*), from confusing an idea with what it is of.[51] The claim is that, in conceiving that T exists unconceived, one conceives T only in the sense of conceiving an *idea of* T. Were we to conceive T itself, rather than just an idea of T, we would be conceiving something that is both conceived and unconceived. But we do not in fact conceive T itself: what we conceive is only an idea of T. And there is no contradiction in supposing that we are conceiving an idea of something that we are conceiving to exist unconceived.

---

[50] For evidence that Berkeley accepts the thesis that conceivability and possibility coincide, see Winkler (1989, 30–3). Ott (2004, 411) claims that Berkeley denies the thesis that inconceivability entails impossibility, for there is a passage in DHP in which Philonous is made to say this: "Many things, for ought I know, may exist, whereof neither I nor any other man hath or can have any idea or notion whatsoever" (DHP 3; W2: 232–3). But the principle that Berkeley denies here is not the claim that inconceivable *states of affairs* (including states of affairs involving conceivable *things*) are impossible, but rather the different claim that the inability to form an idea or notion of a *thing* entails that it is impossible for it to exist.

That Berkeley does not accept the thesis that everything that exists is perceived by him is evident from the fact that he argues that there are other minds that have ideas that he himself does not perceive (see PHK 140, 145; W2: 105, 107 and DHP 3; W2: 233).

[51] See Pitcher (1977, 113).

But it is surely unlikely that Berkeley, who is otherwise so attuned to the cogency of his own reasoning, would proffer such an *obviously* fallacious piece of reasoning.[52] So some Berkeley scholars have tried to reconstruct the Master Argument in a more charitable way. Before laying out what I take to be the proper reconstruction of Berkeley's reasoning, let me briefly consider two influential proposals in this vein.

One proposal, due to Bolton (1987), is that Berkeley infers the impossibility of conceiving a book's existing unconceived from his theory of ideas, according to which ideas are their own objects. As she puts the point:

An idea of books that omits their being conceived is logically impossible; it would be books that are conceived (by you) and not conceived (being conceived is omitted from the idea-object).[53]

The reasoning runs as follows. Suppose that I conceive of a book (say, B) that exists unconceived. In doing this, I conceive an idea of B, where B itself is unconceived. But if ideas are their own objects, then everything that is true of the idea is also true of its object. Thus, from the fact that I conceive an idea of B, it follows that B itself is conceived. And given that B is unconceived, it would follow that B is both conceived and unconceived. This, then, is the contradiction that follows from the supposition that it is possible to conceive sensible objects existing unconceived. Unfortunately, this is almost certainly not how Berkeley himself reasons. For, as we have already seen, the theory that ideas are their own objects would give Berkeley too easy an argument for idealism and does not fit with what he says about ideas of memory and imagination.

On another proposal, due to Szabó (2005), the Master Argument amounts to a challenge that derives from reflection on one's own conception when one conceives a sensible object that is unconceived. According to Szabó, the thought that one conceives a sensible object that is

---

[52] Lennon makes a similar point with greater *panache*: "The strategic problem with [the standard criticisms of the Master Argument], and thus with the interpretations on which they are based, is that they make Berkeley out to be a philosophical nitwit" (Lennon 1988, 233). In defense of Berkeley, Lennon argues that "the Master Argument...turns out to be no argument at all, but rather the expression of a fundamental intuition of [Berkeleian nominalism]" (Lennon 1988, 246). As I argue below, the Master Argument *is* an argument. And though I agree with Lennon that the argument relies on a fundamental intuition, the intuition on which I claim it relies is not nominalism, but rather the thesis that all objects of conception are ideas.

[53] Bolton (1987, 74).

unconceived is not self-contradictory; nor is what one conceives in conceiving an unconceived sensible object self-contradictory. Self-contradiction occurs only when one performs the second-order act of reflecting on one's conception of an unconceived sensible object. As Szabó sees it, Berkeley assumes the following Reflection Principle (where $N$ is a name and $NP$ is a noun phrase):

> (Reflection Principle) If $N$ conceives $NP$, then, by reflecting on this, $N$ can come to conceive $NP$ which $N$ conceives.[54]

Thus, if Hylas conceives a tree that is not conceived, then, by the Reflection Principle, if Hylas reflects on this very act of conceiving, he thereby conceives an unconceived tree that he conceives. So reflection on his act of conception leads Hylas to conceive a thought that is self-contradictory. It is the self-contradictory nature of *this* thought that leads Berkeley to say that it is manifestly repugnant to conceive of an unconceived sensible object.

The main problem with this reconstruction is that Berkeley makes it quite clear where the purported repugnancy is supposed to lie. Recall that in order to fend off the Materialist's Argument, Berkeley must establish that it is impossible for anyone to conceive of an unconceived sensible object. As an answer to the Materialist's Argument, it simply will not do to answer that it is impossible for anyone to *self-reflectively* conceive of an unconceived sensible object. For it is surely possible to conceive of something without doing so self-reflectively. So if the repugnancy that Berkeley seeks is to serve his purpose, it must lie in the very thought that one conceives of an unconceived sensible object.

Thus far, we have seen that Berkeley uses the Conception Schema to infer that X conceives T from the fact that X conceives that T exists unconceived. If the point of Berkeley's answer to the Materialist's Argument is to challenge the premise that it is possible to conceive that T exists unconceived, then the point of Berkeley's inference must be to initiate a *reductio* of the claim that (for any arbitrary X) X conceives that T exists unconceived. But what does Berkeley think follows from the fact that X conceives T? The answer, left implicit in the passage from PHK, is made explicit in the corresponding passages from DHP 1.

---

[54] Szabó (2005, 469).

At various points in PHK 23, Berkeley states that when one tries to conceive a tree's existing unconceived one is actually only conceiving an idea (presumably, a complex idea) to which one gives the name of "tree." For example, in section (A), Berkeley writes that, in imagining books and trees with nobody by to perceive them, one is doing no more than "framing in [one's] mind certain ideas which [one] calls *books* and *trees*." In section (C), he says that the attempt to conceive books and trees existing unconceived shows no more than that one has "the power of imagining or forming ideas in [one's] mind." And in section (E), he writes that "[w]hen we do our utmost to conceive the existence of external bodies, we are all the while only contemplating our own ideas." What these passages strongly suggest is that Berkeley takes the fact of one's conceiving T to entail that T is an idea. That Berkeley accepts the entailment is confirmed by the following exchange from DHP 1:

Philo: And what is conceived is surely in the mind.
Hyl: Without question, that which is conceived is in the mind. (DHP 1; W2: 200)

Let us then call this assumption "The Idea Schema":

(Idea Schema) If X conceives T, then T is an idea.

Given the Idea Schema, it is simple to derive a contradiction from the assumption that X conceives that T exists unconceived. For Berkeley assumes that the nature of ideas is such that it is not possible for them to exist unconceived. Ideas, after all, are "inert, fleeting, dependent beings, which subsist not by themselves, but are supported by, or exist in minds or spiritual substances" (PHK 89; W2: 79–80), and "the existence of an idea consists in being perceived" (PHK 2; W2: 42). So, from the fact that T is an idea it follows that it is impossible that T exists unconceived. But, as we have seen, Berkeley assumes that conceivability (or imaginability) entails possibility, and hence that impossibility entails inconceivability. So, from the fact that it is impossible that T exists unconceived, it follows that it is impossible to conceive that T exists unconceived. But the assumption for *reductio* is that X conceives that T exists unconceived. Given that the assumption entails its negation, it follows that the assumption is self-contradictory.

This, then, is Berkeley's Master Argument (where X is an arbitrary mind and T is an arbitrary sensible object):

(1)  X conceives that T exists unconceived. [Assumption for *reductio*]

(2)  If X conceives that T is F, then X conceives T. [Conception Schema]

So,  (3)  X conceives T. [From 1, 2]

(4)  If X conceives T, then T is an idea. [Idea Schema]

So,  (5)  T is an idea. [From 3, 4]

(6)  If T is an idea, then it is impossible that T exists unconceived. [Nature of Ideas]

So,  (7)  It is impossible that T exists unconceived. [From 5, 6]

(8)  If it is impossible that *p*, then it is impossible to conceive that *p*. [Impossibility entails Inconceivability]

So,  (9)  It is impossible to conceive that T exists unconceived. [From 7, 8]

So, (10)  X does not conceive that T exists unconceived. [From 9]

So, (11)  X does and does not conceive that T exists unconceived. [From 1, 10]

As the reconstruction makes clear, the argument is simple, straightforward, and, importantly, deductively valid. It is based on four premises: the Conception Schema, the Idea Schema, the thesis that ideas cannot exist unconceived, and the thesis that impossibility entails inconceivability. As Berkeley sees it, the last two premises are both obvious to, and uncontested by, his philosophical opponents. So the dialectical success of the argument hinges on the truth-value of the Conception Schema and the Idea Schema.

Could a materialist provide some reason for denying the Conception Schema? To deny the Conception Schema is to claim that it is possible for someone to conceive that T is F without conceiving T. But how could such a claim be true? Consider the book (call it "Ben") that you are now reading. (Let us assume that you are not reading this online.) Now try to imagine Ben's being closed, instead of open. Can you imagine this without imagining Ben itself? I dare say, not. This phenomenon seems perfectly general. So how could the Conception Schema be false?

One way to attack the Conception Schema is to claim that conceiving and imagining are different mental processes that Berkeley mistakenly fails to distinguish. If they are indeed different, then it might be impossible to *imagine* that T is F without *imagining* T, even as it is possible to *conceive* that T is F without *conceiving* T. But how could conceiving and imagining come apart? Berkeley, like Locke, assumes that there is only one faculty that enables the mind to represent states of affairs that are contrary to fact, and this is the imagination. As against this, it might be argued that reason can conceive things that cannot be represented by the imagination. So, for example, in the Sixth Meditation Descartes famously claims that the unimaginability of a chiliagon is no bar to its conceivability by means of the pure understanding (AT 7: 72–3; CSM 2: 50–1). If Descartes's mental economy is correct, then it may be necessary for Berkeley to grant that the Conception Schema is, if not false, at least less than self-evident. But let us distinguish between two claims: (i) that it is impossible to conceive that T is F without *conceiving* T, and (ii) that it is impossible to conceive that T is F without *imagining* T. What Descartes invites us to accept entails the falsity of (ii) but does not *by itself* entail the falsity of (i). So even if Descartes is right, it may yet be that the Conception Schema is true.

As I see it, the most vulnerable premise of the Master Argument is the Idea Schema. Berkeley assumes, completely without argument, that every object of conception is an idea, and hence, given the mind-dependent nature of ideas, that every object of conception cannot exist unperceived. But why? A materialist might well accept that every *immediate* object of conception (or perception) is an idea without thereby conceding that every *mediate* object of conception (or perception) is an idea. If Berkeley cannot rule out the possibility of mediately conceiving a mind-*independent* object O by conceiving a mind-*dependent* idea that is in some way related to O, then the Master Argument fails on its own terms. It is, I believe, in large part to rule out this sort of objection that Berkeley pens DHP 1.

# 4

# The Argument for Idealism in the First *Dialogue*

Our investigation into Berkeley's reasons for accepting idealism in the early sections of PHK has yielded the following results. First, Berkeley's Semantic Argument for idealism in PHK 3 succeeds only if it is supplemented with an argument for the claim that perceivable (sensible) things are ideas. Second, Berkeley does not rest his argument for idealism in PHK on immaterialism, anti-abstractionism, or the likeness principle. Rather, Berkeley provides two Simple Arguments for idealism, the first resting on the claim that sensible objects are perceived by sense and the claim that ideas are the only things perceived by sense, the second resting on the claim that sensible objects are collections of sensible qualities and the claim that sensible qualities are ideas. Unfortunately, the latter three claims beg the question against materialists unless independent reason can be given for accepting them. Third, Berkeley does not use the Master Argument to establish idealism, but rather to rebut anti-idealist reasoning (the Materialist's Argument) designed to show that sensible objects can exist unperceived; and although the Master Argument is valid, it too begs the question against materialists unless Berkeley can provide independent support for his assumption that all objects of conception (perception) are ideas.

In this chapter, I argue that the most important function of DHP 1 is to remedy the defects of the two Simple Arguments and the Master Argument (thereby remedying the defects of the Semantic Argument) in PHK. Once it is understood what DHP 1 is designed to accomplish, it becomes impossible to read it as anything other than a deliberate attempt to shore up the earlier arguments for idealism by defending the very principles that Whiston and Clarke had so breezily dismissed.

# 1 Defending the Two Simple Arguments

At the very beginning of DHP 1, Hylas complains of skeptics who profess "an entire ignorance of all things, or [advance] such notions as are repugnant to plain and commonly received principles" (DHP 1; W2: 172). Philonous agrees. Hylas then charges Philonous with skepticism on the basis of the latter's denial of the existence of matter. Philonous replies that although he does indeed deny the existence of matter, he himself is not a skeptic, and that those who affirm the existence of matter "are by virtue of that opinion [greater skeptics], and maintain more paradoxes and repugnancies to common sense" than those who affirm the opposite (DHP 1; W2: 172). The topic then shifts to a discussion of the nature of skepticism, and after a brief discussion both Hylas and Philonous agree that it is sufficient to be denominated a skeptic that one deny "the reality of sensible things, or [profess] the greatest ignorance of them" (DHP 1; W2: 173). This introductory exchange sets the stage for the rest of DHP, which is designed to show that whereas materialism leads to skepticism (DHP 3; W2: 228–9), idealistic immaterialism does not (DHP 3; W2: 229–30).

Immediately following the introductory exchange on skepticism, the topic shifts to a discussion of the nature of sensible things. This discussion frames the rest of DHP 1, and provides the key to understanding how Berkeley proposes to shore up the Simple Arguments of PHK. Given its critical importance, I now quote the relevant passage in full, dividing it up into chunks for ease of reference:

[A]  Phil: What mean you by sensible things?
  Hyl: Those things which are perceived by the senses. Can you imagine that I mean anything else?
  Phil: Pardon me, Hylas, if I am desirous clearly to apprehend your notions, since this may much shorten our inquiry. (DHP 1; W2: 174)

[B1]  Phil: Suffer me then to ask you this farther question. Are those things only perceived by the senses which are perceived immediately? Or may those things properly be said to be *sensible*, which are perceived mediately, or not without the intervention of others?
  Hyl: I do not sufficiently understand you. (DHP 1; W2: 174)

[B2]  Phil: In reading a book, what I immediately perceive are the letters, but mediately, or by means of these, are suggested to my mind the notions of God, virtue, truth, etc. Now, that the letters are truly sensible things, or perceived by sense, there is no doubt: but I would know whether you take the things suggested by them to be so too.

Hyl: No certainly, it were absurd to think *God* or *Virtue* sensible things, though they may be signified and suggested to the mind by sensible marks, with which they have an arbitrary connexion.

Phil: It seems then, that by *sensible things* you mean those only which can be perceived immediately by sense.

Hyl: Right. (DHP 1; W2: 174)

[B3]   Phil: Doth it not follow from this, that though I see one part of the sky red, and another blue, and that my reason doth thence evidently conclude there must be some cause of that diversity of colours, yet that cause cannot be said to be a sensible thing, or perceived by the sense of seeing?

Hyl: It doth.

Phil: In like manner, though I hear variety of sounds, yet I cannot be said to hear the causes of those sounds.

Hyl: You cannot.

Phil: And when by my touch I perceive a thing to be hot and heavy, I cannot say with any truth or propriety, that I feel the cause of its heat or weight.

Hyl: To prevent any more questions of this kind, I tell you once for all, that by *sensible things* I mean those only which are perceived by sense, and that in truth the senses perceive nothing which they do not perceive immediately: for they make no inferences. The deducing therefore of causes or occasion from effects and appearances, which alone are perceived by sense, entirely relates to reason.

Phil: This point then is agreed between us, that *sensible things are those only which are immediately perceived by sense.* (DHP 1; W2: 174–5)

[C]   Phil: You will farther inform me, whether we immediately perceive by sight any thing beside light, and colours, and figures: or by hearing, any thing but sounds: by the palate, any thing beside tastes: by the smell, beside odours: or by the touch, more than tangible qualities.

Hyl: We do not. (DHP 1; W2: 175)

[D]   Phil: It seems therefore, that if you take away all sensible qualities, there remains nothing sensible.

Hyl: I grant it.

Phil: Sensible things therefore are nothing else but so many sensible qualities, or combinations of sensible qualities.

Hyl: Nothing else. (DHP 1; W2: 175)

The general structure of passages [A]–[D] taken as a whole is clear. In [A], Philonous and Hylas agree that to be a sensible thing (or object) is to be perceived by the senses. This assumption immediately entails the first premise of the First Simple Argument:

Sensible objects are perceived by means of the senses.

In [B1], Philonous raises the question whether all things that are perceived by the senses are immediately perceived. In [B3], Hylas answers Philonous's question in the affirmative:

Whatever is perceived by means of the senses is immediately perceived.

From these two propositions, Philonous (in [B2]) and Hylas (in [B3]) both conclude that "sensible things are those only which are immediately perceived by sense," that is, that all sensible objects are immediately perceived by means of the senses.[1] In [C], Philonous and Hylas agree that the objects of immediate sense perception are all sensible qualities (light, colors, figures, sounds, tastes, odors, and tangible qualities) or combinations thereof:

Whatever is immediately perceived by the senses is a sensible quality or combination of sensible qualities.

Finally, in [D], Philonous and Hylas agree on the following conclusion (explicitly introduced by "therefore"):

Sensible things are sensible qualities or combinations thereof.

Given that the proposition that sensible things are sensible qualities or combinations thereof follows logically from the three premises identified above, it is clear that Berkeley means to use [A]–[D] as an argument for it. The reasoning is simple: sensible things are perceived by sense; anything that is perceived by sense is immediately perceived; anything that is immediately perceived by sense is a sensible quality or combination of sensible qualities; therefore, sensible things are all sensible qualities or combinations thereof.[2]

---

[1] In [B2] Hylas does not say (i) that sensible things *are* perceived immediately by sense, but rather (ii) that sensible things *can be* perceived immediately by sense. Is this significant? I think not. For one thing, Hylas makes plain his acceptance of (1) in [B1] and (2) in [B3], from which it follows, not merely that (ii) is true, but also that (i) is true. So Hylas's commitment to (1) and (2) commits him logically to (i) in addition to (ii). For another thing, Philonous makes plain at the very end of [B3] that both he and Hylas accept (i). Thanks to Daniel Schwartz for bringing this issue to my attention.

[2] It is therefore a mistake for Muehlmann (1992, 124) to claim that "Berkeley's nominalism ... underlies his claim that a sensible thing consists of nothing but sensible qualities." Although, as I argue below, nominalism *does* play a (somewhat limited) role in Berkeley's argument for idealism, it is not *here* that Berkeley appeals to it. The important premise *here* is the claim that everything that is perceived by sense is immediately perceived.

Immediately following passages [A]–[D], Philonous raises the question whether "the reality of sensible things consist[s] in being perceived [or is] something distinct from their being perceived" (DHP 1; W2: 175). Given that Philonous has just shown that sensible things are sensible qualities or combinations thereof, this question reduces to the question whether the being of sensible qualities or combinations of sensible qualities consists in being perceived. For much of the rest of DHP 1 (about which more below), Philonous argues that "heat and cold are only sensations existing in our minds" (DHP 1; W2: 179), that "sweetness and bitterness [as well as all other tastes] do not exist without the mind" (DHP 1; W2: 180), that smells "cannot exist in any but a perceiving substance or mind" (DHP 1; W2: 181), that sounds "have no real being without the mind" (DHP 1; W2: 183), that colors "have certainly no existence without the mind" (DHP 1; W2: 187), that it is impossible for figure or extension to "subsist in that which doth not perceive it" (DHP 1; W2: 190), and that any quality that presupposes extension (including motion, solidity, and gravity) has "no existence without the mind" (DHP 1; W2: 191). Philonous concludes that all sensible qualities, both secondary and primary, are nothing but sensations, ideas existing in the minds that perceive them. This is no more than the second premise of the Second Simple Argument for idealism:

> Sensible qualities are ideas.

The conjunction of this proposition and the previous conclusion that sensible things are sensible qualities or combinations thereof then entails the following conclusion:

> Sensible things are ideas or combinations thereof.

And given that the *esse* of an idea is *percipi*, it follows directly from this conclusion that the being of a sensible thing consists in its being perceived.[3]

---

[3] It might be suggested that the reasoning for the claim that sensible things are sensible qualities/ideas or combinations thereof is endorsed by Hylas, but not by Philonous (and hence not by Berkeley); indeed, that the entirety of DHP 1 is to be read as an *ad hominem* against Hylas (and hence as an *ad hominem* against materialism). In that case, it would be false that *Berkeley* endorses the claim that anything perceived by the senses is immediately perceived. The suggestion derives its plausibility from the fact that Philonous gets Hylas to endorse this claim *before* saying that he and Hylas are *agreed* on its truth.

But the suggestion is false. For it is not Hylas but rather Philonous who explicitly endorses the reasoning for the claim that sensible things are sensible qualities/ideas or combinations thereof at the beginning of DHP 3. Clearly speaking in his own voice, and not merely

Consider now the two Simple Arguments for idealism:

> Sensible objects are perceived by means of the senses.
> Everything that is perceived by means of the senses is an idea.
> So, Sensible objects are ideas.

> Sensible objects are collections of sensible qualities.
> Sensible qualities are ideas.
> So, Sensible objects are collections of ideas.

As we have seen, Berkeley appeals to the proposition that sensible objects are perceived by means of the senses in passage [A]. That he does not argue for it there (or anywhere else) strongly suggests that he treats the assumption as obvious, indeed true as a matter of definition; for what it is to be a sensible object is to be something that is perceived by sense. More interesting is the fact that the assumptions extracted from passages [B3] and [C], namely that whatever is perceived by means of the senses is immediately perceived and that whatever is immediately perceived by the senses is a sensible quality or combination of sensible qualities, can be used to argue validly for both the premise that everything that is perceived by means of the senses is an idea and the premise that sensible objects are collections of sensible qualities.

Consider first the argument for the claim that sensible objects are collections of sensible qualities. By the first premise of the First Simple Argument, sensible objects are perceived by sense. But we are given that anything that is perceived by sense is immediately perceived, and that anything that is immediately perceived by sense is a sensible quality or combination of sensible qualities. These three assumptions together entail that sensible objects are sensible qualities or combinations thereof. But Berkeley assumes that sensible *objects* (i.e., sensible things

---

echoing Hylas's thoughts, Philonous says: "Wood, stones, fire, water, flesh, iron, and the like things . . . are things that I know. And I should not have known them, but that I perceived them by my senses; and things perceived by the senses are immediately perceived; and things immediately perceived are ideas; and ideas cannot exist without the mind; their existence therefore consists in being perceived; when therefore they are actually perceived, there can be no doubt of their existence. Away then with all that scepticism, all those ridiculous philosophical doubts" (DHP 3; W2: 230). This passage recapitulates the reasoning of DHP 1 to a tee. So, although there are indeed numerous pieces of purely *ad hominem* reasoning in DHP 1, the reasoning establishing that sensible things are sensible qualities/ideas or collections thereof is not among them.

such as tables and chairs, mountains and cherries) cannot be identified with *individual* sensible qualities: a chair is not identical to a color or a shape, a cherry is not identical to a taste or a texture. But then, given that sensible things are sensible qualities or combinations thereof, it follows that sensible objects are combinations (or collections) of sensible qualities.

Now consider the argument for the second premise of the First Simple Argument, the claim that everything perceived by means of the senses is an idea. We have already shown that anything that is perceived by sense is a sensible quality or combination of sensible qualities. By the second premise of the Second Simple Argument, all sensible qualities are ideas. It follows that anything that is perceived by sense is an idea or combination of ideas. But, as we have seen, Berkeley identifies combinations of ideas with complex ideas. Consequently, anything that is perceived by sense is an idea.

Unsurprisingly, then, the main argument of DHP 1, which is designed to establish that the being of a sensible object consists in being perceived, is based on premises that explain Berkeley's acceptance of the two Simple Arguments in the early sections of PHK. The structure of the reasoning is this. Taking it for granted that sensible objects are perceived by sense, Berkeley uses three assumptions to argue for the claim that everything that is perceived by sense is an idea: that everything that is perceived by sense is immediately perceived, that everything that is immediately perceived by sense is a sensible quality or collection of sensible qualities, and that every sensible quality is an idea. Combining this result with the premise that sensible objects are perceived by sense, he then derives the conclusion of the First Simple Argument, that all sensible objects are ideas.

Having argued that all sensible qualities are ideas, Berkeley argues for the claim that sensible objects are collections of sensible qualities as follows: sensible objects are perceived by sense, whatever is perceived by sense is immediately perceived, and whatever is immediately perceived by sense is a sensible quality or combination of sensible qualities. But from the claim that sensible objects are collections of qualities and the claim that qualities are ideas, it follows directly that sensible objects are collections of ideas. This is the conclusion of the Second Simple Argument. Ultimately, Berkeley's reasoning relies on the principle that all sensible objects are perceived by sense, the principle that whatever is perceived by sense is immediately perceived, the principle that everything that is immediately perceived is either a sensible quality or a collection of sensible qualities, and the principle that all sensible qualities are ideas.[4] Of these premises, Berkeley takes it to be self-evident that sensible objects are perceived by sense and that everything that is immediately perceived is either a sensible quality or a collection of sensible qualities. The premises he thinks require support are the principle that whatever is perceived by sense is immediately perceived and the principle that sensible qualities are ideas. The purpose of the next two sections is to consider Berkeley's reasons for accepting these premises. Once those reasons are understood, we will be able to reconstruct the entirety of Berkeley's sophisticated argument for idealism.

## 2 Why All Things Perceived by Sense are Immediately Perceived

Let's call the proposition that whatever is perceived by sense is immediately perceived, the "Principle of Immediate Perception":

(PIP)   Whatever is perceived by sense is immediately perceived.

On what grounds does Berkeley accept the truth of (PIP)? In [B1], Philonous raises the question whether (PIP) is true: "Are those things only perceived by the senses which are perceived immediately?" And at the end of both [B2] and [B3], Philonous concludes that the principle is indeed true. For, given the assumption that sensible objects are perceived by sense, it is the acceptance of (PIP) that explains Philonous's insistence at the end of both [B2] and [B3] that "sensible things are those only which are immediately perceived by sense"; and Hylas himself insists in [B3] that "in truth the senses perceive nothing which they do not perceived immediately." So if there is any reasoning for (PIP), it is contained in [B2] or [B3]. Let us consider each of these passages in turn.

---

[4]  Flage (2004, 31) claims, as I think rightly, that "questions of immediacy are not needed to reconstruct the arguments in the opening seven sections of the *Principles*." But it is worth emphasizing that questions of immediacy *are* needed to reconstruct the arguments of DHP 1 that are designed to *fill in* the arguments in the opening seven sections of PHK.

Recall [B2]:

[B2]   Phil: In reading a book, what I immediately perceive are the letters,
       but mediately, or by means of these, are suggested to my mind
       the notions of God, virtue, truth, etc. Now, that the letters are
       truly sensible things, or perceived by sense, there is no doubt: but
       I would know whether you take the things suggested by them to
       be so too.

       Hyl: No certainly, it were absurd to think *God* or *Virtue* sensible things,
       though they may be signified and suggested to the mind by sensible
       marks, with which they have an arbitrary connexion.

       Phil: It seems then, that by *sensible things* you mean those only which can be
       perceived immediately by sense.

       Hyl: Right. (DHP 1; W2: 174)

The purpose of this passage is to illustrate (PIP) by means of an example.
Philonous and Hylas both agree that the words "God," "virtue," and
"truth" are composed of letters that together suggest or signify the notions
of God, virtue, and truth respectively.[5] When one sees the word "God"
(or "virtue," or "truth") in a book, says Philonous, the string of letters that
constitute the word is *immediately* perceived by sight, while the notion
suggested by the word is thereby *mediately* perceived. It is then agreed that
notions are not perceived by sense, and hence that notions are not
themselves sensible things.[6] This result is a corollary of the claim that no
mediate object of perception is perceived by sense, and hence that all
sensible objects must be immediately perceived. As such, it corroborates
the claim of which it is the corollary.

---

[5]   It may appear as if Hylas endorses the claim that what the word "God" suggests is not the
notion of God, but rather God himself. For he says that "*God . . .* is signified and suggested to
the mind by sensible marks." But in placing the word "God" in italics, Berkeley may well be
using the word to refer to the notion suggested by it rather than to the Supreme Being to
which the unitalicized word is commonly used to refer.

   Notions (at least in the technical sense of "notion" that Berkeley emphasizes in the
1734 editions of DHP and PHK) are active thinking images, and hence are numerically
distinct from ideas, which are passive. Whether Berkeley is using the word "notion"
at DHP 1; W2: 174 to refer to notions *in the technical sense* emphasized in the 1734
editions of DHP and PHK is unclear. But he *could* be. For he explicitly claims in the 1713
edition of DHP that he has a notion of God that is distinct from any idea (DHP 3; W2:
231–2)—see chapter 3, note 41.

[6]   We may presume that Berkeley takes notions to be perceived by reflection, a form of
introspection which enables the mind to represent its own activities.

It might be thought that [B2] contains more of an argument for (PIP) than a kind of corroboration grounded in a single instance. For it may seem that Berkeley argues as follows:

(1)     All notions are mediate objects of perception.
(2)     Nothing that is perceived by means of the senses is a notion.
So, (PIP)  Nothing that is perceived by means of the senses is a mediate object of perception.

But if this were Berkeley's argument, then it would be a dismal failure, a failure he would almost surely have noticed. For the reasoning from (1) and (2) to (PIP) is an instance of a well-known syllogistic fallacy, the fallacy of illicit major:

(1)     All F are G.
(2)     No H is F.
So, (3)  No H is G.

To see that the argument is invalid, one need only consider an obviously invalid argument that has the same form:

(1)     All dogs are mammals.
(2)     No cat is a dog.
So, (3)  No cat is a mammal.

The premises of this argument are true but the conclusion is false. The fallacy was well known in Berkeley's day, and it is difficult in the extreme to believe that Berkeley himself would have succumbed to it.

Let us now turn to [B3]. As we have already seen, the argument of [B3] may be represented as follows:

(1)     Sensible things are perceived immediately by sense. [By (PIP) and the assumption that sensible things are perceived by sense]
(2)     The causes of our ideas of sense are perceived by inference.
(3)     Anything that is perceived by inference is mediately perceived.
(4)     Whatever is mediately perceived is not immediately perceived.
So, (5)  The causes of our ideas of sense are not sensible things.

The argument, which is straightforwardly valid, depends on (PIP), and cannot therefore be read as an argument for (PIP). And although at the end of [B3] Hylas appears to summarize the reasoning of [B3] as an argument for (PIP) premised on the assumption that "the senses make no inferences," we have seen that the appearance is inaccurate and misleading. I conclude that Berkeley's only reasons for (PIP) are contained in [B2], and that the function of [B3] is to draw one particularly salient anti-materialist conclusion from (PIP), namely that the causes of our sensations are not themselves sensible things.

## 3  Why Sensible Qualities are Ideas

On what grounds does Berkeley accept the claim that all sensible qualities are ideas? In chapter 3, we saw that PHK 10 and PHK 14 do not provide us with any reason to accept the claim. Rather, the function of these sections is entirely *ad hominem*, the point being that the same relativity arguments that have succeeded in convincing some materialists (e.g., the Cartesians) that secondary qualities are ideas should be sufficient to convince them that primary qualities are ideas too. (Berkeley is careful to avoid saying that these arguments *do* establish the mind-dependence of secondary qualities. For, as he makes clear in PHK 15, the opposite is true.) Does Berkeley offer us in DHP the kind of argument for the claim that is missing from PHK?

As most commentators recognize, Berkeley appears to offer two lines of reasoning in DHP 1 for the claim that sensible qualities are ideas. The first line of reasoning (which is widely known as the "Identification Argument") depends on the identification of secondary qualities with mind-dependent hedonic sensations (pleasures and pains). The second line of reasoning (which is widely known as the "Argument from Percep-tual Relativity") depends on the observation that it is possible for the same thing to appear to have contrary qualities to the same observer (or to different observers) at the same time. The standard view is that the Identification Argument is both inherently implausible and does not establish that *all* secondary qualities are sensations, and that the reasoning of the Identification Argument must therefore be supplemented with the Argument from Perceptual Relativity if it is to establish the truth of the claim that sensible qualities are ideas in all generality.[7] My purpose in this section is to establish that the standard picture gets it almost exactly backwards: whereas Berkeley's main (indeed, his only) argument for the ideational nature of secondary qualities is the Identification Argument,

---

[7]  See, for example, Tipton (1974, 226–55), Pitcher (1977, 100–6), and Winkler (1989, 161–75).

Berkeley's use of the Argument from Perceptual Relativity in DHP 1 remains just as *ad hominem* as it was in PHK 14 and is not intended to provide conclusive reasons for the claim that sensible qualities are ideas.[8]

### 4.3.1 The Identification Argument

The Identification Argument begins shortly after passage [A]–[D] leaves off. The argument has the following structure. First, it is shown that all secondary qualities are hedonic sensations, and hence that all secondary qualities are ideas. Second, it is shown that secondary qualities and primary qualities are inseparable in reality, and hence that primary qualities must be ideas as well. It is then concluded that all qualities, both primary and secondary, are ideas.

The identification of secondary qualities with hedonic sensations begins with the case of intense heat:

[E]   Phil: But is not the most vehement and intense degree of heat a very great pain?
      Hyl: No one can deny it. (DHP 1; W2: 176)

The argument, then, is this:

   (IH = P) Intense heat is a pain.
   (P = I)   Pain is an idea.
So, (IH = I)  Intense heat is an idea.

Hylas then questions (IH = P), claiming that "pain is something distinct from heat, and the consequence or effect of it" (DHP 1; W2: 176). This prompts Philonous to offer the following defense of (IH = P):

[F]   Phil: Upon putting your hand near the fire, do you perceive one simple uniform sensation, or two distinct sensations?
      Hyl: But one simple sensation.
      Phil: Is not the heat immediately perceived?
      Hyl: It is.
      Phil: And the pain?
      Hyl: True.
Phil: Seeing therefore they are both immediately perceived at the same time, and the fire affects you only with one simple, or uncompounded idea, it follows that this same simple idea is both the intense heat immediately perceived, and the pain;

---

[8]   The idea that the Argument from Perceptual Relativity is purely *ad hominem* is suggested by Jessop (192, n. 1). Much of what I say in this section recapitulates some of the points rightly emphasized by Muehlmann (1992, chapter 5). But Muehlmann and I disagree on some important details, and I will make a point of emphasizing the differences between our interpretations in the footnotes as the discussion progresses.

and consequently, that the intense heat immediately perceived, is nothing distinct from a particular sort of pain. (DHP 1; W2: 176)

The argument for (IH = P) has the following structure (where T is the time at which we may suppose that I put my hand near a roaring fire):

> (F1)  I immediately perceive exactly one simple sensation at T.
> (F2)  I immediately perceive intense heat and a particular sort of pain at T.

So, (IH = P) The intense heat I immediately perceive at T is identical to the particular sort of pain that I immediately perceive at T.[9]

Crucial to this argument is the assumption that the intense heat and the pain are immediately perceived at the very same time. Pitcher takes issue with this assumption:

[T]here is no credibility at all in the idea that [the heat of the fire] might actually *be* a pain; because, for one thing, I feel the heat of the fire for some time before I begin to feel the pain—and since the heat of the fire, which is presumably unchanging, cannot be the pain *before* the pain begins, it is wildly implausible to suggest that it might be the pain *after* the pain begins.[10]

---

[9] Muehlmann (1992, 140) claims that Berkeley does not, in the end, think that intense heat and pain are the same simple sensation: "The way Berkeley has Philonous express [the Identification Argument] in [F] presupposes that we *can*, at least in less extreme cases, selectively attend to either the heat or the pain: while Philonous urges that we 'perceive one simple uniform sensation,' he also says (my italics) 'they are *both* immediately perceived at the same time.' He could not say the latter if, in every thermal perception, 'heat' and 'pain' referred to one and the same *utterly simple* sensation." But Muehlmann here clearly overreads Berkeley's use of "both" in [F], a loose use that does not in the least presuppose that heat and pain are mentally separable or not numerically identical. Saying that intense heat and pain are *both* immediately perceived at the same time no more presupposes that intense heat is numerically distinct from pain than saying that 2 + 2 and 2 × 2 are *both* integers between 3 and 5 presupposes that 2 + 2 is numerically distinct from 2 × 2.

Muehlmann (1992, 144) also claims that the argument of [F] "at best establishes only that, in the midst of experiencing a very great pain, one does *not* experience an intense heat . . . And this then, by parity of phenomenological reasoning, leaves the door open to one who would argue that in some cases of experiencing very mild degrees of heat and cold . . . one does not experience hedonic sensations of *any* kind." But this involves a misreading of the argument of [F]. There Berkeley says quite plainly that one *does* experience intense heat at the same time as one experiences great pain of a certain kind. Indeed, it is on the basis of this claim that Berkeley purports to establish that intense heat is *identical to* a particular sort of pain. Perhaps Muehlmann's point is a criticism, rather than an interpretation, of the argument of [F], for he writes that "beyond a certain range of temperature, the immediate experience resulting from contact is one of intense pain *simpliciter*" (Muehlmann 1992, 146). But it seems to me that by itself this amounts to no more than a denial of (F2) without argument.

[10] Pitcher (1977, 101). For a similar objection, see Luce (1967, 80), quoted in Tipton (1974, 229).

Pitcher's main claim here is that the heat of the fire is immediately perceived before the pain. Although Pitcher does not elaborate, we may assume that he accepts this because he is thinking of a situation in which one brings one's hand slowly towards the fire until, let us say, it is in the very middle of the flames. Pitcher must be assuming that before one's hand reaches deep into the fire, the sensations that are immediately perceived cannot be described as painful. One immediately perceives warmth in an increasing degree, perhaps, but not pain.

But this objection misses the mark. Before the hand arrives in the center of the fire, what the mind immediately perceives is not *intense* heat, but only a moderate degree of heat. Berkeley's claim is *not* that the *moderate* degree of heat is identical to a pain, but only that the *intense* heat that is immediately felt at the end of the process is identical to a pain. (Indeed, Philonous identifies "a more gentle degree of heat" as a pleasure (DHP 1; W2: 178).) So whether a moderate degree of heat is immediately perceived before the pain is immediately felt is neither here nor there. Moreover, Pitcher assumes that the heat of the fire is unchanging, but this presupposes that as one's hand moves, the heat that one is immediately feeling belongs to a single thing, namely the fire. But, as we saw in chapter 2, Berkeley's considered view is that one's hand immediately perceives many different objects (indeed, many different fires) as it moves. At first, what one immediately perceives is a fire that consists of sensible qualities one of which is the sensation of moderate heat. One then immediately perceives a succession of fires, each of which is a collection of sensible qualities that includes a degree of heat more intense than the degree of heat included by its predecessor. At the end of the process, one immediately perceives a fire that is partially constituted by a very intense heat that is identical to a pain. As Berkeley sees it, Pitcher falls into the vulgar error of supposing that the very same fire is immediately perceived in different ways at different times. But in matters like these, we ought to think (and speak) with the learned.

Pitcher, following Henze (1965, 177), mounts a different objection, this time to (IH = P) itself:

[I]f Berkeley says that the heat of the fire is identical with your pain, then he must also say that your pain, like the heat, is in the fire![11]

---

[11] Pitcher (1977, 101).

The problem for Berkeley takes the form of the following instance of Leibniz's Law:

(1)    The intense heat that I immediately perceive at T is in the fire.

(2)    The particular sort of pain that I immediately perceive at T is not in the fire.

So, (IH≠P)  The intense heat that I immediately perceive at T is not identical to the particular sort of pain that I immediately perceive at T.

On Berkeley's behalf, it might be argued that (1) is false, i.e., that the fire is not intensely hot. According to Tipton (1974, 233–4), this is in fact how Berkeley argues in the following passage:

Phil: To make the point still clearer; tell me, whether in two cases exactly alike, we ought not to make the same judgment?

Hyl: We ought.

Phil: When a pin pricks your finger, doth it not rend and divide the fibres of your flesh?

Hyl: It doth.

Phil: And when a coal burns your finger, doth it any more?

Hyl: It doth not.

Phil: Since therefore you neither judge the sensation itself occasioned by the pin, nor any thing like it to be in the pin; you should not, conformably to what you have now granted, judge the sensation occasioned by the fire, or any thing like it, to be in the fire. (DHP 1; W2: 179)

Tipton then criticizes Berkeley for giving up (1), an important tenet of common sense that Berkeley had previously and emphatically endorsed (e.g., at N 19; W1: 10).

Unfortunately, Tipton has misread the passage. At first reading, it may seem that Philonous endorses the conclusion to which he claims Hylas is committed, namely that the sensation of heat occasioned by the fire is not in the fire. But this is a mistake. The argument that Philonous raises here is *ad hominem*. Philonous's point is that Hylas's own admission that the pain of the pinprick is not in the pin should, by parity of reasoning, commit him to the admission that the sensation of heat occasioned by the fire is not in the fire. Given that the latter admission contradicts common sense, Hylas's own views turn out to be more out of line with commonly accepted principles than Philonous's views. For, indeed, Philonous sets himself up as a champion of common sense, at least with respect to this issue. Philonous takes his own immaterialism to be perfectly compatible with the claim that the fire is hot. What Philonous must reject, if anything, is the notion that the pain of the pinprick is not in the pin.

The objection based on (1) and (2) fails, not because Berkeley rejects (1), but because (2) begs the question against him. As Berkeley sees it, to say that a sensible quality is "in" a sensible object is just to say that the quality is among the qualities that compose the object. The qualities are connected inasmuch as they "are observed to accompany each other" (PHK 1; W2: 41). So if indeed the sensation of pain is found to accompany the other qualities (such as yellowness, motion, and angular shape) that are taken to compose the fire, then there is no bar to saying that the pain is in the fire.[12] (Similarly for the pain's being in the pin.) Pitcher finds it odd to say that my pain is in the fire. This may be because Pitcher assumes an inherence model of property possession. On the inherence model, to say that property F is in X is to say that F inheres in X. And, indeed, Berkeley would admit that it is a mistake to suppose that my pain *inheres in* the fire. But Berkeley rejects the inherence model of property possession. So one cannot presuppose the model in arguing against him. It may also be that Pitcher finds it odd to say that my pain is in the fire because he assumes that my pain is in my mind while the fire is external to my mind. But this too would beg the question against Berkeley, inasmuch as the question as to whether or not the fire is in my mind is precisely the point at issue in the argument for idealism.

Finally, Pitcher objects to (F1), claiming that it is far from clear whether what I immediately perceive at T is a simple sensation or a complex sensation. Pitcher rightly points out that Berkeley's contemporaries are happy to accept the "by no means unreasonable" assumption that introspection is sufficient to determine whether one's sensation is simple or compound.[13] But, says Pitcher:

It now seems obvious that one and the same thing can be classified as simple *or* complex, depending on what our particular interests happen to be with respect to that issue and on what scheme of classification we adopt. (cf. Wittgenstein (1953, §§ 47–8)) . . . If this Wittgensteinian way of looking at simplicity and complexity is right, as I think it is, then Berkeley and all his contemporaries are wrong in assuming that one can tell just by inspection whether a thing is simple or complex.[14]

---

[12] Here I agree with Lennon (1988, 235), who writes: "But color can be in the die as a member of the bundle of sensations composing it. Thus understood pain too should be capable of being in the die."

[13] Pitcher (1977, 102).      [14] Pitcher (1977, 102–3).

Wittgenstein's point at *Philosophical Investigations* §47 is that "[t]he question 'Is what you see composite?' makes good sense if it is already established what kind of complexity...is in question."[15] As Pitcher points out, this claim makes perfect sense. But there is no reason at all why Berkeley cannot take it on board. All he needs to say is that the kind of complexity at issue here is *phenomenological* complexity. The relevant question is whether the intense heat of the fire *feels different* from the particular sort of pain that is experienced at the same time. There is nothing mysterious about this question. In the ordinary course of our experience, we are able to distinguish between phenomenal feels by introspection. Berkeley simply asks us to reflect on our sensations at T to determine whether what we are immediately perceiving is one sensation or two. And the clear answer seems to be that there is no phenomenal distinction between the sensation of intense heat and the sensation of pain.

Thus far we have been discussing Philonous's reasons in [F] for thinking that intense heat is nothing more than a particular sort of pain. But [F] is not the only passage in which Philonous defends something akin to this claim. Immediately following [F], Berkeley writes:

[G]   Phil: Again, try in your thoughts, Hylas, if you can conceive a vehement sensation to be without pain, or pleasure.
Hyl: I cannot.
Phil: Or can you frame to yourself an idea of sensible pain or pleasure in general, abstracted from every particular idea of heat, cold, tastes, smells? Etc.
Hyl: I do not find that I can.
Phil: Doth it not therefore follow, that sensible pain is nothing distinct from those sensations or ideas, in an intense degree?
Hyl: It is undeniable. (DHP 1; W2: 176–7)

The argument of [G] presupposes the claim that inconceivability entails impossibility:

(G1)   It is impossible to conceive pain apart from an intense degree of some secondary quality.

(G2)   Inconceivability entails impossibility.

So, (G3)   It is impossible for pain to exist apart from some intense degree of some secondary quality. [From G1, G2]

(G4)   If it is impossible for X to exist apart from Y, then X is identical to Y.

So, (G5)   Every pain is identical to some intense degree of some secondary quality. [From G3, G4]

---

[15] Wittgenstein (1953, 22).

This argument, which provides reason to identify the pain immediately perceived at T with the intense heat that is immediately perceived at T, is vulnerable to several objections. First, there are good reasons for thinking that (G1) is false, i.e., that it is *possible* to conceive pain apart from an intense degree of some secondary quality. As Pitcher rightly notes, there are many pains that can be conceived apart from an intense degree of any secondary quality, including "stomach aches, tooth aches, the pain of a knife wound, [and] the pain of a heart attack."[16] Second, and perhaps more importantly, there are good reasons for thinking that (G4) is false, for from the fact that X cannot exist apart from Y it does not follow that X is identical to Y. Consider, for example, the case of color and extension. It is clear, to Berkeley at least, that it is impossible to conceive extension without color or color without extension. And yet it is also clear that extension is not identical to color. Whether sensible quality F and sensible quality G are identical depends not on whether F can be conceived apart from G or whether G can be conceived apart from F, but rather on whether F and G are phenomenally indistinguishable.

However, it is possible to reconstruct a more powerful argument for a generalization of the conclusion that intense heat is an idea that is based on the first exchange of [G] and the principle that inconceivability entails impossibility. The argument is this:

(G1★)   It is impossible to conceive any intense degree of a secondary quality apart from pain.

(G2)   Inconceivability entails impossibility.

So, (G3★)   It is impossible for any intense degree of a secondary quality to exist apart from pain. [From G1★, G2]

(G4★)   If Y is an idea and it is impossible for X to exist apart from Y, then X is an idea.

(P = I)   Pain is an idea.

So, (G5★)   Every   intense degree of a secondary quality is an idea. [From G3★, G4★, P = I]

---

[16] Pitcher (1977, 103).

It is clear that Berkeley endorses all of the premises of this argument. (G1★) is the upshot of the first exchange of [G]; (G2) and (G4★) are familiar Berkeleian claims, which play an important role in Berkeley's argument that primary qualities are ideas (see below);[17] and (P = I) is one of the two premises of Berkeley's argument for (IH = I). The argument is stronger than the argument that relies on (G1) and (G4), because (G1★) and (G4★) are not vulnerable to the same sorts of objections. While it seems possible to conceive a pain apart from any intense degree of a secondary quality, it does indeed seem impossible to conceive an intense degree of a secondary quality without pain; and while it seems possible for two things to be numerically distinct even though they cannot exist apart, it does indeed seem impossible for something that cannot exist apart from an idea to be anything other than an idea.

The problem with this argument is that it is unclear that it adds anything to the argument for (IH = P) based on (F1) and (F2). Recall the argument for (IH = P):

> (F1)    I immediately perceive exactly one simple sensation at T.
> (F2)    I immediately perceive intense heat and a particular sort of pain at T.
> So, (IH = P) The intense heat I immediately perceive at T is identical to the particular sort of pain that I immediately perceive at T.

If we apply this form of reasoning to all cases in which I immediately perceive an intense degree of some secondary quality at T, we arrive at the following argument:

> (F1)   I immediately perceive exactly one simple sensation at T.
> (F2-gen)  I immediately perceive an intense degree of some secondary quality and a particular sort of pain at T.
> So, (IH = P-gen) The intense degree of some secondary quality that I immediately perceive at T is identical to the particular sort of pain that I immediately perceive at T.

---

[17] See chapter 3, notes 22 and 50, and accompanying text, for evidence that Berkeley presupposes the truth of (G2) in other passages.

If we now ask why (G1★) is true, that is, if we ask why it is impossible to conceive any intense degree of some secondary quality apart from pain, the obvious answer is that (i) the intense degree of any secondary quality *is identical to* a pain, and (ii) where X is identical to Y it is impossible to conceive X apart from Y. But if one of the reasons for accepting (G1★) is that every intense degree of a secondary quality is identical to a pain, then the argument from (G1★) to the conclusion that every intense degree of a secondary quality is an idea is superfluous.[18,19]

---

[18] Muehlmann (1992, 139) writes that "Berkeley seems to vacillate between two possible conclusions: [the Identification Argument] is supposed to prove either that ($c_1$) any determinate thermal quality is *identical with* a sensation or that ($c_2$) any determinate thermal quality is *inseparable from* a sensation." As I have argued in the text, there is no vacillation here. Berkeley provides one argument for ($c_1$) and another argument for ($c_2$). From both of these arguments Berkeley concludes that any determinate thermal quality is an idea. Muehlmann goes on to claim (rightly, in my view) that Berkeley advances these arguments in the context of a negative attack on materialism and a positive argument for idealism. But Muehlmann also claims (wrongly, as I see it) that "if he wants to use [the Identification Argument] in support of a positive conclusion, in support of his idealism, only ($c_2$) can be congenial to Berkeley. The reason for this is that, if ($c_1$) is true, then the plain man's view—that the heat is in the fire and the pain is in that part of one's body which comes into contact with the fire—cannot be sustained." In defense of this comment, Muehlmann cites two passages from the *Notebooks*, one in which Berkeley endorses the view that "simple ideas [are] in the things themselves" (N 222; W1: 29) and one in which he endorses the view that "the pain is in my finger etc" (N 444; W1: 55). Muehlmann (1992, 141) also cites the fact that the second and subsequent editions of PHK 5 do not contain the claim that "the object and the sensation are the same thing, and cannot therefore be abstracted from each other" as pointing to Berkeley's recognition of the fact that ($c_1$) "is impossible to reconcile with the plain man's view."

My own view here, as I argue in the text, is that the best way for Berkeley to defend ($c_2$) is by means of premises that are sufficient to establish ($c_1$). So, if anything is more congenial to Berkeley, it is ($c_1$) rather than ($c_2$). First, it should be noted that the two claims from the *Notebooks*, N 222 and N 444—that heat is in the fire and that pain is in the finger—are not in any way inconsistent with Berkeley's view that heat and pain are sensations. After all, on Berkeley's ontology of sensible objects, the fire and the finger are nothing but collections of sensations themselves. Second, Berkeley's excision of the claim that "the object and the sensation are the same thing" from the second and subsequent editions of PHK 5 proves no more than that he thought the sentence either otiose or stylistically infelicitous. (As Muehlmann (1992, 142) himself recognizes, even as Berkeley removes the claim that "the object and the sensation are the same thing," he *retains* the claim that "I might as easily divide a thing from itself.") So it is pure speculation to claim that Berkeley had some weightier *philosophical* reason for removing the relevant sentence.

[19] Muehlmann (1992, 139–40) claims that, because of its dependence on (G1★), the Identification Argument depends on Berkeley's anti-abstractionism: "The claim that intense heat is inseparable from great pain must rest on the fact that we *cannot* be aware of one without the other. Since we cannot be aware of one without the other, the distinction between them

Having established that intense heat is a pain, and hence an idea, Philonous shifts his focus to moderate degrees of heat, i.e., to the various degrees of warmth. As Philonous sees it, warmth is the very opposite of pain:

Phil: And is not warmth, or a more gentle degree of heat than what causes uneasiness, a pleasure?
Hyl: What then?
Phil: Consequently it cannot exist without the mind in any unperceiving substance, or body.
Hyl: So it seems. (DHP 1; W2: 178)

The argument is this:

(MH = PL) Moderate heat is a pleasure.
(PL = I)   Pleasure is an idea.
So, (MH = I)   Moderate heat is an idea.

The kind of pleasure Berkeley has in mind in this argument is to be identified with a pleasurable sensation, rather than with the kind of pleasure that one might experience as a result of some intellectual accomplishment. So, in this sense, (PL = I) seems true. The important issue is whether (MH = PL) is true, i.e., whether moderate heat is a pleasure, and here Philonous does not elaborate. We may assume that the reason for this is that his defense of (MH = PL) would mimic his defense of (IH = P). Thus, he might point to the soothing warmth of the water immediately perceived when taking a shower, or the soothing warmth of the fire immediately perceived after having walked one's dog in sub-zero temperatures, as being phenomenally indistinguishable from the pleasant sensation immediately perceived at the time.[20]

---

is merely apparent: we cannot abstract, we 'cannot conceive in our thoughts,' a *real* distinction of one from the other." But, as I argue in the text, Berkeley's claim that intense heat is inseparable from great pain *need not*, and probably in the end *does not*, rest ultimately on the claim that there are no abstract ideas. For the fact that we cannot abstract intense heat from pain derives from the fact that intense heat is identical to a particular sort of pain, an identity claim that is not itself based on anti-abstractionism.

[20] Stoneham (2002, 63) claims that "one can clearly see that the pleasures caused by mild temperatures, or the pains caused by bright lights or loud noises, are more easily separable [in the imagination] from the associated sense perception [than great pain is from the intense heat associated with it]." But it seems to me to beg the question against Berkeley to claim that the pleasure of a soothing bath *is caused by* the warmth of the water. The mistake here lies in the thought that pleasure has some distinctive phenomenal quality, that there is a distinctive way that pleasure feels. But this is precisely what Berkeley is at pains to deny.

Interestingly, however, Hylas simply denies that moderate heat is a pleasure:

Hyl: On second thoughts, I do not think it so evident that warmth is a pleasure, as that a great degree of heat is a pain.

Phil: I do not pretend that warmth is as great a pleasure as heat is a pain. But if you grant it to be even a small pleasure, it serves to make good my conclusion.

Hyl: I could rather call it an *indolence*. It seems to be nothing more than a privation of both pain and pleasure. (DHP 1; W2: 178)

Hylas's claim is that warmth is neither pleasure nor pain, but rather "a privation of both pain and pleasure."[21] If this were true, then Berkeley's attempt to use the Identification Argument to establish the mind-dependence of warmth would fail. Philonous does not attempt to *prove* that this suggestion of Hylas's is mistaken, but points out instead that introspection should be sufficient to establish its falsity:

Phil: If you are resolved to maintain that warmth, or a gentle degree of heat, is no pleasure, I know not how to convince you otherwise, than by appealing to your own sense. (DHP 1; W2: 178)

This exchange is, at least superficially, puzzling.[22] The claim that warmth is a privation seems to deserve more attention than Philonous gives it. However, the fact that he gives it short shrift may simply reflect Berkeley's view that there is very little to be said in its favor.[23] If warmth is something

---

[21] Muehlmann (1992, 145) endorses Hylas's line of thought here. He claims that Berkeley "really has no ground for holding, on the basis of [the Identification Argument], that some mild degrees of heat are in the mind of the perceiver... [For] within some thermal experiences there are, phenomenologically, no hedonic sensations to be found and therefore nothing mental to which they can be inseparably tied."

[22] At N 833 (W1: 99), Berkeley suggests that a mild degree of heat or cold might be "an equal mixture of pleasure and pain." This would explain why we are often indifferent to mild degrees of heat and cold. However, as Muehlmann (1992, 146–7) rightly notes, the suggestion conflicts with Berkeley's commitment to the transparency of the mental. For we are often unaware that we are perceiving a balance of pleasure and pain when we are perceiving a mild degree of heat (or cold); so if such a balance exists, Berkeley must abandon his claim in PHK 25 (W2: 51) that "there is nothing in [our ideas] but what is perceived." This conflict may explain why Berkeley never actually makes the suggestion in his published work.

[23] It is tempting to think (indeed, it might even be the standard view) that Philonous's admission that he cannot find a way of convincing Hylas that warmth is not an indolence other than by appealing to Hylas's own sense reveals that Berkeley himself thinks that the Identification Argument cannot establish that *all* degrees of heat and cold are ideas. Those who succumb to this temptation may also be tempted to think that Berkeley moves from the Identification Argument to the Argument from Perceptual Relativity because he thinks that the latter argument succeeds exactly where the former argument fails. But we should, I think,

sensed, as it seems it is when one takes a shower or comes in from the cold, then it is as much of a sensible quality as color or taste. Perhaps this is the sort of consideration to which Philonous later alludes in saying that "an indifferent sensation is as truly a *sensation* as one more pleasing or painful" (DHP 1; W2: 192).[24]

More importantly, Hylas might be asked how the privation account of warmth could be extended to cover moderate coldness. Once it is admitted that intense heat is a pain, parity of reasoning suggests that intense cold is a pain too, as Hylas readily admits:

Phil: What think you of cold?

Hyl: The same that I do of heat. An intense degree of cold is a pain; for to feel a very great cold, is to perceive a great uneasiness: it cannot therefore exist without the mind. (DHP 1; W2: 178)

But what of moderate coldness? We may assume that Berkeley's view is that moderate cold, like moderate heat, is a pleasure. (Think of walking into an air-conditioned room from the intense heat and humidity of a tropical summer.) If Hylas refuses to accept that moderate heat is a pleasure because moderate heat is a privation, then we may assume that he has no other reason to deny that moderate cold is a pleasure than that it too is a privation. But what kind of privation? There seems no other choice but to identify moderate cold with a privation of pain and pleasure. But then moderate heat and moderate cold would both be privations of pain and pleasure. The problem here is that privations are such that, for any properties F and G, there cannot be more than one privation of F and G.[25] It follows that if X is a privation of F and G and Y is a privation of

---

resist this temptation. When Philonous admits that he knows not how to convince Hylas that warmth is not an indolence other than by appealing to Hylas's own sense, he does not thereby accept that more argument (say, in the form of the Argument from Perceptual Relativity) is needed to prove that warmth is not a privation of pain and pleasure: what he claims is that this conclusion is to be established by introspection rather than by argument.

[24] Muehlmann (1992, 138) claims that this kind of response "seems to beg the question," for "Philonous assumes that indifferent sensible qualities are identical to (or inseparable from) sensations, and this is the very thing the argument is supposed to prove." But notice that Philonous does not say that indifferent *sensible qualities* are identical to sensations. What he says is that indifferent *sensations* are sensations nonetheless. Philonous's point, I take it, is that moderate heat and moderate coldness are still *felt*, even if we find ourselves indifferent to them. This is what makes it difficult to maintain the view that moderate heat and moderate coldness are privations.

[25] This just follows from the logic of privations. In scholastic metaphysics, a privation, such as blindness in humans, is a lack of something that an object is supposed to have. Berkeley is almost surely using "privation" here in a looser sense, as meaning a simple lack. (It doesn't

F and G, then X is identical to Y. On Hylas's account, then, it turns out that moderate heat is identical to moderate cold. But this is absurd. If it were true, then my warm shower would be a cold shower, and the fire in front of which I warm my hands after coming in from the cold would be a cold fire.[26]

Berkeley's considered view, then, is that intense heat and intense cold are pains, while moderate heat and moderate cold are pleasures. By the Identification Argument, it follows directly that heat and cold, whether intense or moderate, are both ideas. Philonous later extends the very same reasoning, first to tastes, and then to odors:

make sense to suppose that sensible objects are *supposed to be* cold or *supposed to be* hot.) But whether Berkeley is using "privation" in the scholastic sense or in the looser sense, it is logically impossible that when an object fails to have a property, there are two or more such property-possession-failures.

It might be argued that it is not that, in Hylas's mouth, the word "privation" possesses a technical meaning that is looser than the technical meaning of the scholastics, but rather that it possesses a completely *non-technical* meaning. On this reading, to say that moderate heat/cold is a privation of pain and pleasure is just to say that moderate heat/cold is neither pleasurable nor painful. But on this reading it would follow from the fact that chairs are neither pleasurable nor painful that chairs are privations of pain and pleasure. Yet the claim that chairs are privations of plain and pleasure is surely not something that any of Berkeley's characters would endorse. In the end, it is too much to believe that Berkeley is not so much as thinking of the long and established *philosophical* history of the term "privation" (e.g., in the work of Descartes, Malebranche, and Locke, as well as scholastic philosophers) in penning Hylas's suggestion that warmth might be a privation.

[26] It might be suggested on Hylas's behalf that moderate heat might be a privation of a *particular kind* of pain and a *particular kind* of pleasure, while moderate cold might be a privation of a *different kind* of pain and a *different kind* of pleasure. Call the kind of pain one lacks when one experiences moderate heat, "$KP_{MH}$," and the kind of pleasure one lacks when one experiences moderate heat, "$KL_{MH}$." And call the kind of pain one lacks when one experiences moderate cold, "$KP_{MC}$," and the kind of pleasure one lacks when one experiences moderate cold, "$KL_{MC}$." On this suggestion, whenever one lacks any pain belonging to $KP_{MH}$ and any pleasure belonging to $KL_{MH}$, then one experiences moderate heat; and whenever one lacks any pain belonging to $KP_{MC}$ and any pleasure belonging to $KL_{MC}$, then one experiences moderate cold. In order to avoid the objection outlined in the text, the suggestion must be that either $KP_{MH} \neq KP_{MC}$ or $KL_{MH} \neq KL_{MC}$. (For if $KP_{MH} = KP_{MC}$ and $KL_{MH} = KL_{MC}$, then moderate heat would be identical to moderate cold.) Suppose, then, that $KP_{MH} \neq KP_{MC}$ and that a subject, say Sally, experiences no pleasure of any kind. In that case, whenever Sally experiences a pain belonging to $KP_{MC}$, she experiences moderate heat (for she experiences neither a pain belonging to $KP_{MH}$ nor a pleasure belonging to $KL_{MH}$). This seems counterintuitive (i.e., contrary to common sense). Suppose, then that $KL_{MH} \neq KL_{MC}$ and that Sally experiences no pain of any kind. In that case, whenever Sally experiences a pleasure belonging to $KL_{MC}$, she experiences moderate heat (for, again, she experiences neither a pain belonging to $KP_{MH}$ nor a pleasure belonging to $KL_{MH}$). This too seems counterintuitive. So counterintuitive consequences follow, whether one assumes $KP_{MH} \neq KP_{MC}$ or $KL_{MH} \neq KL_{MC}$.

Phil: What think you of tastes, do they exist without the mind, or no?

Hyl: Can any man in his senses doubt whether sugar is sweet, or wormwood bitter?

Phil: Inform me, Hylas. Is a sweet taste a particular kind of pleasure or pleasant sensation, or is it not?

Hyl: It is.

Phil: And is not bitterness some kind of uneasiness or pain?

Hyl: I grant it. (DHP 1; W2: 179–80)

Phil: In the next place, odours are to be considered. And with regard to these, I would fain know, whether what hath been said of tastes doth not exactly agree to them? Are they not so many pleasing or displeasing sensations?

Hyl: They are. (DHP 1; W2: 180–1)

The reasoning is the same as it is in the case of heat and cold. Phenomenally, the taste of a luscious peach or the smell of a new rose is indistinguishable from the relevant pleasurable experience, and the taste of spoiled milk or the smell of rancid cheese is indistinguishable from the relevant painful experience. Given the parallels with the case of heat and cold, it is not surprising to find that Berkeley's discussion of the Identification Argument in the case of tastes and smells is relatively brief. No doubt similar objections might be offered to the identification of tastes and smells with pleasurable and painful sensations, but these would presumably be followed by similar replies. Rather than rehearse the same objections and replies, Berkeley (for reasonable stylistic reasons) simply omits them.

The real question here is why Berkeley fails to apply the Identification Argument to the case of the two remaining sets of secondary qualities, namely colors and sounds. Two hypotheses immediately present themselves. The first hypothesis is that Berkeley thinks that the Identification Argument does not apply to colors and sounds. In that case, he needs a completely different sort of argument to establish that colors and sounds are ideas. (Those who take this road will find it natural to suppose that Berkeley intends the considerations about perceptual relativity that occupy him a great deal in DHP 1 as just this kind of argument. More on this below.) The second hypothesis is that although Berkeley thinks that the Identification Argument applies to colors and sounds, he also thinks it would be tiresome to wheel out the argument five times, once for each of the five types of secondary qualities.

There are several reasons to favor the second hypothesis over the first. In the first place, as I argue below, the Argument from Perceptual

Relativity is an *ad hominem* attack on a very particular kind of materialism, rather than a positive argument for the claim that secondary qualities are ideas. Second, if the Identification Argument is actually applied to colors and sounds, it is no less convincing than the same argument as applied to heat, cold, tastes, and odors. As Muehlmann aptly remarks:

> [I]f one hears an intensely loud sound, one feels a great pain; and if one stares at a very brilliant light (e.g., the sun), one feels a great irritation.[27]

The point here is that intense sounds and colors are experienced as pains, while more moderate sounds and colors are experienced as pleasures. (Think of the difference between Beethoven's Fifth cranked up to maximum volume and the same piece played at moderate volume.)[28] Finally, there is already evidence that Berkeley employs stylistic considerations to shorten discussions that might have been pursued at greater length in DHP 1. For example, as we have seen, Berkeley does not reproduce the objections and replies involved in his application of the Identification Argument to the case of heat when it comes time for him to discuss tastes

---

[27] Muehlmann (1992, 138). This is not to say that I agree with all of Muehlmann's remarks on the subject. One of his claims is that "Berkeley observes that [the Identification Argument] does not so readily apply to sounds, colors, and the primary qualities" (1992, 137–8). Muehlmann cites no passages in defense of this claim. I dare say that this is in large part because there are none to be found. As far as I am aware, Berkeley never explicitly addresses the issue of whether the Identification Argument applies or does not apply to colors, sounds, or primary qualities.

[28] It might be suggested that a brilliant or intense shade of red, for example, may carry with it neither irritation nor pleasure. But here we must be careful to distinguish between brilliance and intensity. A brilliant shade of red is strong and attention-grabbing, but not necessarily intense. The intensity of a color (as distinguished, say, from its saturatedness) depends on the total amount of light involved. My claim is not that Berkeley thinks that *brilliant* colors are pains. My claim is that Berkeley thinks that *intense* colors are pains.

It might also be objected that many people experience colors such as puke yellow, chartreuse, and teal as disagreeable, even when they are not intense, and that this is a fact of which Berkeley must have been aware. But here we must be careful to make an important distinction. Sensible qualities that are pains are *intrinsically* disagreeable, and sensible qualities that are pleasures are *intrinsically* agreeable; sensible qualities that are neither pains nor pleasures are neither intrinsically agreeable nor intrinsically disagreeable, but may be *extrinsically* agreeable/disagreeable by virtue of being associated with something agreeable/disagreeable. This, I believe, is what Berkeley would tell us about the perception of puke yellow or green (as well as other "disagreeable" colors). Though not pains, and so not disagreeable *in themselves*, these colors may suggest (and so be associated with) painful experiences of other sorts, and hence rightfully qualify as *extrinsically* disagreeable. Indeed, this is compatible with such colors being pleasures, and hence intrinsically agreeable!

and odors. Rather, his discussion of tastes and odors is severely truncated, for what are clearly reasons of style and exposition.[29]

So I think we should read Berkeley as intending to apply the Identification Argument to all the secondary qualities. But what should we say of the primary qualities? Does Berkeley mean us to read the Identification Argument as applying to them too? Muehlmann thinks that Berkeley "could have applied [the Identification Argument], with equal plausibility, to *all* of the sensible qualities," including primary qualities. As an example, Muehlmann suggests that, in defense of the application of the Identification Argument to solidity, one might point out that "if one intensely touches (say, by falling off one's horse) the solidity of the ground, one feels, perhaps, a whole barrage of very great pains."[30] But the application of the Identification Argument to primary qualities *is* problematic in the way that the application of the very same argument to secondary qualities is not. Consider first the fact that primary qualities (such as solidity, size, shape, and motion) are not gradable on a scale of intensity: whereas one odor can be more intense than another, it makes no sense to say that one shape or magnitude is more intense than another. This makes it impossible for Berkeley to argue that intense shape (or magnitude, or motion, or solidity) is a pain while moderate shape (or magnitude, or motion, or solidity) is a pleasure. (Muehlmann's reference to the intense touching of solidity obscures this point. In order for the Identification Argument to work, the relevant intensity should qualify the quality itself rather than the action that occasions one's perception of it.) There is also the following problem.

---

[29] Muehlmann (1992, 137) suggests that the reason Berkeley does not apply the Identification Argument to colors and sounds is that "by the time sounds and colors become the subject of discussion, Berkeley has moved Hylas from his initial naïve materialism [according to which sound and color are *sensed*] to a more sophisticated materialism according to which sound and color are described in the terminology of a mathematico-corpuscular theory of reality." As Muehlmann sees it, "Berkeley understands that he cannot defeat sophisticated materialism by the use of [the Identification Argument]," which applies "only to *sensed* qualities" and not to the mathematical qualities of the corpuscularians. Now it may be true that Berkeley recognizes that the Identification Argument cannot be used to defeat the mathematico-corpuscular theory of secondary qualities, but this does not explain why Berkeley fails to apply the argument to *sensed* colors and sounds. Before making Hylas switch to the mathematico-corpuscular theory of sounds and colors, Berkeley might have forced him to recognize that *sensed* colors and *sensed* sounds are nothing but painful, pleasurable, or indifferent sensations. Muehlmann's hypothesis does not explain why Berkeley chooses not to do so.

[30] Muehlmann (1992, 138).

Even accepting the claim that the "intense" touching of solid objects occasions pain, it often happens that the pain is immediately perceived some time *after* the episode of intense touching. A few years ago, my seven-year-old daughter, Alice, was bouncing up and down on a trampoline with a friend of hers, Megan. As Megan bounced upwards, Alice bent her head to say something. Alice's lip met Megan's head. For a few moments after the collision, Alice was surprised but clearly not in pain. Then she suddenly felt pain and started to cry. The point is that the intense touching preceded (even if only by a few seconds) her immediately felt sensation of pain. With facts like these it becomes particularly difficult to hold that the "intense touching of solidity" should be *identified* with great pain.[31]

## 4.3.2 The Argument from Perceptual Relativity

On the most widely accepted interpretation of Berkeley's reasons for accepting that all sensible qualities are ideas, the Identification Argument is a very weak piece of reasoning for this conclusion. In the first place, the argument seems a poor reason for thinking that secondary qualities are sensations. And in the second place, the argument does not even purport

---

[31] It might be suggested that extending the Identification Argument to primary qualities would be even more problematic than I am making it out to be. For Berkeley holds that it is impossible to conceive (or perceive) a primary quality in separation from all secondary qualities (see section 4.3.3 below). This means that every perception of a primary quality is necessarily accompanied by a perception of a secondary quality. So if every secondary quality is a pain or a pleasure, then every perception of a primary quality (including size, shape, and motion) would be accompanied by a sensation of pain or pleasure. And yet this seems false.

This problem is as much an objection to Berkeley's application of the Identification Argument to secondary qualities as it is an objection to Berkeley's extending the application of the same argument to primary qualities. But I think that Berkeley has a ready answer to it, namely that there is nothing wrong with the conclusion. Although there is no *direct* evidence bearing on this issue either way, there is *indirect* evidence that Berkeley thinks that all of our experience is accompanied by pleasures or pains. Close to the beginning of DHP 2, Philonous waxes lyrical about the beauty of nature: "Look! Are not the fields covered with a delightful verdure? Is there not something in the woods and groves, in the rivers and clear springs, that soothes, delights, that transports the soul? At the prospect of the wide and deep ocean, or some huge mountain whose top is lost in the clouds, or of an old gloomy forest, are not our minds filled with a pleasing horror? Even in rocks and deserts, is there not an agreeable wildness? How sincere a pleasure is it to behold the natural beauties of the earth!" (DHP 2; W2: 210). And on and on, for what is one of Philonous's longest speeches of DHP. The message here, I submit, is that *all* of our experience of moderate degrees of secondary qualities, along with the primary qualities with which they are combined, is pleasurable; a pleasurable experience that is only broken by occasional bouts of intense degrees of secondary qualities, which are pains, caused in us by God to help us attain greater pleasure in the long run.

to establish the mind-dependence of primary qualities. Aware of the Identification Argument's non-probative nature, so the interpretation goes, Berkeley turns to a completely different argument for the same conclusion, a piece of reasoning (already foreshadowed in PHK 14) that depends on the observation that the same sensible object can appear to have contrary sensible qualities to the same observer (or to different observers) at the same time. This is widely known as the *positive* interpretation of the Argument from Perceptual Relativity. It is a distinctly minority view (defended most extensively and carefully by Muehlmann) that Berkeley's Argument from Perceptual Relativity is no more than an *ad hominem* attack on materialism.[32] The minority view is widely known as the *negative* interpretation of the Argument from Perceptual Relativity. My purpose in this section is to explain why the *negative* interpretation of the argument fits the text far better than does its *positive* alternative.

Philonous introduces the first instance of the Argument from Perceptual Relativity immediately after acknowledging that he "know[s] not how to convince [Hylas that warmth is not a mere privation of pain and pleasure] otherwise than by appealing to [Hylas's] own sense" (DHP 1; W2: 178). The set-up involves some discussion of the nature of coldness:

[H] Phil: But what think you of cold?
Hyl: The same that I do of heat. An intense degree of cold is a pain; for to feel a
   very great cold, is to perceive a great uneasiness: it cannot therefore exist without
   the mind; but a lesser degree of cold may, as well as a lesser degree of heat.
Phil: Those bodies therefore, upon whose application to our own, we perceive a
   moderate degree of heat, must be concluded to have a moderate degree of heat
   or warmth in them: and those, upon whose application we feel a like degree of
   cold, must be thought to have cold in them.
Hyl: They must. (DHP 1; W2: 178)

In the first part of [H], Hylas insists that there is a difference between intense cold and moderate cold: whereas intense cold (like intense heat) is a particular sort of pain, moderate cold (like moderate heat) is nothing but an indolence, a privation of pain and pleasure. Seemingly on the basis of this admission (notice the use of "therefore"), Philonous gets Hylas to admit that we are entitled to conclude from our (immediate) perception of

---

[32] Muehlmann (1992, 149 ff.). For a partial but extensive list of commentators who endorse the positive interpretation, see Muehlmann (1992, 150, n. 11). A variant of the positive interpretation is also defended in Harris (1997).

a body as being moderately hot that the body is indeed moderately hot, and from our (immediate) perception of a body as being moderately cold that the body is indeed moderately cold. The further admission is odd, in large part because it does not actually follow from the first. Why then does Hylas so readily make it?

The answer is to be found in one of Hylas's very first claims about the relationship between sensible qualities and our perception of them. When Philonous first brings up the case of heat, Hylas insists that heat is a real being that exists without the mind. Philonous then wonders whether the same is true for all degrees of heat, and Hylas answers in the affirmative:

Phil:  Tell me, Hylas, is this real existence equally compatible to all degrees of heat, which we perceive: or is there any reason why we should attribute it to some, and deny it to others? And if there be, pray let me know that reason.
Hyl:  *Whatever degree of heat we perceive by sense, we may be sure the same exists in the object that occasions it.*
Phil:  What, the greatest as well as the least?
Hyl:  I tell you, the reason is plainly the same in respect of both: they are both perceived by sense; nay, the greater degree of heat is more sensibly perceived; and consequently, if there is any difference, we are more certain of its real existence than we can be of the reality of a lesser degree. (DHP 1; W2: 175–6— emphasis added)

Philonous is interested in the ontological question of whether all degrees of heat exist without the mind, and wants to know what Hylas's reasons are for answering it affirmatively. Hylas's answer is that he is entitled to infer that a body has such-and-such degree of heat from his sensory perception of the body as having that degree of heat. This claim is based on the italicized principle, that *whatever degree of heat we perceive by sense, we may be sure the same exists in the object that occasions it.*

Consider now a generalization of this principle, which I will call "the Principle of Attribution":

*The Principle of Attribution*
If X perceives by sense at time T that object O has sensible quality F, then O has F at T.

It is on the basis of the Principle of Attribution that Hylas admits at the end of [H] that "those bodies therefore, upon whose application to our own, we perceive a moderate degree of heat [cold], must be concluded to have a moderate degree of heat [cold] in them." The Principle of Attribution is part and parcel of Hylas's common-sense materialism, which involves not only the claim that matter exists but also straightforward claims about what individual portions of matter are like on the basis of one's sensory awareness of them. Just as ordinary folk assume that fire engines are red on the basis of their sensory perception of them as red and that sugar is sweet on the basis of their sensory perception of it as sweet, so Hylas assumes that snow is cold on the basis of his sensory perception of it as cold.

Having foregrounded the Principle of Attribution and its application to all degrees of heat and cold in particular, Philonous runs the first instance of the Argument from Perceptual Relativity:

[J]    Phil: Can any doctrine be true that necessarily leads a man into an absurdity?
       Hyl: Without a doubt it cannot.
       Phil: Is it not an absurdity to think that the same thing should be at the same time both cold and warm?
       Hyl: It is.
       Phil: Suppose now one of your hands hot, and the other cold, and that they are both at once put into the same vessel of water, in an intermediate state; will not the water seem cold to one hand, and warm to the other?
       Hyl: It will.
       Phil: Ought we not therefore by your principles to conclude, it is really both cold and warm at the same time, that is, according to your own concession, to believe an absurdity.
       Hyl: I confess it seems so.
       Phil: Consequently, the principles themselves are false, since you have granted that no true principle leads to an absurdity.
       Hyl: But after all, can any thing be more absurd than to say, *there is no heat in the fire*? (DHP 1; W2: 178–9)

The argument is easy to state. Let the relevant expanse of water be W:

(J1)    If X perceives by sense at T that object O has sensible quality F, then O has F at T. [Principle of Attribution]

(J2)    At T, Hylas perceives by sense through his left hand that W is cold.

(J3)    At T, Hylas perceives by sense through his right hand that W is warm.

So, (J4)    At T, W is both cold and warm. [From J1, J2, J3]

(J5)    It is impossible for the same thing to be at the same time both cold and warm.

So, (J6)    It is not the case that at T, W is both cold and warm. [From J5]

The argument of [J] is clearly a *reductio ad absurdum* of the Principle of Attribution. For from the Principle and the facts of the hypothetical case, Berkeley infers that the same water is at the same time both cold and warm, a result that contradicts the self-evident proposition that nothing can be both cold and warm at the same time. As should be evident, the falsity of the Principle of Attribution does not entail that cold and warmth are sensations or ideas. For the falsity of the Principle is consistent both with the proposition that cold is a property of mind-independent things and with the proposition that warmth is a property of mind-independent things. All that follows from the falsity of the Principle of Attribution is that from the fact that a body is perceived by sense to have a quality it does not follow that the body actually possesses that quality, and, in particular, that from the fact that a body is perceived by sense to be warm [cold] it does not follow that the body is warm [cold]. This means that there are at least possible circumstances in which a body is perceived by sense to have a quality that it does not actually have.[33]

Seen from Berkeley's perspective, this is a strange result. As the passage about the crooked stick illusion indicates (see chapter 2), Berkeley himself clearly endorses the claim that sensible objects have the properties they are immediately perceived to have: for there is no such thing as an illusion in the realm of immediate perception. Given that Berkeley insists that all sense perception is immediate, how, then, does he avoid endorsing the falsity of the Principle of Attribution? The answer is that the premises of the argument presuppose something that Berkeley denies. According to the materialist, there is only one expanse of water in the hypothetical scenario, water that is immediately perceived by both hands at the same time. The fact that there is only one expanse of water is needed to validly infer that the same thing is both cold and warm at the same time. But the fact that there is only one expanse of water is something Berkeley would

---

[33] Concerning Philonous's application of the Argument from Perceptual Relativity to the case of warmth and coldness, Tipton (1974, 240–1) writes: "The way out of this difficulty may seem obvious. Hylas should withdraw his claim that any object must have any quality it appears to have. Philonous, though, insists he should make a different move. Rather than saying, for example, that the water *is* warm but only *appears* cool (to the hand that has been in the pocket) he should recognise that the warmth and coolness are equally *appearances*, that neither can be in an external substance, and that both must be in the mind." But this is to misread the text. It is Hylas, not Philonous, who concludes at the end of [J] that heat cannot be in an external substance. All that Philonous says is that the Argument from Perceptual Relativity shows the absurdity of Hylas's own principles.

deny. On his view, what is immediately perceived to be cold by means of one hand is not numerically identical to what is immediately perceived to be warm by means of the other hand: the water that is immediately perceived to be cold is a collection of sensible qualities, one of which is the property of being cold, while the water that is immediately perceived to be warm is a different collection of sensible qualities, one of which is the property of being warm. Berkeley's ontology of sensible objects therefore enables him to avoid what would otherwise be a very problematic admission to the effect that the Principle of Attribution is false. Not having a similar ontology, the materialist cannot avoid making this admission, an admission that puts him on a collision course with common sense.[34]

It is plain, then, that the very first instance of the Argument from Perceptual Relativity is designed as an *ad hominem* criticism of materialism. At no point in this argument does Philonous draw the conclusion that cold and warmth are sensations or ideas.[35] Hylas, it is true, feels compelled to

---

[34] It might be objected that the claim that there are two expanses of water, rather than one, is also contrary to common sense. So if Berkeley's hot-and-cold-water argument against the materialist is that the premises of the argument lead to a conclusion that conflicts with common sense, then Berkeley's own way of preserving the claim that sensible objects possess the qualities they are immediately perceived to have does not fare any better. However, as Berkeley sees it, common sense does not require that there be only one expanse of water in the hot-and-cold-water scenario. As argued above in chapter 2, the view that there is only one such object when there are in fact many is the product of a prejudice deriving from practical considerations related to effective linguistic communication.

[35] Harris (1997, 110–11) accepts that the Argument from Perceptual Relativity is designed as a *reductio* of a principle close to the Principle of Attribution, namely (PA'):

(PA')  Sensible things have those qualities they are perceived to have as parts.

Harris also claims that (PA') follows from the conjunction of (III), (IV), and (V):

(III) Sensible things are mind-independent.
(IV) Sensible qualities are parts of sensible things.
(V) Sensible qualities are immediately perceived.

He then argues that Philonous, taking (IV) and (V) for granted, infers the falsity of (III) from the falsity of (PA'). This is a positive (and not merely an *ad hominem*) result, for the claim that (III) is false amounts to the claim that sensible things are mind-dependent.

The main problem with Harris's interpretation is that (PA') does not in fact follow logically from the conjunction of (III), (IV), and (V). Harris rightly notices that (III) and (IV) together logically entail (1):

(1)  Sensible qualities are parts of mind-independent things.

But Harris then wrongly claims that (PA') follows from the conjunction of (1) and (V). This dooms his attempt to extract a positive moral from the Argument from Perceptual Relativity.

draw the conclusion that "*there is no heat in the fire.*"[36] Why? This is a bit of a mystery. From the fact that the same water cannot be both cold and warm, it follows that the water is not cold *or* the water is not warm. This state of affairs is compatible (i) with the water's being warm and not cold and (ii) with the water's being cold but not warm.[37] Given the facts of the case, then, it is possible that the water is really warm even though it feels cold to the left hand. How could this be? The materialist might well hypothesize that cold is perceived when the corpuscles in one's hand start moving more slowly, and that this is exactly what happens when a hand in which corpuscles are moving at great speed (perhaps a hand that was originally placed in a bucket of *hot* water) is placed in warm water. So there is no need for Hylas to draw the extreme conclusion that "there is no heat in the fire," and hence, by parity of reasoning, that the water is not warm. Similarly, the materialist might hypothesize that warmth is perceived when the corpuscles in one's hand start moving more quickly, and that this is what happens when a hand in which corpuscles are moving very slowly (perhaps a hand that was originally placed in a bucket of *very cold* water) is placed in cold water. So there is also no need for Hylas to draw the extreme conclusion that the water is not cold.[38] It appears, then, that there is nothing to explain Hylas's response other than his lack of philosophical sophistication.

---

[36] Tipton (1974, 238) claims that one main reason for thinking that Berkeley's use of the Argument from Perceptual Relativity is not merely *ad hominem* is that "initially, Hylas has no use for the argument at all." "It is Philonous (the Berkeleian)," continues Tipton, "who convinces [Hylas] he should accept it in the case of the secondary qualities and who then forces him to extend its use." But this is to misread the text (see note 33, and also Muehlmann (1992, 168)). At the end of [J], Philonous merely points out that Hylas's principles are false in that they lead to absurdity. It is *Hylas*, not *Philonous*, who takes the extra step of concluding that "there is no heat in the fire." What Philonous takes pains to point out is that, *if* this is the appropriate reaction in the case of the secondary qualities, *then* it is also the appropriate reaction in the case of the primary qualities. But Philonous does not himself endorse the claim that Hylas's reaction is appropriate. Indeed, as Berkeley recognizes at PHK 15, it is not.

[37] Winkler (1989, 167–9) makes a similar point.

[38] Winkler (1989, 167) writes that "there is . . . every reason to treat the heat and cold we perceive when our hands are in the water as if they were on a par, and if it is not the case that *both* are in the water, parity demands that neither is." But, at least from the materialist point of view, it is just not true that there is every reason to treat the heat and cold we perceive when our hands are in the water as if they were on a par. Suppose that before being placed in the water, one hand was placed in a bucket of very hot water but the other one was not. In that sort of situation, materialists might well argue that the perception of the water as cold is the product of an illusion whereas the perception of the water as warm is not.

However, lack of sophistication seems at most only part of the correct explanation of Hylas's response. For later, as we will see, Hylas's response remains the same even as his level of sophistication rises. The best explanation I can think of for Hylas's mistake is a particular form of scope confusion. Recall the Principle of Attribution:

(PA)   If X perceives by sense at T that O is F, then O is F at T.

Philonous claims that the Argument from Perceptual Relativity establishes the falsity of the Principle of Attribution. The negation of the Principle of Attribution is this:

(~PA)   It is not the case that if X perceives by sense at T that O is F then O is F at T.

In (~PA), the negation has scope over the entire conditional. That is to say, the logical form of (~PA) is this:

$$\sim (P \rightarrow Q)$$

But, as legions of logic students will readily testify, it is easy for the logically unsophisticated to confuse this negation with the following conditional:

$$(P \rightarrow \sim Q)$$

The difference between both of these logical forms concerns the scope of the negation. In the first statement, the negation has scope over the entire conditional; in the second statement, the negation has scope over the consequent. Suppose, then, that Hylas confuses these two logical forms. In that case, he will treat (~PA) as logically equivalent to the following statement:

(B)   If X perceives by sense at T that O is F, then it is not the case that O is F at T.

But (B) entails that if Hylas perceives by sense at T that the water W is warm, then it is not the case that W is warm at T; and (B) also entails that if Hylas perceives by sense at T that W is cold, then it is not the case that W is cold at T. Given that Hylas *does* perceive by sense at T that W is warm and that W is cold, it follows from (B) that W is neither warm nor cold at T. It is this, I suggest, that explains Hylas's extreme reaction to Philonous's first application of the Argument from Perceptual Relativity, namely that the argument compels acceptance of the absurd conclusion that there is no warmth in the water, and, by parity of reasoning, that "there is no heat in the fire."[39]

The fact that Philonous does not conclude from the first instance of the Argument from Perceptual Relativity that cold and warmth are ideas is not surprising. For, as Berkeley himself notes in PHK 15, arguments that are based on facts about perceptual relativity do not establish that sensible qualities are ideas (see chapter 3). It would be odd in the extreme for Berkeley to recognize explicitly in 1710 that the Argument from Perceptual Relativity does not entail that sensible qualities are ideas and then, three years later, publish a dialogue in which his spokesman insists that the entailment holds. From all of this we must conclude that, at least in the case of coldness and warmth, the negative interpretation of the Argument from Perceptual Relativity is far superior to its positive counterpart.

Should we say the same about Philonous's application of the Argument from Perceptual Relativity to other sensible qualities? Consider Philonous's application of the argument to the primary qualities, particularly figure, extension and motion. First, figure and extension:

Phil: Is it your opinion, the very figure and extension which you perceive by sense, exist in the outward object or material substance?

Hyl: It is.

Phil: Have all other animals as good grounds to think the same of the figure and extension which they see and feel?

Hyl: Without doubt, if they have any thought at all.

Phil: Answer me, *Hylas*. Think you the senses were bestowed upon all animals for their preservation and well-being in life? or were they given to men alone for this end?

Hyl: I make no question but they have the same use in all other animals.

Phil: If so, is it not necessary they should be enabled by them to perceive their own limbs, and those bodies which are capable of harming them?

Hyl: Certainly.

---

[39] Hylas's confusion here is compatible with two hypotheses about Berkeley's authorial intentions with respect to the confusion. The first is that Berkeley himself succumbs to confusion without being aware of it, and as a result commits Hylas to the view that the Argument from Perceptual Relativity shows that "there is no heat in the fire." The second is that Berkeley is well aware of the confusion, but foists it on Hylas either because he thinks that it is natural for the materialist (or for any philosopher) to succumb to such confusion or because he just wants to make materialists look bad.

Phil: A mite therefore must be supposed to see his own foot, and things equal or even less than it, as bodies of some considerable dimension; though at the same time they appear scarce discernible, or at best as so many visible points.

Hyl: I cannot deny it.

Phil: And to creatures less than the mite they will seem yet larger.

Hyl: They will.

Phil: Insomuch that what you can hardly discern, will to another extremely minute animal appear as some huge mountain.

Hyl: All this I grant.

Phil: Can one and the same thing be at the same time in itself of different dimensions?

Hyl: That were absurd to imagine.

Phil: But from what you have laid down it follows, that both the extension by you perceived, and that perceived by the mite itself, as likewise all those perceived by lesser animals, are each of them the true extension of the mite's foot, that is to say, by your own principles you are led into an absurdity.

Hyl: There seems to be some difficulty in the point. (DHP 1; W2: 188–9)

Again, it is clear that Philonous is mounting a *reductio* of Hylas's own principles. The main relevant principle here is the Principle of Attribution:

If X perceives by sense at time T that object O has sensible quality F, then O has F at T.

The argument is perfectly parallel. The upshot of the relevant thought experiment is that a mite perceives its foot to be large at the same time that Hylas perceives the same foot to be small. By the Principle of Attribution, it follows that largeness and smallness exist in the same foot at the same time, that is, that the same foot is both large and small at the same time. But, as Philonous insists and Hylas accepts, this result is absurd, for no object can possess largeness and smallness at the same time. The conclusion Philonous draws from this is *not* that extension and size are ideas or sensations, but rather that the Principle of Attribution is false. And the falsity of this principle tells us no more than that, from the fact that someone perceives by sense that an object possesses a particular extension (size) it does not follow that the object actually possesses that extension (size).

Next, consider Philonous's application of the Argument from Perceptual Relativity to motion:

Phil: Figures and extension being dispatched, we proceed next to *motion*. Can a real motion in any external body be at the same time both very swift and very slow?

Hyl: It cannot.

Phil: Is not the motion of a body swift in a reciprocal proportion to the time it takes up in describing any given space? Thus a body that describes a mile in an hour, moves three times faster than it would in case it described only a mile in three hours.

Hyl: I agree with you.

Phil: And is not time measured by the succession of ideas in our minds?

Hyl: It is.

Phil: And is it not possible ideas should succeed one another twice as fast in your mind, as they do in mine, or in that of some spirit of another kind?

Hyl: I own it.

Phil: Consequently the same body may to another seem to perform its motion over any space in half the time that it doth to you. And the same reasoning will hold as to any other proportion: That is to say, according to your principles (since the motions perceived are both really in the object) it is possible one and the same body shall be really moved the same way at once, both very swift and very slow. How is this consistent either with common sense, or with what you just now granted?

Hyl: I have nothing to say to it. (DHP 1; W2: 190)

Clearly the argument is parallel here too. According to Hylas's principles, which include the Principle of Attribution, if I perceive by sense that my hand is moving quickly at T, then my hand is indeed moving quickly at T. But if you perceive by sense that my hand is moving slowly at T, then my hand is moving slowly at T. Unfortunately, Hylas also grants that an object's apparent speed is fixed by how quickly the ideas connected with the object succeed each other in one's mind. Thus it can happen that the same object at the same time seems to me to be moving quickly but seems to you to be moving slowly. If the Principle of Attribution is true, then under such circumstances it follows that the same object is moving both quickly and slowly at the same time. But, as Hylas grants, this result is absurd: it is not possible for the same object to move quickly and slowly at the same time. Consequently Hylas must grant that the Principle of Attribution is false, in particular, that from the fact that an object is perceived by sense to be moving quickly (slowly) at T it does not follow that the object is actually moving quickly (slowly) at T.

Thus far, we have seen that the passages in which Philonous applies the Argument from Perceptual Relativity to temperature, size (shape, extension), and motion suggest that the argument is merely *ad hominem*. But there are also various passages that suggest otherwise. Careful examination of these passages will help us evaluate the relative merits of the negative and positive interpretations of the argument.

In the first place, there is Philonous's application of the Argument from Perceptual Relativity to tastes:

> Phil:  That which at other times seems sweet, shall to a distempered palate appear bitter. And nothing can be plainer, than that divers persons perceive different tastes in the same food, since that which one man delights in, another abhors. And how could this be, if the taste was something really inherent in the food?
> Hyl:  I acknowledge I know not how. (DHP 1; W2: 180)

Second, there is Philonous's application of the Identification Argument and the Argument from Perceptual Relativity to odors:

> Phil:  In the next place, odours are to be considered. And with regard to these, I would fain know, whether what hath been said of tastes doth not exactly agree to them? Are they not so many pleasing or displeasing sensations?
> Hyl:  They are.
> Phil:  Can you then conceive it possible that they should exist in an unperceiving thing?
> Hyl:  I cannot.
> Phil:  Or can you imagine, that filth and ordure affect those brute animals that feed on them out of choice, with the same smells which we perceive in them?
> Hyl:  By no means.
> Phil:  May we not therefore conclude of smells, as of the other forementioned qualities, that they cannot exist in any but a perceiving substance or mind?
> Hyl:  I think so. (DHP 1; W2: 180-1)

Third, there is Philonous's application of the Argument from Perceptual Relativity to colors:

> Phil:  Besides, it is not only possible but manifest, that there actually are animals, whose eyes are by nature framed to perceive those things, which by reason of their minuteness escape our sight. What think you of those inconceivably small animals perceived by glasses? Must we suppose they are all stark blind? Or, in case they see, can it be imagined their sight hath not the same use in preserving their bodies from injuries, which appears in that of all other animals? And if it hath, is it not evident, they must see particles less than their own bodies, which will present them with a far different view in each object, from that which strikes our senses? Even our own eyes do not always represent objects to us after the same manner. In the *jaundice*, every one knows that all things seem yellow. Is it not therefore highly probable, those

animals in whose eyes we discern a very different texture from that of ours, and whose bodies abound with different humours, do not see the same colours in every outward object that we do? From all which, should it not seem to follow, that all colours are equally apparent, and that none of those which we perceive are really inherent in any outward object?

Hyl: It should. (DHP 1; W2: 185)

And finally there is Philonous's summary of his application of the Argument from Perceptual Relativity to temperature, with an extension of the argument to the case of extension and shape:

Phil: Was it not admitted as a good argument, that neither heat nor cold was in the water, because it seemed warm to one hand, and cold to the other?

Hyl: It was.

Phil: Is it not the very same reasoning to conclude, there is no extension or figure in an object, because to one eye it shall seem little, smooth, and round, when at the same time it appears to the other, great, uneven, and angular?

Hyl: The very same. But doth this latter fact ever happen?

Phil: You may at any time make the experiment, by looking with one eye bare, and with the other through a microscope. (DHP 1; W2: 189)

In the first three passages, Philonous gets Hylas to accept that tastes are not "really inherent in" food, that smells "cannot exist in any but a perceiving substance or mind," and that no perceived colors "are really inherent in any outward object." It would seem, then, that Philonous (and hence Berkeley) holds that the Argument from Perceptual Relativity entails that some sensible qualities are mind-dependent sensations. To see that this is a mistake, one need only consider the fourth passage. There Philonous makes it quite clear that it was Hylas who admitted that the Argument from Perceptual Relativity established that "neither heat nor cold was in the water." Pointedly, Philonous does not say that he himself endorses this conclusion. Rather, Philonous insists that one who thinks (as it happens, mistakenly) that considerations of perceptual relativity establish the mind-dependence of heat and cold should, by parity of reasoning, also think that considerations of perceptual relativity establish the mind-dependence of extension and shape. This is no more than an echo of the point that Berkeley himself makes in PHK 14 (see chapter 3). In order to make this point, Philonous need not himself endorse the view that the Argument from Perceptual Relativity establishes the mind-dependence of sensible qualities. And, indeed, as I have argued, he does not (and should not).[40]

It might be thought that, in addition to the Argument from Perceptual Relativity, Philonous explicitly deploys an argument that is designed to establish the mind-dependence of at least some sensible qualities. This is the argument from change, first described in Philonous's discussion of color. Philonous begins by considering the point that "all colours are equally apparent, and that none of those which we perceive are really inherent in any outward object." He continues:

> Phil: The point will be past all doubt, if you consider, that in case colours were real properties or affections inherent in external bodies, they could admit of no alteration, without some change wrought in the very bodies themselves: but is it not evident from what hath been said, that upon the use of microscopes, upon a change in the humours of the eye, or a variation of distance, without any manner of real alteration in the thing itself, the colours of any object are either changed, or totally disappear? (DHP 1; W2: 185–6)

The argument seems to fit the following pattern:

(1)  If colors were real properties of external bodies, they could not be changed without the bodies' suffering real alteration.

(2)  The color of a body can be changed without the body's suffering real alteration.

So, (3)  Colors are not real properties of external bodies. [From 1, 2]

If this is indeed how Philonous argues, then we have strong evidence for the claim that Berkeley endorses the conclusion that colors are not real properties of external bodies, from which it appears to follow that colors must be mind-dependent entities.

But, in fact, this is not how Philonous actually argues. To see this, consider what Philonous says in defense of the argument's second premise:

> Phil: Nay all other circumstances remaining the same, change but the situation of some objects, and they shall *present* different colours to the eye. The same thing happens *upon viewing an object* in various degrees of light. And what is more known, than that the same bodies *appear* differently coloured by candle-light, from what they do in the open day? Add to these the experiment of a prism, which separating the heterogeneous rays of light, alters the colour of any object; and will cause the whitest to *appear* of a deep blue or red to the naked eye. (DHP 1; W2: 186—emphasis added)

---

[40]  Muehlmann (1992, 159) makes a similar point in criticizing Lambert (1982).

As this passage makes plain, Philonous does not actually argue for the claim that *the color of a body* can be changed without the body's suffering any real alteration. The proposition for which Philonous offers evidence is the claim that *the perceived color of a body* can be changed without the body's suffering any real alteration. If this is so, then (2) must be replaced by (2'):

(2') The perceived color of a body can be changed without the body's suffering any real alteration.

The problem is that the argument from (1) and (2') to (3) is now straight-forwardly invalid. One way to turn Philonous's reasoning into a valid argument for (3) would be to replace (1) with (1*):

(1*) If colors were real properties of external bodies, bodies' perceived colors could not be changed without the bodies' suffering real alteration.

The problem is that there is no reason to think that (1*) is true: it seems perfectly conceivable (at least from the materialist point of view) that the *perceived* color of a body could change without the body's suffering real alteration *even as the body's actual color is a real property of it*; for it may be that a body's *perceived* color differs from its *actual* color. In order to avoid *this* problem, then, it might be suggested that (1*) should be replaced by (1'):

(1') If all external bodies actually possess the colors they are perceived to have, then their perceived colors could not be changed with-out their suffering real alteration.

This solves the problem with (1*), because (1') now seems eminently reasonable. But there is now a new problem, which is that (3) does not follow from the conjunction of (1') and (2'). In order to avoid *this* problem, it might then be suggested that (3) be replaced by (3'):

(3') It is not true that all external bodies actually possess the colors they are perceived to have.

And, indeed, if (3) is replaced by (3'), then the resulting argument from (1') and (2') to (3') is valid.

On reflection, then, it seems that Philonous's argument should be represented as follows:

(1')    If all external bodies actually possess the colors they are perceived to have, then their perceived colors could not be changed without their suffering real alteration.

(2')    The perceived color of a body can be changed without the body's suffering any real alteration.

So, (3')    It is not true that all external bodies actually possess the colors they are perceived to have. [From 1', 2']

But if this is the correct way to represent Philonous's argument, then it is not in fact an argument for the claim that colors are not real properties of external bodies (and hence mind-dependent). Rather, it is an argument for the claim that one is not entitled to infer, from the fact that an external body is perceived to have such-and-such a color, that the body actually possesses that color. And this is exactly the negation of the Principle of Attribution as applied to the case of color. So Philonous's argument, properly understood, is another *argumentum ad hominem* directed at the materialist, rather than a defense of the mind-dependence of colors.

That this is the point of Philonous's argument is confirmed by his deployment of it in the case of extension:

Phil: Again, have you not acknowledged that no real inherent property of any object can be changed, without some change in the thing itself?
Hyl: I have.
Phil: But as we approach to or recede from an object, the *visible extension* varies, being at one distance ten or an hundred times greater than at another. Doth it not therefore follow from hence likewise, that it is not really inherent in the object?
Hyl: I own I am at a loss what to think. (DHP 1; W2: 189—emphasis added)

Notice that here too Philonous emphasizes that it is the *visible* (that is, the perceived) extension that varies when one approaches to or recedes from an object. From this, Philonous is not entitled to conclude that extension is mind-dependent. What he *is* entitled to conclude is that an external object's real extension (if it has one) cannot be inferred from the extension it is perceived to have.

I conclude that a close and careful examination of all the relevant texts reveals that the negative interpretation of the Argument from Perceptual Relativity is far better supported than the positive interpretation.[41] It

---

[41] It might be argued that there is evidence from DHP 2 suggesting that Berkeley thinks of the Argument from Perceptual Relativity as having a positive, rather than a negative, upshot.

follows that Berkeley's one and only positive argument for the mind-dependence of *secondary* qualities is the Identification Argument. How, then, does Berkeley argue for the mind-dependence of *primary* qualities?

### 4.3.3 Why Primary Qualities are Ideas

Berkeley's argument for the mind-dependence of primary qualities depends on the claim, already established by means of the Identification Argument, that secondary qualities are ideas. The basic thrust of the argument is that primary qualities cannot be conceived, and hence cannot exist, apart from secondary qualities, and thus that if secondary qualities are in the mind, so likewise must primary qualities be in the mind. The argument appears in both PHK and DHP 1. Here is the first passage:

[K] They who assert that figure, motion, and the rest of the primary or original qualities do exist without the mind, in unthinking substances, do at the same time acknowledge that colours, sounds, heat, cold, and such like secondary qualities, do not, which they tell us are sensations existing in the mind alone . . . Now if it be certain, that those original qualities are inseparably united with the other sensible qualities, and not, even in thought, capable of being abstracted from them, it plainly follows that they exist only in the mind. But I desire any one to reflect and try, whether he can by any abstraction of thought, conceive the extension and motion of a body, without all other sensible qualities. For my own part, I see evidently that it is not in my power to frame an idea of a body extended and moved, but I must withal give it some colour or other sensible quality which is acknowledged to exist only in the mind. In short, extension, figure, and motion, abstracted from all other qualities, are inconceivable. Where therefore the other sensible qualities are, there must these be also, to wit, in the mind and no where else. (PHK 10; W2: 45)

Here is the second passage:

[L]  Phil: But for your farther satisfaction, try if you can frame the idea of any figure, abstracted from all particularities of size, or even from other sensible qualities.
   Hyl: Let me think a little—I do not find that I can.

---

At W2: 212, Philonous tells Hylas: "To me it is evident, *for the reasons you allow of*, that sensible things cannot exist otherwise than in a mind or spirit" (emphasis added). It might be suggested that the relevant reasons here encompass *all* the main reasoning of DHP 1, including both the Identification Argument *and* the Argument from Perceptual Relativity. In reply, I would note that, although the relevant passage *could* be read in this way, it *need not* be so read. For it could be that Philonous is gesturing at the Identification Argument *only*, and not at the Argument from Perceptual Relativity. Certainly, the text does not *by itself* determine to which "reasons" Philonous is alluding.

> Phil: And can you think it possible, that should really exist in Nature, which implies a repugnancy in its conception?
>
> Hyl: By no means.
>
> Phil: Since therefore it is impossible even for the mind to disunite the ideas of extension and motion from all other sensible qualities, doth it not follow, that where the one exist, there necessarily the other exist likewise?
>
> Hyl: It should seem so.
>
> Phil: Consequently the very same arguments which you admitted, as conclusive against the secondary qualities, are without any farther application of force against the primary too. (DHP 1; W2: 194)

In passages [K] and [L], Berkeley argues from the mind-dependence of secondary qualities and the impossibility of conceiving primary qualities existing apart from secondary qualities to the conclusion that primary qualities are mind-dependent. The reasoning is clear:

(1)  It is impossible to abstract primary qualities from all secondary qualities in thought (i.e., it is impossible to conceive a primary quality existing apart from any secondary quality).

(2)  If it is impossible to abstract X from Y in thought, then it is impossible for X to exist apart from Y in reality (i.e., if it is impossible to conceive X existing apart from Y, then it is impossible for X to exist apart from Y).[42]

So, (3)  Primary qualities cannot exist apart from secondary qualities. [From 1, 2]

(4)  Secondary qualities are in the mind.

(5)  If Y is in the mind and X cannot exist apart from Y, then X is in the mind.

So, (6)  Primary qualities are in the mind. [From 3, 4, 5][43]

---

[42]  This assumption follows from the already familiar Berkeleian claim that inconceivability entails impossibility: see Chapter 3, note 22; Chapter 3, note 50; this chapter, note 17; and accompanying text.

[43]  Muehlmann (1978, 96) argues that Berkeley's argument for the mind-dependence of primary qualities relies on two theses: (I) two entities can be abstracted from each other in thought only if they can exist apart from each other in reality, and (II) two entities can exist apart from each other in reality only if they have been observed apart from each other in experience. As Muehlmann sees it, Berkeley notices that primary qualities have not been observed apart from secondary qualities in experience, infers from (II) that primary qualities cannot exist apart from each other in reality, and finally infers from (I) that primary qualities cannot be abstracted from secondary qualities in thought. But this representation of Berkeley's reasoning gets matters almost exactly backwards. As the first DHP passage makes clear, Berkeley begins by noticing that primary qualities cannot be abstracted from secondary

So, for example, Berkeley invites us to imagine a particular extension E that has no color. Noticing that this is something that we cannot imagine or conceive, we must conclude on the basis of (2) that E cannot exist apart from color in reality. But then, if color is an idea, then (given (5)) so too must E be an idea.[44]

In both [K] and [L] Berkeley emphasizes that this piece of reasoning can be used *ad hominem* against materialists (such as Descartes and Galileo) who think that secondary qualities, but not primary qualities, are mind-dependent. The problem for these theorists, as Berkeley reasons, is that his argument shows that their position is incoherent: if secondary qualities are in the mind, then so too must primary qualities be in the mind. (The argument does not work against materialists, such as Locke, who hold that both primary and secondary qualities exist in material objects that are external to the mind.) But the fact that the argument can be used to attack a certain kind of materialist does not entail that it can only be employed *ad hominem*. Indeed, when Philonous later recapitulates the reasoning that led him to insist on the mind-dependence of primary qualities, he says this:

> Phil: Indeed in treating of figure and motion, we concluded they could not exist without the mind, because it was impossible even in thought to separate them from all secondary qualities, so as to conceive them existing by themselves. (DHP 1; W2: 200)

So it is clear that Berkeley means the argument of [K] and [L] to work as much in favor of his own claim that all sensible qualities are ideas as it works against the Galilean–Cartesian claim that some, but not all, sensible qualities are ideas.

---

qualities in thought, and then, relying on the *converse* of (I), infers that primary qualities cannot exist apart from secondary qualities in reality. Moreover, principle (II) plays no role in Berkeley's reasoning. (This is a good thing, too, given that it is plainly false, even for Berkeley: as McKim (1997–8, 6) points out, although I have never witnessed the roof of my house apart from the walls of my house in my experience, it is certainly possible for the roof to exist apart from the walls in reality—in case of a hurricane, say.)

[44] It is true that in [K] Berkeley says no more than that, in framing an idea of an extended body, "I must withal give it some color *or other sensible quality*" (emphasis added). This may suggest that Berkeley thinks it possible to conceive an extended thing that has no color (even as he thinks it impossible to conceive an extended thing that has no secondary qualities whatso-ever). But in the Introduction to PHK, as we saw in chapter 3, Berkeley goes further: "[W]hatever hand or eye I imagine, it must have some particular . . . colour. Likewise the idea of man that I frame to myself must be either of a white, or a black, or a tawny . . . man" (I10; W2: 29). So Berkeley really does think that it is impossible to frame an idea of colorless extension.

In chapter 3, section 3 I argued that Berkeley does not employ anti-abstractionism as a premise in an argument for idealism in PHK. And, up until passage [L], Berkeley has not appealed to anti-abstractionism in filling out his two Simple Arguments for idealism in PHK. But in [L] Berkeley's anti-abstractionism plays a crucial role in the reasoning. Berkeley does not infer that extension cannot be mentally separated from color from the fact that extension cannot actually exist apart from color; rather he argues that extension cannot actually exist apart from color because extension cannot be mentally separated from color. Admittedly, Berkeley does not need to appeal to the claim that *all* abstract ideas are impossible in order to establish the truth of premise (1). For one thing, (1) does not follow from the impossibility of *generalizing* abstraction. (Recall that, in generalizing abstraction, the mind mentally separates a general quality from its particular determinations.) And although (1) *does* follow from the impossibility of *singling* abstraction (where singling abstraction is the mental separation of one particular quality from another), (1) might still be true even if singling abstraction were possible for *some* pairs of qualities. Still, it is both significant and important that the impossibility of mentally separating primary qualities from secondary qualities plays a critical role in establishing the truth of the general claim that all sensible qualities are ideas, and hence plays a critical role in establishing the truth of idealism generally.

One of the more interesting facts that Berkeley's employment of the argument of [K] and [L] points up is that Berkeley's hostility to abstractionism cannot depend *wholly* on the claim that impossibility entails inconceivability. For if Berkeley's claim that it is impossible to conceive extension existing apart from color depends on his claim that it is impossible for extension to exist apart from color in reality, then he would be arguing in a circle if he then argued (as he does) that the latter claim follows from the former. It follows that Winkler's account of Berkeley's argument for anti-abstractionism cannot be correct. In chapter 3, we saw that Berkeley's hostility to *generalizing* abstraction is grounded in the thought that the mind's powers are inadequate to the task: try as one might, one simply cannot mentally separate a general idea from its particular determinations. Passages [K] and [L] reveal that Berkeley *at least sometimes* relies on the limited nature of the mind's powers to establish the impossibility of *singling* abstraction as well. Reflection, says Berkeley, shows that "it is not in [one's] power to frame an idea of a body extended and moved" that has no color; and when asked to "frame the idea of [a] figure, abstracted from . . . other sensible qualities," Hylas replies, after a little thought, that he does not find that he can. This is not to say that Berkeley *never* argues from the fact that one quality cannot exist apart from another to the claim that the one cannot be mentally separated from the other. As Winkler rightly points out, there are places in which Berkeley argues against singling abstraction on just these grounds. But this strategy could not be used in [K] and [L] without rendering Berkeley's reasoning straightforwardly circular.

How good is Berkeley's argument for the claim that primary qualities are ideas given that secondary qualities are ideas? I think it is difficult to deny Berkeley's assumption that it is impossible to conceive of a colorless extension, as long as conception reduces to a kind of imagination. This reduction, which Berkeley takes for granted, might be questioned, particularly by rationalists, whose inventory of mental faculties differs from Berkeley's in allowing for the existence of an intellectual power distinct from the power of the imagination. But having granted the accuracy of Berkeley's inventory of mental faculties, the only reasonable way to criticize his argument is to take issue with the assumption that inconceivability entails impossibility. Berkeley assumes that if extension cannot be mentally separated from color, then extension cannot exist apart from color in reality. Here Berkeley's equation of inconceivability with unimaginability hurts, rather than helps, his case. For whereas it seems difficult to deny that the pure intellect's inability to represent a state of affairs as possible indicates that the state of affairs cannot obtain, it seems much easier to deny that impossibility follows from unimaginability: though it might be impossible to represent an infinite series of numbers by means of the imagination, infinite series of numbers are possible (indeed, actual) for all that. The main problem for Berkeley, then, is that in arguing for the mind-dependence of primary qualities, he wants to have it both ways: on the one hand, he wants the faculty of conceiving to work like the faculty of imagination; on the other hand, he wants the faculty of conceiving to work like the (putative) faculty of pure intellection. If he cannot have it both ways, then his argument fails.

## 4 Summary of the Argument for Idealism

It should now be clear that Berkeley wrote DHP 1 in large part to fill in the two Simple Arguments for idealism he had proposed in the early sections of PHK. The strategy is clear. First, Berkeley argues that sensible objects are nothing but collections of sensible qualities. He does this by reasoning that sensible objects are perceived by sense, that everything that is perceived by sense is immediately perceived, and that the only things that are immediately perceived are sensible qualities or collections thereof. Given that sensible objects (such as tables and chairs) cannot be identified with individual sensible qualities, it follows that they must be identified with collections of sensible qualities. Second, Berkeley uses the Identification Argument to establish that all secondary qualities are nothing but pleasures and pains, and hence must be identified with ideas in minds. The Identification Argument has two parts. According to the first part, intense secondary qualities (such as intense heat or cold, putrid odors, disgusting tastes, very loud sounds, etc.) are nothing but particular sorts of pains, for such qualities and such pains are immediately perceived at a time when what one perceives is a phenomenological unity; according to the second part, moderate secondary qualities (such as moderate heat or cold, the smell of baked bread, the taste of honey, euphonious sounds, etc.) are nothing but particular sorts of pleasures. Third, Berkeley argues that it is impossible to mentally separate primary qualities from secondary qualities, that consequently primary qualities cannot exist apart from secondary qualities in reality, and hence primary qualities must be where secondary qualities are. Given that the Identification Argument has shown that secondary qualities are in the mind, it follows directly that primary qualities are in the mind, and hence that all sensible qualities (whether primary or secondary) are in the mind. Finally, from the fact that sensible objects are collections of sensible qualities and the fact that sensible qualities are all ideas of various kinds, Berkeley concludes that sensible objects are nothing but collections of ideas. This is the structure of Berkeley's sophisticated and elegant argument for idealism.

As should now be clear, Berkeley's argument for idealism in DHP 1 does not rely on immaterialism, the Aristotelian Dictum, or the likeness principle. Rather, the argument relies on four crucial claims: (i) that whatever is perceived by sense is immediately perceived, (ii) that whatever is immediately perceived is either a sensible quality or a combination of sensible qualities, (iii) that secondary qualities are pleasures and pains, and (iv) that primary qualities cannot be abstracted from secondary qualities. Of these four claims, only the fourth appears in PHK, and its main function there is merely *ad hominem*. As it turns out, Berkeley's anti-abstractionism plays a limited role in the argument. First, it is only one of several important assumptions without the assistance of which idealism simply would not follow. Second, the relevant anti-abstractionist premise concerns only singling abstraction, and not generalizing abstraction. And third, it is only one very particular kind of singling abstraction that the relevant anti-abstractionist premise refuses to countenance, namely the mental separation of primary from secondary qualities. Given the structure of his argument, it is open to Berkeley to argue, *on the basis of the truth of idealism*, that other forms of abstraction are impossible. And, indeed, this is what he does. When, in PHK 5 (W2: 42–3), Berkeley claims that it is impossible to abstract "the existence of sensible objects from their being perceived, so as to conceive them existing unperceived," it is on the basis of the claim that one "might as easily divide a thing from it self," that one's "conceiving or imagining power does not extend beyond the possibility of real existence or perception." The argument here is not, as proponents of the argument from anti-abstractionism would have it, that idealism is true because it is impossible to abstract the existence of a sensible object from its being perceived. Rather, the argument runs exactly in reverse. Berkeley's point is that the existence of a sensible object cannot be abstracted from its being perceived because idealism is true. The operant principle here is not that inconceivability entails impossibility, but rather that impossibility entails inconceivability. And because Berkeley's argument for idealism rests on the impossibility of abstracting primary qualities from secondary qualities and *not* on the impossibility of abstracting the existence of a sensible object from its being perceived, there is no circularity in Berkeley's appeal to the impossibility of one kind of abstraction to establish the impossibility of another kind of abstraction.

# Conclusion

Berkeley's argument for idealism is clearly valid. But is it sound? From the perspective of the twenty-first century, it is not clear that it is. Thanks in part to the efforts of Berkeley's successors, Reid and Leibniz, many philosophers have abandoned the way of ideas and the transparency of the mental. Without these background assumptions, Berkeley's argument fails to get off the ground. But it is worth asking whether Berkeley's argument is *dialectically* successful, whether it should have convinced his intellectual predecessors and contemporaries. And here, I think, the answer is that the argument ends up posing a significant challenge to those who would dispute its conclusion. Exactly how Berkeley's argument represents such a challenge is what I now wish to explain.

Berkeley's argument rests on two crucial premises, (OP) and (PIP):

(OP)    Sensible things are perceived by sense.

(PIP)    Everything that is perceived by sense is immediately perceived.

If at least one of these premises is false, the argument is unsound. If Berkeley's materialist opponents have no good reason to reject them, then they will find it difficult to deny the argument's conclusion, namely that sensible things are nothing but collections of ideas.

There is considerable evidence that Berkeley struggled with these premises over the course of his life. The problem lies in the fact that the premises are ambiguous, because the phrase "perceived by sense" can be understood in two different ways. On one interpretation, to perceive something by sense is to perceive it *wholly* by sense. (Call this the "Whole" interpretation.) On another interpretation, to perceive something by sense is to perceive it *partly* (but not wholly) by sense. (Call this the "Part" interpretation.)[1] According to the "Whole" interpretation, to perceive something wholly by sense is to perceive it by sense *and not by means of any other mental faculty* (whether this be reason, memory, or imagination). According to the "Part" interpretation, by contrast, it is possible to perceive something by sense even if it is perceived at least in part by means of another mental faculty. The existence of ambiguity threatens the soundness of Berkeley's argument because it makes it vulnerable in principle to the fallacy of equivocation. The important thing, for Berkeley's purposes, is to secure an interpretation of (OP) and (PIP) that makes them both true and preserves the argument's validity.

Berkeley's corpus reveals that his understanding of the phrase "perceived by sense" shifted over time, indicating a struggle to secure the argument against the threat of equivocation. Early on, at the time of NTV (1709), Berkeley insists, as we have seen, that distance, magnitude, and situation are perceived mediately by sight, and that other persons' passions are also mediately perceived by sight, namely by seeing their facial expressions. This insistence almost surely reflects Berkeley's desire to maintain an interpretation of "perceived by sense" on which premise (OP) comes out true. For, on the one hand, Berkeley wants to agree with the proponents of the geometrical theory of vision that distance, magnitude, and situation are sensible things, and wants to agree with ordinary folk that we can perceive another person's anger (or disappointment, or elation) by sight. But, on the other hand, Berkeley argues that distance, magnitude, and situation are not perceived *wholly* by sight, but can only be perceived with the aid of the imagination through the mechanism of suggestion. And, similarly, Berkeley understands that the means by which we recognize the passions in other minds require a kind of suggestion driven by a connection between passions and facial expressions. The way to achieve complete consistency in these matters is to adopt the "Part" interpretation. For this interpretation makes it possible to say without contradiction that distance (or magnitude, or situation) is sensible, that distance (or magnitude, or situation) is perceived in part (but not wholly) by sense, and (OP) that all sensible things are perceived by sense. Had Berkeley adopted the "Whole" interpretation instead of the "Part" interpretation at the time of NTV, he would have found himself forced to deny (OP) on the basis of numerous

[1] I thank Michael Hardimon and Clinton Tolley for raising this possibility with me.

counterexamples. For distance (or magnitude, or situation) and the passions in other minds appear to be sensible things that are not *wholly* perceived by sense.

By the time of DHP (1713), Berkeley has become aware of the fact that the "Part" interpretation is problematic. The difficulty now is that the "Part" interpretation has enabled him to purchase the truth of (OP) only at the cost of being committed to the falsity of (PIP). For it is false that everything that is perceived in part (but not wholly) by sense is immediately perceived. Berkeley's recognition of this comes out quite clearly at the very end of DHP 1. There Philonous makes the following important admission:

I grant we may, in one acceptation, be said to perceive sensible things mediately by sense—that is, when, from a frequently perceived connection, the immediate perception of ideas by one sense suggests to the mind others, perhaps belonging to another sense, which are wont to be connected with them. For instance, when I hear a coach drive along the streets, immediately I perceive only the sound; but from the experience I have had that such a sound is connected with a coach, I am said to hear the coach. It is nevertheless evident that, in truth and strictness, nothing can be *heard* by *sound* and the coach is not then properly perceived by sense, but suggested from experience. So likewise when we are said to see a red-hot bar of iron; the solidity and heat of the iron are not the objects of sight, but suggested to the imagination by the color and figure which are properly perceived by that sense. (DHP 1; W2: 204)

The nub of Philonous's admission is that some of the things perceived by sense are mediately perceived: we perceive the coach by hearing, and yet the coach is perceived by perceiving something else (namely, a sound) that suggests the coach to the imagination; we perceive the heat of the iron by sight, and yet the iron's heat is perceived by perceiving something else (namely, its red color) that suggests the heat to the imagination. But if this is the right way to understand Philonous's admission, then (PIP) is false.

Does it follow that, at the time of DHP 1, Berkeley has come to the realization that the "Part" interpretation should be abandoned as an interpretation of the phrase "perceived by sense"? The answer is "no." The text suggests, rather, that Berkeley thinks he can have his cake and eat it too. First, there is no indication in DHP that Berkeley has given up the "Part" interpretation. More importantly, though, Berkeley's reaction to the falsity of (PIP) is that, for the purposes of an argument for idealism that depends on the "Part" interpretation, it doesn't matter: this interpretation secures the truth of (OP), and the counterexamples to (PIP) that Berkeley accepts do not vitiate his argument for idealism. The reason for this is that in each of the counterexamples Berkeley accepts (including the mediate perception of the coach by hearing, and the mediate perception of the iron's heat by sight), what grounds the relevant mediate perception is "a frequently perceived connection." What makes mediate perception of the coach through hearing possible is that in the past one's (immediate) perception of the relevant type of sound (of wheels on cobblestones) was cotemporaneous with *immediate* perception of a coach; and what makes mediate perception of the iron bar's heat possible is that in the past one's (immediate) perception of a bar's red color was cotemporaneous with *immediate* perception of its heat. In each of these cases, what is mediately perceived now (the coach, the heat) is the kind of thing that can be immediately perceived, namely (as another premise in Berkeley's argument for idealism tells us) a sensible quality or combination of sensible qualities, which (as the rest of Berkeley's argument tells us) are to be identified with ideas or collections of ideas. Berkeley's position at the end of DHP 1, then, is that although it is possible to mediately perceive sensible things, those things are themselves no more than ideas or collections of ideas.

That this is Berkeley's considered view in DHP 1 is confirmed by his treatment of Hylas's "Julius Caesar" counterexample to (PIP). The example arises as follows:

Phil: How! Is there anything perceived by sense which is not immediately perceived?
Hyl: Yes, Philonous, in some sort there is. For example, when I look on a picture or statue of Julius Caesar, I may be said, after a manner, to perceive him (though not immediately) by my senses. (DHP 1; W2: 203)

Hylas's claim, then, is that (PIP) is false because he perceives Julius Caesar by sight (and hence by sense) and yet perceives him only mediately (by perceiving the picture or statue that represents him). On Hylas's view, Julius Caesar (as well as any material thing), though perceived by sense, is not the sort of thing that could be *immediately* perceived:

Phil: In the same way that Julius Caesar, in himself invisible, is nevertheless perceived by sight, real things, in themselves imperceptible, are perceived by sense.
Hyl: In the very same. (DHP 1; W2: 203)

Berkeley's reaction to this counterexample is swift and uncompromising: notwithstanding Hylas's protestations to the contrary, the fact is that Julius Caesar is *not* perceived by sense at all:

> Phil: Tell me, Hylas, when you behold the picture of Julius Caesar, do you see with your eyes any more than some colors and figures, with a certain symmetry and composition of the whole?
>
> Hyl: Nothing else.
>
> Phil: And would not a man who had never known anything of Julius Caesar see as much?
>
> Hyl: He would.
>
> Phil: Consequently, he has his sight and the use of it in as perfect degree as you?
>
> Hyl: I agree with you.
>
> Phil: Whence comes it then that your thoughts are directed to the Roman Emperor, and his are not? This cannot proceed from the sensations or ideas of sense by you then perceived, since you acknowledge you have no advantage over him in that respect. It should seem therefore to proceed from reason and memory, should it not?
>
> Hyl: It should.
>
> Phil: Consequently, it will not follow from that instance that anything is perceived by sense which is not immediately perceived. (DHP 1; W2: 203–4)

Berkeley's point, here, is that Julius Caesar is not perceived by sense, but rather by some other mental faculty (namely, reason or memory). For if Julius Caesar were perceived by sense when one (immediately) perceived his picture, then someone who had no knowledge of what Julius Caesar looked like (or who had no knowledge of Julius Caesar at all) would, *per impossibile*, be able to perceive (i.e., think of) Julius Caesar when looking at his picture. What this shows is that Berkeley refuses to accept counter-examples to (PIP) that involve the mediate perception of things that are not themselves immediately perceivable by sense.

In DHP 1, then, Berkeley strives to preserve the validity of his argument for idealism by using the "Part" interpretation to assure the truth of (OP) and by restricting the admissible counterexamples to (PIP) to cases that support the argument's conclusion. This is a clever dialectical strategy, but, as Berkeley later comes to realize, it is also fragile and ultimately unsustainable. The problem is that there remain counterexamples to (PIP) that differ from both the sound–coach/red–heat examples and the Julius Caesar examples. These are cases in which X perceives something mediately by sight, something that X cannot immediately perceive. To Berkeley, these sorts of cases are quite familiar.

Recall that, in NTV, Berkeley insists that it is possible for me to perceive your emotions mediately by sight, namely by perceiving your facial expression. The problem is that even if your facial expression is something I can immediately perceive, your emotions are not immediately perceivable by me. Try as I may, I cannot immediately experience your anger, your resentment, your envy, or your elation. What happens in your mind is not something that I can perceive *immediately* (even if it is something that *you* can perceive immediately). Nor is mediate perception of your passions grounded in a "frequently perceived connection" between my immediate perception of your facial features and my immediate perception of your passions. Thus, my mediate perception of your passions is relevantly like my mediate perception of Julius Caesar. Just as Julius Caesar is not (on Hylas's view) the sort of thing that I can perceive immediately by sense, so your passions are not (on Hylas's view) the sorts of things that I can perceive immediately by sense. By parity of reasoning, then, the Berkeley of DHP 1 is committed to the view that I do *not* perceive the passions in others' minds *by sense*, but rather that I perceive them by *reason* (by inferring them by analogy with my own case).[2]

The bottom line is that there is no way for Berkeley to retain everything he wants to say about all the relevant cases if he assumes the "Part" interpretation. The clearest way out of this conundrum is to jettison this assumption, which, as I will now argue, is precisely what Berkeley ends up doing in the later TVV (1733). There Berkeley writes: "By a sensible *object* I understand that which is *properly* perceived by sense" (emphasis added), where *proper* perception by faculty X (as we saw in chapter 1) is understood to be perception by no faculty other than X (TVV 9; W1: 255). On *this* reading of "X is perceived by sense," it would *not* be true that distance is perceived by sight, for the perception of distance that relies on vision also relies on the faculty of imagination to suggest the idea of distance whenever certain forms of visual confusion or eye strain are immediately perceived. Similarly, it would *not* be true that the passions of other

---

[2] At PHK 140 (W2: 105), Berkeley writes that "as we conceive the ideas that are in the minds of other spirits by means of our own, which we suppose to be resemblances of them, so we know other spirits by means of our own soul—which in that sense is the image or idea of them." And at PHK 145 (W2: 107), he writes that "the knowledge I have of other spirits is not immediate, as is the knowledge of my ideas, but depending on the intervention of ideas, by me referred to agents or spirits distinct from myself, as effects or concomitant signs."

minds are perceived by sight, for the perception of passions that relies on vision also relies on the faculty of imagination to suggest them whenever certain colors are immediately perceived on the countenance. So TVV arguably involves the rejection (or restatement) of the "Part" interpretation and other central claims of NTV, even as it defends *other* central claims of NTV, such as the Heterogeneity Thesis.

Thus, instead of saying, as he does in NTV, that distance, magnitude, and situation are mediately perceived by sight, in TVV Berkeley says that these properties are perceived by the imagination only. For instance, Berkeley writes:

Besides things properly and immediately perceived by any sense, there may be also other things [e.g., distance, magnitude, and situation] suggested to the mind by means of those proper and immediate objects; *which things so suggested are not objects of that sense, being in truth only objects of the imagination*, and originally belonging to some other sense or faculty. (TVV 9; W1: 255–6—emphasis added)

And later, he writes:

Ideas which are observed to be connected with other ideas come to be considered as signs, by means whereof things not actually perceived by sense are signified or suggested to the imagination; *whose objects they are, and which alone perceives them.* (TVV 39; W1: 264—emphasis added)

All of this strongly suggests that, by the time of TVV, Berkeley has abandoned the "Part" interpretation for the "Whole" interpretation. As he sees matters in 1733, it is false to say that objects that are perceived *in part but not wholly* by sense are immediately perceived. In order to preserve the truth of (PIP), it is therefore best to adopt the "Whole" interpretation. For if "X is perceived by sense" is read to mean "X is perceived *wholly* by sense," then there should be no objection to accepting the truth of (PIP): for it is clear that anything that is perceived by sense *and not by means of any other mental faculty* is immediately perceived. This result follows directly from Berkeley's conception of immediate perception. For, as we saw in chapter 1, to say that an object is immediately perceived is to say that it is perceived without intermediary, i.e., without being suggested to the mind by the faculty of bare representation that belongs to the imagination, where such representation is underwritten by stipulation, comparison, or deduction. So whenever an object is perceived by sense without the assistance of the imagination or of any other faculty that underwrites the faculty of bare representation, that object *cannot* be mediately perceived, and must therefore be immediately perceived.

The problem with the "Whole" interpretation, if there is one, concerns (OP) rather than (PIP). If Berkeley's argument for idealism is to avoid the fallacy of equivocation, then adoption of the "Whole" interpretation as providing the reading of "perceived by sense" in (PIP) requires adoption of the same interpretation as providing the reading of the same phrase in (OP). Now, according to the "Whole" interpretation, (OP) says that sensible things are perceived *wholly* by sense. The initial difficulty with this interpretation of (OP) is that it is not an assumption that Berkeley's realist opponents will be happy to accept. One issue on which realists might balk concerns the proper individuation of mental faculties and their operations. Locke, for one, claims that "the *Ideas we receive by sensation, are often* in grown People *alter'd by the Judgment*, without our taking notice of it," as when the sensation "of a flat Circle variously shadow'd" is turned into "the perception of a convex Figure, and an uniform Colour" (E II. ix.8: 145). Here Locke contrasts the faculty of judgment with the faculty of sensation, claiming that at least some of the ideas we *take to be* ideas acquired wholly by sensation are actually acquired by the operation of sensation and judgment. Berkeley might suggest in response that Locke is confusing the operation of judgment with the operation of suggestion, whereby an idea of sensation is mentally associated with a numerically distinct idea of touch. But the bone of contention here, such as it is, is left unresolved. More generally, while realists and idealists alike suppose that sensible objects such as chairs and cherries are sensible things, realists may insist that reason plays an important role in the perception of chairs and cherries. As Locke might say, although chairs and cherries are sensible things (inasmuch as sensation is needed to perceive them), they cannot be perceived without being inferred to exist on the basis of the immediately perceived sensations they produce in our minds.[3]

---

[3] Here it might be thought that Locke's account of sensitive knowledge is non-inferential. But, as I argue in Rickless (2008, 96–7), this is a mistake.

Descartes's account in the *Meditations* is clearly inferential. In the *Second Meditation*, Descartes writes: "We say that we see the wax itself, if it is there before us, not that we judge it to be there from its colour or shape; and this might lead me to conclude without more ado that knowledge of the wax comes from what the eye sees, and not from the scrutiny of the mind alone. But then if I look out of the window and see men crossing the square, as I just happen to have done, I normally say that I see the men themselves, just as I say that I see the wax. Yet do I see any more than hats and coats which could conceal automatons? I *judge* that

There is therefore *a* sense in which Berkeley's argument for idealism results in a kind of philosophical stalemate. Berkeley had hoped to be able to produce a valid argument for idealism grounded in premises that his realist opponents could not reasonably deny. This is clearly the aspiration behind DHP, in which the materialist Hylas does not quarrel with the suggestion that what it is for a thing to be sensible is for it to be perceived by sense and is brought to accept on the basis of rigorous dialectically persuasive argumentation that things perceived by sense, whether immediately or mediately, must be mind-dependent ideas. On reflection, this was too much to hope for.

However, it is also possible to read Berkeley's argument as posing a significant challenge to his realist opponents. Understood this way, the argument is, I believe, successful. For the only dialectically acceptable way to reject Berkeley's argument is to reject premise (OP), as read in accordance with the "Whole" interpretation. That is, the only reasonable way to avoid the conclusion that sensible objects are collections of ideas is to claim that sensible objects are perceived at least in part by the operation of some faculty other than the senses. For Berkeley's opponents (including most notably Descartes and Locke), this faculty is reason. As they see it, the fact that tables and chairs are the objects of sense perception is justified by an inference to the best explanation: if everything has a cause, then there must be something causing our table-sensations and chair-sensations; given that we perceive these sensations regardless of whether we will to do so (and, indeed, sometimes against our will), we ourselves are not the causes of these sensations; therefore, something outside our minds must be causing these sensations; and if our sensations represent (and hence, at least with respect to primary qualities, resemble) what is causing them, their causes must have the primary qualities we represent them to have; that is, the causes of our sensations must be mind-independent tables and chairs.

At this point, Berkeley will insist that, although it is true that our table-sensations and chair-sensations are being caused by something outside our minds, there is no reason to suppose (and every reason *not* to suppose) that the cause of our sensations is anything other than a mind. For, by the likeness principle, nothing can be like an idea but another idea, and hence, if our table-sensations were to represent (and hence resemble) tables, then

they are men. And so something which I thought I was seeing with my eyes is in fact grasped solely by the faculty of judgement which is in my mind" (AT 7:21; CSM 2:21).

tables would be (collections of) ideas. Moreover, tables could not be the causes of our table-sensations, given that ideas are, in and of themselves, inert and passive beings.[4] And even if Berkeley's opponents found a good reason to reject the likeness principle, it appears both contrary to common sense and to one's experience to suppose that the exercise of *reason* is required for the production of perceptual beliefs. I am not aware of inferring on the basis of my sensations of vision and touch that I am typing this sentence on a laptop computer; and given the transparency of the mental (a thesis to which most of Berkeley's realist contemporaries, apart from Leibniz, subscribed), this lack of awareness provides strong evidence for Berkeley's claim that my perceptual beliefs are not produced with the assistance of reason or judgment.

Much as he would have liked it to be otherwise, Berkeley does not in the end provide a knock-down argument for idealism. Looking back at his intellectual corpus, we should not count this against him. Knock-down arguments are famously difficult to come by in philosophy, and this case is no exception. But Berkeley's argument for idealism should, I think, leave us in awe. It is, without a doubt, one of the most impressive examples of pure a priori ratiocination in defense of an immensely important onto-logical thesis ever devised. The argument should have been taken far more seriously than it was by his intellectual contemporaries and immediate successors, including Hume, for whom it produced no more than "momentary amazement and irresolution and confusion."[5] Even as it stands, it represents a forceful challenge to realists and materialists of all stripes. The way of ideas, Berkeley tells us, leads to a world of ideas. In saying this, he may well be right.

---

[4] Notice here that the likeness principle and the thesis of the inertness of ideas do not play the role of premises in Berkeley's argument for idealism. What they do is make it difficult, perhaps impossible, for Berkeley's realist opponents to reasonably deny one of the argument's most important premises, understood in accordance with the "Whole" interpretation.

Berkeley's opponents might also balk at the likeness principle. But if they do so, then they have a hard row to hoe. For if our table-sensations resemble tables that are not themselves sensations, then, given that the tables have shape and size, it would follow that our table-sensations have shape and size too. It would then be left to Cartesians and Lockeans to explain how the contents of an unextended mind could be extended themselves.

[5] Hume (1999, 203, fn. 32).

# Bibliography

Adams, Robert M. 1994. *Leibniz: Determinist, Theist, Idealist*. New York: Oxford University Press.

——2007. "Idealism Vindicated." In *Persons: Human and Divine*, ed. Peter van Inwagen and Dean Zimmerman. New York: Oxford University Press, 35–54.

Allaire, Edwin B. 1963. "Berkeley's Idealism." *Theoria* 29: 229–44.

——1982. "Berkeley's Idealism Revisited." In Turbayne 1982, 197–206.

——1995. "Berkeley's Idealism: Yet Another Visit." In Muehlmann 1995, 23–38.

Armstrong, D. M. 1960. *Berkeley's Theory of Vision*. Parkville, VI: Melbourne University Press.

Atherton, Margaret. 1987. "Berkeley's Anti-Abstractionism." In Sosa 1987, 45–60.

——1990. *Berkeley's Revolution in Vision*. Ithaca: Cornell University Press.

——1995. "Berkeley Without God." In Muehlmann 1995, 231–48.

——2007. "The Objects of Immediate Perception." In *New Interpretations of Berkeley's Thought*, ed. Stephen H. Daniel. Amherst, NY: Humanity Books, 107–19.

Ayers, Michael R. (ed.). 1975. *George Berkeley: Philosophical Works, Including the Works on Vision*. London: J. M. Dent.

——1978. "Review of George Pitcher's *Berkeley*." *Times Literary Supplement*, June 16, 680.

Barnes, Jonathan (ed.). 1984. *The Complete Works of Aristotle*. Revised Oxford Translation. Princeton: Princeton University Press.

Baxter, Donald L. M. 1991. "Berkeley, Perception, and Identity." *Philosophy and Phenomenological Research* 51: 85–98.

Beierwaltes, Werner. 1972. "Die Wiederentdeckung des Eriugena im Deutschen Idealismus" In *Platonismus und Idealismus*. Frankfurt: Klostermann, 188–201.

——1985. *Denken des Einen: Studien zur neuplatonischen Philosophie und ihrer Wirkungsgeschichte*. Frankfurt: Klostermann.

——1994. "Zur Wirkungsgeschichte Eriugenas im Deutschen Idealismus und danach: Eine kurze, unsystematische Nachlese." In *Eriugena: Grundzüge seines Denkens*. Frankfurt: Klostermann, 313–30.

Bennett, Jonathan F. 1988. *Events and Their Names*. Oxford: Clarendon Press.

——1998. *The Act Itself*. Oxford: Clarendon Press.

Bolton, Martha Brandt. 1987. "Berkeley's Objection to Abstract Ideas and Unconceived Objects." In Sosa 1987, 61–84.

Boswell, James. 1791/2008. *The Life of Samuel Johnson*, ed. David Womersley. London: Penguin Classics.

Bracken, Harry M. 1964. "Some Problems of Substance Among the Cartesians." *American Philosophical Quarterly* 1: 129–37.

Burnyeat, Miles. 1982. "Idealism and Greek Philosophy: What Descartes Saw and Berkeley Missed." *Philosophical Review* 91: 3–40.

Collier, Arthur. 1713. *Clavis Universalis*. London: Robert Gosling.

Cummins, Phillip D. 1963. "Perceptual Relativity and Ideas in the Mind." *Philosophy and Phenomenological Research* 24: 204–14.

——1975. "Berkeley's Ideas of Sense." *Noûs* 9: 55–72.

——and Guenter Zoeller (eds.). 1992. *Minds, Ideas, and Objects: Essays in the Theory of Representation in Modern Philosophy*, North American Kant Society Studies in Philosophy, Volume 2. Atascadero, CA: Ridgeview.

Daniel, Stephen H. 2001a. "Berkeley's Christian Neoplatonism, Archetypes, and Divine Ideas." *Journal of the History of Philosophy* 39: 239–58.

——2001b. "Berkeley's Pantheistic Discourse." *International Journal for Philosophy of Religion* 49: 179–94.

——2007. "Berkeley's Stoic Notion of Spiritual Substance." In *New Interpretations of Berkeley's Thought*, ed. Stephen H. Daniel. Amherst, NY: Humanity Books, 203–30.

Descartes, René. 1985. *The Philosophical Writings of Descartes, Volume 2*, ed. John Cottingham, Robert Stoothoff, and Dugald Murdoch. Cambridge: Cambridge University Press. Abbreviated as CSM2.

Dicker, Georges. 1982. "The Concept of Immediate Perception in Berkeley's Immaterialism." In Turbayne 1982, 48–66.

——1992. "Berkeley on the Immediate Perception of Objects." In Cummins and Zoeller 1992, 201–13.

——2006. "Berkeley on Immediate Perception: Once More Unto the Breach." *The Philosophical Quarterly* 56: 517–35.

Doney, Willis. 1983. "Berkeley's Argument Against Abstract Ideas." In *Midwest Studies in Philosophy VIII: Contemporary Perspectives on the History of Philosophy*, ed. Peter A. French, Theodore E. Uehling, Jr., and Howard K. Wettstein. Minneapolis: University of Minnesota Press, 295–308.

Emilsson, Eyjólfur Kjalar. 1996. "Cognition and its Object." In *The Cambridge Companion to Plotinus*, ed. Lloyd P. Gerson. Cambridge: Cambridge University Press, 217–49.

Flage, Daniel E. 2004. "Berkeley's Epistemic Ontology: *The Principles*." *Canadian Journal of Philosophy* 34: 25–60.

Fogelin, Robert J. 2001. *Routledge Philosophy Guidebook to Berkeley and the Principles of Human Knowledge*. New York: Routledge.

Gallois, Andre. 1974. "Berkeley's Master Argument." *Philosophical Review* 83: 55–69.

Grayling, A. C. 1986. *Berkeley: The Central Arguments*. La Salle, IL: Open Court.

Hacking, Ian. 1975. *Why Does Language Matter to Philosophy?* Cambridge: Cambridge University Press.

Harris, Stephen. 1997. "Berkeley's Argument from Perceptual Relativity." *History of Philosophy Quarterly* 14: 99–120.

Hausman, Alan. 1984. "Adhering to Inherence: A New Look at the Old Steps in Berkeley's March to Idealism." *Canadian Journal of Philosophy* 14: 421–43.

Henze, Donald F. 1965. "Berkeley on Sensations and Qualities." *Theoria* 31: 174–80.

Hibbs, Darren. 2005. "Was Gregory of Nyssa a Berkeleyan Idealist?" *British Journal for the History of Philosophy* 13: 425–35.

Hight, Marc and Walter Ott. 2004. "The New Berkeley." *Canadian Journal of Philosophy* 34: 1–24.

Hume, David. 1999. *An Enquiry Concerning Human Understanding*, ed. Tom L. Beauchamp. Oxford: Oxford University Press.

Jessop, T. E. (ed.). 1952. *Berkeley: Philosophical Writings*. Edinburgh: Nelson.

Lambert, Richard T. 1982. "Berkeley's Commitment to Relativism." In Turbayne 1982, 22–32.

Lennon, Thomas M. 1988. "Berkeley and the Ineffable." *Synthese* 75: 231–50.

Locke, John. 1975. *An Essay Concerning Human Understanding*, ed. Peter H. Nidditch. Oxford: Clarendon Press. Abbreviated as *Essay*, and cited by book number, chapter number, and section number, followed by page number.

Lodge, Paul. 2001. "Leibniz's Notion of an Aggregate." *British Journal for the History of Philosophy* 9: 467–86.

Luce, A. A. 1963. *The Dialectic of Immaterialism*. London: Hodder & Stoughton.

——1966. "Berkeley's New Principle Completed." In Steinkraus 1966, 1–12.

——1967. "Sensible Ideas and Sensations." *Hermathena* 105: 74–83.

——and T. E. Jessop (eds.). 1948–57. *The Works of George Berkeley, Bishop of Cloyne*. London: Thomas Nelson.

Mackie, John L. 1976. *Problems From Locke*. Oxford: Clarendon Press.

McKim, Robert. 1992. "Berkeley on Private Ideas and Public Objects." In Cummins and Zoeller 1992, 215–33.

——1997–8. "Abstraction and Immaterialism: Recent Interpretations." *The Berkeley Newsletter* 15: 1–13.

Mill, John Stuart. 1861/1979. *Utilitarianism*, ed. George Sher. Indianapolis: Hackett.

Molyneux, William. 1692. *Dioptrica Nova*. London: Benj. Tooke.

Moran, Dermot. 1989. *The Philosophy of John Scottus Eriugena: A Study of Idealism in the Middle Ages*. Cambridge: Cambridge University Press.

Moran, Dermot. 1999. "Idealism in Medieval Philosophy: The Case of Johannes Scottus Eriugena." *Medieval Philosophy and Theology* 8: 53–82.

Muehlmann, Robert G. 1978. "Berkeley's Ontology and the Epistemology of Idealism." *Canadian Journal of Philosophy* 8: 89–111.

——1992. *Berkeley's Ontology*. Indianapolis: Hackett.

——(ed.). 1995. *Berkeley's Metaphysics: Structural, Interpretive, and Critical Essays*. University Park, PA: Pennsylvania State University Press.

Newman, Lex. 2002. "Review of George S. Pappas's *Berkeley's Thought*." *Philosophical Review* 111: 314–18.

——(ed.). 2007. *The Cambridge Companion to Locke's "Essay Concerning Human Understanding."* Cambridge: Cambridge University Press.

Oaklander, L. Nathan. 1977. "The Inherence Interpretation of Berkeley: A Critique." *The Modern Schoolman* 54: 261–9.

Ott, Walter R. 2004. "The Cartesian Context of Berkeley's Attack on Abstraction." *Pacific Philosophical Quarterly* 85: 407–24.

Pappas, George S. 1980. "Ideas, Minds, and Berkeley." *American Philosophical Quarterly* 17: 181–94.

——1985. "Abstract Ideas and the *Esse* is *Percipi* Thesis." *Hermathena* 139: 47–62.

——1986. "Berkeley on the Perception of Objects." *Journal of the History of Philosophy* 24: 99–105.

——2000. *Berkeley's Thought*. Ithaca: Cornell University Press.

——2002. "Abstraction and Existence." *History of Philosophy Quarterly* 19: 43–63.

Pitcher, George. 1977. *Berkeley*. London: Routledge & Kegan Paul.

Priest, Graham. 1995. *Beyond the Limits of Thought*. Cambridge: Cambridge University Press.

Prior, Arthur N. 1955. "Berkeley in Logical Form." *Theoria* 21: 117–22. Reprinted in Prior 1976, 33–8.

——1976. *Papers in Logic and Ethics*, ed. Peter T. Geach and Anthony J. P. Kenny. London: Duckworth.

Reid, Thomas. 1785. *Essays on the Intellectual Powers of Man*. Edinburgh: J. Bell.

Rickless, Samuel C. 1997. "Locke on Primary and Secondary Qualities." *Pacific Philosophical Quarterly* 78: 297–319.

——2008. "Is Locke's Theory of Knowledge Inconsistent?" *Philosophy and Phenomenological Research* 77: 83–104.

Roberts, John R. 2007. *A Metaphysics for the Mob: The Philosophy of George Berkeley*. New York: Oxford University Press.

Rutherford, Donald. 2008. "Leibniz as Idealist." *Oxford Studies in Early Modern Philosophy* 4: 141–90.

Sorabji, Richard. 1983. "Gregory of Nyssa: The Origins of Idealism." In *Time, Creation and the Continuum: Theories in Antiquity and the Early Middle Ages*, Ithaca: Cornell University Press, 287–96.

Sosa, Ernest (ed.). 1987. *Essays on the Philosophy of George Berkeley*. Dordrecht: D. Reidel.

Steinkraus, Warren E. (ed.). 1966. *New Studies in Berkeley's Philosophy*. New York: Holt, Rinehart and Winston.

Stoneham, Tom. 2002. *Berkeley's World: An Examination of the* Three Dialogues. Oxford: Clarendon Press.

——2006. "Berkeley's 'Esse is Percipi' and Collier's 'Simple' Argument." *History of Philosophy Quarterly* 23: 211–24.

——2007. "When Did Collier Read Berkeley?" *British Journal for the History of Philosophy* 15: 361–4.

Szabó, Zoltán Gendler. 2005. "Sententialism and Berkeley's *Master Argument*." *Philosophical Quarterly* 55: 462–74.

Thomson, Judith Jarvis. 1977. *Acts and Other Events*. Ithaca: Cornell University Press.

Tipton, Ian C. 1974. *Berkeley: The Philosophy of Immaterialism*. London: Methuen.

Turbayne, Colin M. 1959. (ed.). 1982. *Berkeley: Critical and Interpretive Essays*. Minneapolis: University of Minnesota Press.

Watson, Richard A. 1963. "Berkeley in a Cartesian Context." *Revue Internationale de Philosophie* 65: 381–94.

Williams, Bernard. 1981. "Philosophy." In *The Legacy of Greece: A New Appraisal*, ed. M. I. Finley. Oxford: Clarendon Press, 202–55.

Wilson, Fred. 1995. "On the Hausmans' 'A New Approach'." In Muehlmann 1995, 67–88.

Winkler, Kenneth P. 1989. *Berkeley: An Interpretation*. Oxford: Oxford University Press.

Wittgenstein, Ludwig. 1953. *Philosophical Investigations*, trans. G. E. M. Anscombe. Oxford: Blackwell.

# Index

Printed and bound by CPI Group (UK) Ltd, Croydon, CR0 4YY